W9-AWB-613

THE MINI ROUGH GUIDE TO

TORONTO

Forthcoming titles include

Devon & Cornwall • Ibiza • Iceland
Malta • Tenerife • Vancouver

Forthcoming reference guides include

Cuban Music • Hip-Hop • Personal Computers
Pregnancy & Birth • Trumpet & Trombone

Rough Guides online

www.roughguides.com

Rough Guide Credits

Text editor: Stephen Timblin
Managing Editor: Andrew Rosenberg
Series editor: Mark Ellingham
Production: Robert McKinlay
Cartography: Maxine Repath and Ed Wright
Proofreading: Margaret Doyle

Publishing Information

This second edition published March 2001
by Rough Guides Ltd,
62–70 Shorts Gardens, London, WC2H 9AH

Distributed by the Penguin Group:

Penguin Books Ltd, 27 Wrights Lane, London W8 5TZ
Penguin Putnam, Inc., 375 Hudson Street, New York 10014, USA
Penguin Books Australia Ltd, 487 Maroondah Highway,
PO Box 257, Ringwood, Victoria 3134, Australia
Penguin Books Canada Ltd, 10 Alcorn Avenue,
Toronto, Ontario, Canada M4V 1E4
Penguin Books (NZ) Ltd,
182–190 Wairau Road, Auckland 10, New Zealand

Typeset in Bembo and Helvetica to an original design by Henry Iles.
Printed in Spain by Graphy Cems.

ISBN 1-85828-760-X

THE MINI ROUGH GUIDE TO

TORONTO

by Phil Lee and Helen Lovekin

ROUGH GUIDES

We set out to do something different when the first Rough Guide was published in 1982. Mark Ellingham, just out of university, was travelling in Greece. He brought along the popular guides of the day, but found they were all lacking in some way. They were either strong on ruins and museums but went on for pages without mentioning a beach or taverna. Or they were so conscious of the need to save money that they lost sight of Greece's cultural and historical significance. Also, none of the books told him anything about Greece's contemporary life – its politics, its culture, its people, and how they lived.

So with no job in prospect, Mark decided to write his own guidebook, one which aimed to provide practical information that was second to none, detailing the best beaches and the hottest clubs and restaurants, while also giving hard-hitting accounts of every sight, both famous and obscure, and providing up-to-the-minute information on contemporary culture. It was a guide that encouraged independent travellers to find the best of Greece, and was a great success, getting shortlisted for the Thomas Cook travel guide award, and encouraging Mark, along with three friends, to expand the series.

The Rough Guide list grew rapidly and the letters flooded in, indicating a much broader readership than had been anticipated, but one which uniformly appreciated the Rough Guide mix of practical detail and humour, irreverence and enthusiasm. Things haven't changed. The same four friends who began the series are still the caretakers of the Rough Guide mission today: to provide the most reliable, up-to-date and entertaining information to independent-minded travellers of all ages, on all budgets.

We now publish more than 150 titles and have offices in London and New York. The travel guides are written and researched by a dedicated team of more than 100 authors, based in Britain, Europe, the USA and Australia. We have also created a unique series of phrasebooks to accompany the travel series, along with an acclaimed series of music guides, and a best-selling pocket guide to the Internet and World Wide Web. We also publish comprehensive travel information on our Web site: **www.roughguides.com**

Help us update

We've gone to a lot of trouble to ensure that this Rough Guide is as up to date and accurate as possible. However, things do change, and any suggestions, comments and corrections are much appreciated. We'll send a copy of the next edition (or any other Rough Guide if you prefer) for the best letters.

Please mark letters **"Rough Guide Mini Toronto Update"** and send to:

Rough Guides, 62–70 Shorts Gardens, London, WC2H 9AH, or Rough Guides, 4th Floor, 345 Hudson St, New York NY 10014.

Or send email to: mail@roughguides.co.uk
Online updates about this book can be found on
Rough Guides' Web site (see opposite)

The authors

Phil Lee first experienced Canada as a bartender in an Ontario water-ski resort. Subsequent contacts have been less chaotic and have given him an abiding interest in the country. Phil has worked as a freelance author with the Rough Guides for more than ten years. Previous titles include *Mallorca & Menorca*, *Norway*, *Belgium & Luxembourg*, *Canada* and *Toronto*.

Helen Lovekin is a Torontonian born and bred, and this is her only Rough Guide. She lives with the love of her life in a "wee hoose" in Cabbagetown.

Acknowledgements

Phil: A very special thanks to Ontario Tourism and, in particular, to Media Co-ordinator Diane Helinski for her unstinting support and lively sense of humour. Thanks also to my editor Stephen Timblin for his enthusiasm and hard work in making this book as good as I think it is.

Helen: Many, many thanks to the legions of friends, colleagues, store owners, restaurateurs, artists and impresarios whose creativity and hard work have given Toronto the wonderful facilities detailed here. Also, a word of gratitude to our editor, Stephen Timblin, whose clear-headed persistence brought this edition to a timely conclusion, to my friend and co-author Phil, and to Rey Stephen for his thoughts on Toronto's gay community. Finally, deepest thanks to John Harnden, whose support, advice and love make all things possible.

ACKNOWLEDGEMENTS

CONTENTS

Contents 279

MAP LIST

Introduction

The economic and cultural focus of English-speaking Canada, **Toronto** is the country's largest metropolis. It sprawls along the northern shore of Lake Ontario, its surprisingly vibrant centre encased by a jangle of satellite townships and industrial zones that cover – as "Greater Toronto" – no less than 100 square kilometres. For decades, Toronto was saddled with unflattering sobriquets – "Toronto the Good", "Hogtown" – that reflected a perhaps deserved reputation for complacent mediocrity and greed. Spurred into years of image-building, the city's post-war administrations have lavished millions of dollars on glitzy architecture, slick museums, an excellent public transport system, and the reclamation and development of the lake-front. As a result, Toronto has become one of North America's most likeable cities, an eminently liveable place with a proud sense of itself.

Huge new shopping malls and skyrise office blocks reflect the economic successes of the last two or three decades, a boom that has attracted immigrants from all over the world, transforming an overwhelmingly Anglophone city into a cosmopolitan one of some sixty significant minorities. Furthermore, the city's multiculturalism goes far deeper than an extravagant diversity of restaurants and sporadic pockets of multilingual street signs: Toronto's schools, for example, have extensive "Heritage Language Programmes", which encourage the maintenance of the immigrants' first cultures.

Getting the feel of Toronto's diversity is one of the city's great pleasures, but there are attention-grabbing sights here as well. Most are conveniently clustered in the city centre, and the most celebrated of them all is the **CN Tower**, the world's tallest freestanding structure, next door to which lies the modern hump of the **SkyDome** sports stadium. The city's other prestige attractions are led by the **Art Gallery of Ontario**, which possesses a first-rate selection of Canadian painting, and the **Royal Ontario Museum**, where pride of place goes to the Chinese collection. But it's the pick of Toronto's smaller, less-visited galleries and period homes that really add to the city's charm. There are superb Canadian paintings at the **Thomson Gallery** and a fascinating range of footwear at the **Bata Shoe Museum**. The Toronto Dominion Bank boasts the eclectic **Gallery of Inuit Art,** and the mock-Gothic extravagances of **Casa Loma**, the Victorian gentility of **Spadina House** along with the replica of **Fort York**, the colonial settlement where Toronto began, all vie for your attention.

Toronto's sights illustrate different facets of the city, but in no way do they crystallise its identity. The city remains opaque – too big and diverse to allow for a defining personality. This, however, adds an air of excitement and unpredictability to the place. Toronto caters to everything, and the city surges with Canada's most vibrant restaurant, performing-arts and nightlife scenes.

Toronto is also a convenient base for exploring southwest Ontario, a triangular tract of land that lies sandwiched between lakes Huron and Erie. Significant parts of the region have been heavily industrialized, but there's also mile upon mile of rolling farmland and a series of first-rate attractions, the pick of which are within a two- to three-hour drive of downtown Toronto. In "Day-trips" we've detailed some of the area's best excursions, beginning with Canada's premier tourist spot, Niagara Falls, and nearby Niagara-on-the-Lake, a beguiling town of leafy streets and charming colonial houses. There's also Goderich and Bayfield, two lovely, small-town places tucked against the bluffs of the Lake Huron shoreline. Finally, Severn Sound is the location of the beautiful Georgian Bay Islands National Park, as well as a pair of top-notch historical reconstructions: Discovery Harbour and Sainte-Marie among the Hurons.

	F°		C°		RAINFALL	
	AVERAGE DAILY		AVERAGE DAILY		AVERAGE MONTHLY	
	MAX	MIN	MAX	MIN	MM	IN
Jan	-1	-8	30	18	55	2.2
Feb	-3	-7	31	19	53	2.1
March	4.2	-3	40	27	65	2.6
April	12	3	53	38	*65	2.6
May	18	8	64	47	68	2.7
June	24	14	75	57	67	2.6
July	27	16	80	62	71	2.8
Aug	26	16	78	61	83	3.3
Sept	22	12	71	54	76	3.0
Oct	15	7	60	45	63	2.5
Nov	8	2	46	35	76	3.0
Dec	1	-4	34	23	77	3.0

When to visit

Toronto has a harsh **climate**. In the winter, it's often bitterly cold with sub-zero temperatures and heavy snowfalls. January and February are usually the coldest months, but real winter conditions can begin in early November and drag on into late March. Summers, on the other hand, are hot and humid. July and August are consistently the hottest months, sometimes uncomfortably so. Spring and autumn offer the city's most enjoyable weather, with lots of warm, sunny days and balmy nights.

THE GUIDE

THE GUIDE

1

Introducing the city

Toronto's city limits are vast, but fortunately for the visitor most of the city's key sights, better restaurants and livelier nightspots are concentrated in the city centre. The centre itself is divided into three clearly defined areas, the most diverse of which is **downtown Toronto**, sandwiched between Front Street to the south, Gerrard Street to the north, Spadina Avenue to the west and Jarvis Street to the east. Here you'll find the city's most visited attractions: the **CN Tower** and the **SkyDome** sports stadium, as well as the **banking district**, whose assorted skyscrapers display some of the city's most striking architecture. Within these dense office blocks are pleasant surprises like the delightful **Gallery of Inuit Art** and **St Andrew's Presbyterian Church**, whose Romanesque stonework is a proud reminder of the nineteenth-century city. The banking district fizzles out at Queen Street, giving way to **Nathan Phillips Square**, site of both the old and new City Halls, and the sprawling **Eaton Centre**, Toronto's main shopping mall, which extends along Yonge as far as Dundas Street. The Bay department store next door holds the charming **Thomson Gallery**, where there's an excellent sample of Canadian paintings. And if this whets your appetite, you can move on to the **Art Gallery of Ontario**, home to an outstanding collection of both European and Canadian works.

Moving north, **uptown Toronto** runs from Gerrard as far as Dupont Street. With the exception of the **Ontario Legislative Assembly Building**, a whopping sandstone pile on University Avenue, the principal attractions here are museums, from the wide-ranging applied art collections of the **Royal Ontario Museum** through to the **Gardiner Museum of Ceramic Art** and the inventive **Bata Shoe Museum**. Also of interest here are a pair of intriguing old houses – **Casa Loma** and **Spadina House** – and you can also dip into two of Toronto's most beguiling neighbourhoods, chi-chi **Yorkville** and fashionable **Cabbagetown**.

The third part of the city centre is the **Harbourfront**, an old industrial strip of wharves and warehouses that has been turned into one of the smartest parts of the city. Deluxe condominiums and bright office blocks now line the lakeshore, and there are open-air performance areas, art galleries, bars and restaurants, too. This is also where ferries leave for the **Toronto Islands**, the low-lying, crescent-shaped sandbanks that protect the harbour and provide opportunities for city folk to go walking, swimming and sailing.

To get a real flavour for Toronto's core, it's best to explore on **foot**, a perfectly feasible option as distances are quite manageable – from Front Street to Bloor Street is about 2km; Spadina Avenue to Jarvis Street 1km. However, visiting some of the more peripheral attractions – like Casa Loma and Spadina House – can be a bit of a trek, especially in the summer when the city is often unbearably humid. To save time and effort, your best bet at these times is to use Toronto's **public transport** system, a comprehensive, safe and inexpensive network of streetcars, buses, and subways that reaches into every nook and cranny of the city.

Toronto's public transport system also brings most of the city's **suburbs** to within easy reach. By and large, these districts are only of limited interest, the main exception being **The Beaches**, a delightful neighbourhood bordering Lake Ontario, a twenty-minute streetcar ride east of downtown.

Toronto now has two area codes, Ⓣ416 and Ⓣ647, the latter reserved for phone numbers created after March 1, 2001. Since the area code split is not based on distinct city areas, all local telephone calls now require that you dial a ten-digit number. All of the Toronto phone numbers in the *Guide* use the Ⓣ416 code unless otherwise specified.

TORONTO'S NEIGHBOURHOODS

For the purpose of this book, Toronto has been divided into three general chapters: downtown, uptown, and the Harbourfront and Toronto Islands (see maps at the back of the book). Peppered throughout the city, however, are enclaves of distinct **neighbourhoods**, slivers that might consist of just a few streets, but that hold a cultural flavour all their own. Many are defined by ethnic origin, others by income level or sexual preference. Street signs identify some of these neighbourhoods, but architecturally one is often indistinguishable from the next. The following rundown will help you get the most from the city's demographic mosaic, whether you want to shop, eat or just take in the atmosphere. But bear in mind that there is a certain artificiality to the nomenclature – Chinatown, for example, has hundreds of Vietnamese residents, Little Italy a large contingent of Portuguese.

The Annex (Map 4, A3 through E4), bounded east–west by Bathurst Street and Avenue Road, and north–south by Bloor and Dupont streets, was in its heyday (1890–1910) the most fashionable part of town. This residential district has since lost much of its allure, but is still dotted with stately old mansions.

The Beaches (see p.82), lying south of Queen Street

East between Woodbine and Victoria Park avenues, is a prosperous and particularly appealing district with chic boutiques, leafy streets and a sandy beach trimmed by a popular boardwalk. Pianist Glenn Gould was born here.

Cabbagetown (see p.67), east of Jarvis Street and roughly bounded by Gerrard Street East on its south side, Wellesley Street East to the north and the Don River to the east, is renowned for its Victorian housing. Its name comes from the district's nineteenth-century immigrants, whose tiny front gardens were filled with cabbages.

Chinatown (see p.51) is concentrated along Dundas Street West between Bay Street and Spadina Avenue. This is one of Toronto's most distinctive neighbourhoods, with busy restaurants and stores selling anything from porcelain and jade to herbs and pickled seaweed.

The Gay and Lesbian Village (see p.215), with its plethora of bars, restaurants and bookshops, is centred on the Church and Wellesley streets intersection.

Greektown (Map 2, H6), a burgeoning neighbourhood along Danforth Avenue, is located between Pape and Woodbine avenues. With scores of authentic restaurants, this is the place to go for Greek food.

High Park (see p.92) takes its name from the park that overlooks the Gardiner Expressway to the west of downtown. Its main drag, Roncesvalles Avenue, is the heart of Toronto's large Polish community.

Kensington Market (see p.51), just north of Dundas Street West between Spadina and Augusta avenues, is the most ethnically diverse part of town, combining Portuguese, West Indian and Jewish Canadians, who pack the streets with a plethora of tiny shops and open-air stalls.

Little India (Map 2, H7) is along Gerrard Street East running one block west from Coxwell Avenue. Visually, it's not too appealing, but the area does have a number of fine restaurants.

Little Italy (Map 4, A8) – the so-called Corso Italia – runs along College Street between Bathurst Street and Clinton Street, and is one of Toronto's liveliest neighbourhoods.

Little Portugal (Map 3, A1), a crowded, vital area packed with shops and neighbourhood food joints, is focused on Dundas Street West, west of Bathurst Street as far as Dovercourt Road.

Queen Street West (see p.43), between University and Spadina, has one of the highest retail rents in the city and is home to all things trendy and expensive. The students and punks who once hung around here have moved on to what is known as Queen West West, between Spadina and Bathurst.

Rosedale (Map 4, I1 through N5) is a byword for prosperity, a well-heeled neighbourhood whose leafy streets and old mansions have traditionally been home to the city's elite. Its boundaries are Yonge Street to the west, the Don Valley Parkway to the east, St Clair Avenue to the north and Bloor Street East to the south.

St Lawrence (Map 3, I5 through K6) enjoyed its first period of rapid growth after the War of 1812 and became one of the most fashionable parts of Victorian Toronto. It went downhill thereafter, but has recently been revived and gentrified. The district possesses a smattering of handsome late nineteenth-century buildings, most notably the neo-Gothic St James Cathedral. The St Lawrence neighbourhood is just to the east of Yonge Street, between King Street East, Frederick Street and The Esplanade.

Yorkville (see p.65), just above Bloor Street West between Yonge and Avenue Road, was "alternative" in the 1960s, with appearances by figureheads of the counterculture like Gordon Lightfoot and Joni Mitchell. Today, the alternative vibe of the place is long gone, and the district holds some of Toronto's most expensive clothing shops and art galleries, as well as several good bars and restaurants.

Arrival

Toronto is extremely easy to get to. Its international airport is linked to almost every major city in the world and there are flights from virtually every corner of Canada. The majority of visitors arrive by **plane**, but Toronto also has reasonably fast and frequent **bus** and **train** services that link the city to many US and Canadian destinations. The train and bus stations are both conveniently located downtown, while the airport is an hour bus ride away. Car drivers will find the city encircled by a number of efficient motorways, and although traffic congestion can be a problem, delays are not usually as severe as in many other large cities.

BY AIR

Arriving by **air**, you'll almost certainly land at Toronto's main airport, **Lester B. Pearson International**, about 25km northwest of the city centre. There are three terminals – terminals 2 and 3 are where most international flights arrive, and terminal 1 handles the majority of domestic flights. Each of the terminals has a full range of facilities, including money-exchange offices, ATMs and free hotel hot lines.

The **Airport Express bus** service (daily: one every twenty minutes 6am–12.30am, every thirty minutes 1am–5.30am; ⓣ905/564-6333; ⓦ *www.torontoairportexpress .com*) picks up passengers outside the terminals and takes between forty and sixty minutes to reach downtown, though heavy traffic can make the journey considerably longer. The bus drops passengers at the bus station (see p.10 for details) and seven of Toronto's major hotels: the *Westin Harbour Castle*, *Royal York*, *Crowne Plaza*, *Sheraton Centre*, *Colony*, *Metropolitan* and the *Delta Chelsea*. Connecting

ARRIVAL

minibuses take passengers to most of the other downtown hotels. Tickets for the airport bus can be purchased either at the kiosks next to the bus stop outside the terminal buildings or from the driver. A one-way fare is $13.75, round-trip $23.65; the minibus service costs an extra $3 (round-trip $5). Round-trip tickets are valid for one year.

Airport Express also operates bus services from the airport to three subway stations – Islington, well to the west of the city centre (daily: one every forty minutes 6am–midnight, every thirty minutes 12.30am–5.30am), and Yorkdale and York Mills to the north (daily: one every forty minutes 6am–midnight). Buses leave from designated stops outside each of the terminal buildings and payment can be made to either the driver or at the company's kiosks. The journey time is around twenty minutes to Islington, forty to Yorkdale, and fifty to York Mills. A one-way fare to Islington is $7.10, round-trip $11.50; Yorkdale $7.60, $13.15; York Mills $8.70, $13.90. Round-trip tickets are valid for one year. The subway operates Mon–Sat 6am–1am, Sun 9am–1am; for further information on the subway system, see p.14.

Alternatively, there's an airport **limo** service (a shared taxi system) next to each terminal's bus platform; limos cost about $30 per person for the journey from the airport to the city centre; they only leave when they're full. Individual **taxis** charge approximately $40 from the airport to downtown Toronto.

Finally, a subsidiary of Air Canada, Air Ontario (T1-888/247-2262, within Toronto T925-2311) operates flights from Montreal, Ottawa and London, Ontario, into the much smaller **Toronto City Centre Airport**, which is on Hanlan's Point in Toronto's harbour, close to downtown. From the airport, there's a free minibus service to the *Royal York Hotel*, on the corner of Front Street West and York Street.

ARRIVAL

BY BUS

Toronto's **bus station** is located on Edward Street at Bay Street, metres from Dundas Street West and a five-minute walk from the subway stop at the corner of Yonge and Dundas streets. If you're arriving late at night, note that the bus station's immediate environs are unsavoury, but it only takes a couple of minutes to reach more reassuring parts of downtown. Nonetheless, if you're travelling alone and late at night, it's probably best to take a taxi to your ultimate destination.

BY TRAIN

All incoming trains arrive at **Union Railway Station**, at the junction of Bay Street and Front Street West and the heart of Toronto's public transport system. The station complex includes a subway station and also holds the main terminal for the GO trains and buses that service the city's suburbs. Details of GO services are available at their ticket offices here, or call toll free ☎1-888/438-6646 (within Toronto call ☎869-3200).

BY CAR

From Niagara Falls and points along Lake Ontario, most traffic arrives via the **QEW** (Queen Elizabeth Way), which funnels into the **Gardiner Expressway**, an elevated motorway that cuts across the southern side of downtown, just south of Front Street.

From the east and west, the quickest approach is on **Hwy-401**, which sweeps through the city's suburbs north of downtown. Driving in from the north, take **Hwy-400**, which intersects with Hwy-401 northwest of the centre, or **Hwy-404**, which meets Hwy-401 northeast of the centre.

Note that on all routes you can expect delays during rush hours (roughly 7.30–9.30am and 4.30–6.30pm).

To relieve congestion on Hwy-401, an alternative motorway, **Hwy-407ETR**, has been built further north on the city's edge. It was North America's first all-electronic toll highway: instead of toll booths, vehicles are identified either by an electronic tag or a license plate photo, and the invoice is posted later. Toll charges vary according to the time of day, the day of the week and the distance travelled. During peak periods (Mon–Fri 5.30–9.30am & 4–7pm), the charge is 10¢ per kilometre, day-time off-peak costs 8¢, night time 4¢. If you rent a car, be aware that rental companies slap on an extra administration charge (of around $10) if you take their vehicles on this road.

Information

The excellent **Ontario Tourism Travel Information Centre** (Mon–Fri 10am–9pm, Sat 9.30am–7pm & Sun noon–5pm; ☎1-800/ONTARIO, within Toronto ☎314-0944; ⓦ*www.ontariotravel.net*), on Level 1 of the Eaton shopping centre at the corner of Yonge and Dundas streets, stocks a comprehensive range of information on all the major attractions in Toronto and throughout Ontario. Of particular interest here are the free city maps; the *Ride Guide* to the city's transport system; and accommodation and entertainment details in the monthly magazine *Where*. They will also book hotel accommodation on your behalf both in Toronto and across all of Ontario.

Alternatively, the Info T.O. visitor information centre (daily: May–Sept 8am–8pm, Oct–April 9am–5pm) is located in the city's Convention Centre at 255 Front St West, a

INFORMATION

TORONTO ON THE INTERNET

Toronto is extremely well represented on the **Internet**. Most of the city's main tourist attractions have their own sites, as do an increasing number of hotels and restaurants. Individual business Web sites are listed throughout the guide: below you'll find a few of the more helpful and interesting general sites on offer.

Art Gallery of Ontario. Ⓦ*www.ago.on.ca*
A comprehensive site providing high-quality reproductions of the gallery's key paintings and details of its temporary exhibitions. Plus, there's information on the museum's many programs, including lectures, art courses and the museum's film schedule.

Beaches International Jazz Festival. Ⓦ*www.beachesjazz.com*
The official site of this free four-day festival held in late July contains a full schedule and performer information, as well as advice for would-be performers on how to get a gig there.

City of Toronto. Ⓦ*www.city.toronto.on.ca*
The City's government site provides links to a series of city maps which you can use to pinpoint local amenities, as well as providing an up-to-the minute guide to events such as the free concerts held from June to September as part of Toronto's Music Garden program.

Gay Toronto. Ⓦ*www.gaytoronto.com*
A useful starting point if you're looking to find out what's where on the male scene, but it has no information for women.

couple of minutes' walk west from Union Station. Privately run, they are more geared up for selling tour tickets than providing information, though they do have a reasonable supply of free literature on the city and its environs. They are not, however, nearly as well organised as the Ontario

There's a useful bulletin board service which has an accommodation section.

Ice hockey. ⓦ*www.canadianhockey.ca*
If you wanted proof that Canadians are passionate about their national sport, this will do; it is operated by the Canadian Hockey Association.

Moltencore – Toronto Club Guide. ⓦ*www.moltencore.com /club.html*
This internet music shop contains an admittedly partisan guide to the city's drinking and live music venues.

Niagara Parks Commission. ⓦ*www.infoniagara.com*
Information on all the major attractions in and around Niagara Falls, and details on accommodation and restaurants. There is also a link to the local *Sheraton Hotel*'s "falls cam", which provides live pictures of the Falls.

Ontario Tourism. ⓦ*www.ontariotravel.net*.
If you're planning a trip around Ontario, surf over to this page for well-organised and regularly updated information on everything from accommodation to tours throughout the region.

Toronto Star. ⓦ*www.thestar.com*
The best bet for Toronto news, sports and weather updates. Plus, there's a well-updated "what's on" section covering local music, film and TV schedules.

Tribe. ⓦ*www.tribe.ca*
This free magazine focusing on the dance music scene in Canada is available in full online and gives frequently updated details on the club and rave scene in Toronto.

Tourism Centre. Finally, Tourism Toronto, the city's official visitor and convention bureau, operates a telephone information line that can handle most city queries and will make hotel reservations (Mon–Fri 8.30am–5pm, Sat 9am–5pm, Sun 10am–5pm; ⓣ203-2500 or 1/800-363-1990; ⓦ*www .torontotourism.com*).

The colour maps at the back of this book should be all you'll need for central Toronto, but if you need something covering the whole of the city, you'll find other maps at most bookshops and newsstands. *MapArt* is the best manufacturer: their comprehensive *Toronto Pocket Street Atlas* costs $7.95, and their large-scale general Toronto map is $2.95. They also publish an excellent *Ontario Road Atlas* book for $19.95.

Getting around

Fast, frequent, safe and efficient, the city's public transport is overseen by the Toronto Transit Commission (TTC; ☏393-4636 daily 8am–5pm; ⓦ*www.ttc.ca*), whose integrated network of subways, buses and streetcars serves virtually every corner of the city. With the exception of downtown, where all the major sights are within easy walking distance of each other, your best option is to use public transport to hop between attractions – especially in the cold of winter or the sultry summertime.

Yonge Street is Toronto's principal north–south artery. Main drags perpendicular to Yonge use this intersection to change from west to east – Queen Street West, for example, becomes Queen Street East when it crosses Yonge. Note, therefore, that 1000 Queen Street West is a long way from 1000 Queen Street East.

THE SUBWAY

Toronto's **subway**, the core of the city's public transport, pivots on a simple, two-line system (see map number 5 at the back of the book). The Bloor-Danforth line cuts east to west along Bloor Street and the Yonge-University-Spadina line forms a loop heading north from Union Station along University Avenue and Yonge Street. Transferring between the two lines is possible at three stations only: Spadina, St George and Bloor-Yonge.

The subway operates Mon–Sat 6am–1am, Sun 9am–1am. A single journey costs $2 (local students and seniors $1.40, and children under two travel free), and **tickets** are available at all subway stations. Metallic **tokens** can also be used, but are impossibly small and difficult to keep track of. More economically, a batch of five tickets or tokens can be bought for $8.50, $17 for ten, at any station and at most convenience stores and newsstands. Each ticket or token entitles passengers to one complete journey of any length on the TTC system. If this involves more than one type of transport, it is necessary to get a paper **transfer** at your point of entry (there are automatic machines that provide transfers at all subway stations). A **day pass** costs $7 and provides one adult with unlimited TTC travel all day on Saturdays and after 9.30am on weekdays. On Sundays, the same pass becomes a terrific deal for families: it covers up to six people – only two of which can be adults.

The TTC also runs several **commuter lines**. The most useful is the **Scarborough Rapid Transit**, a streetcar service that picks up passengers at the eastern terminus of the Bloor-Danforth subway line and makes a five-stop trek to the heart of Scarborough, a Toronto suburb (see p.85). Transfers from the rest of the TTC network are valid on the Scarborough Rapid Transit.

GO trains – express links to the city's various suburbs and neighbouring towns – arrive and depart from Union Station. There are no free transfers from the TTC system to

GO train lines, but they are primarily used by commuters and are of little use for tourists based in the city.

BUSES AND STREETCARS

The subway provides the backbone of the TTC system, but its services are faithfully supplemented by buses and street-cars. The system couldn't be simpler, as a bus and/or street-car station adjoins every major subway stop. Prices are the same as for the subway, and each ticket or token entitles pas-sengers to one complete journey of any length on the TTC system. Transfers to the subway are available from the driver.

The TTC has a **Request Stop Program**, which allows women travelling alone and late at night to get off buses whenever they want, and not necessarily at regular TTC stops.

TAXIS

Taxis cruise the city in abundance and can be hailed from any street corner. Give the driver your destination and ask the approximate price before you start. **Fares** are generally reasonable based on a fixed tariff of $2.50 for the first .235km and 25¢ for every .235km thereafter. Thus, the fare from the airport to downtown will set you back about $40, and a ride from Union Station to the far side of Cabbagetown should cost around $10. Of the multitude of cab companies to choose from, the most reliable tend to be Co-op Cabs (☏504-2667) or Diamond Taxicab (☏366-6868).

Toronto taxi drivers expect a tip of 10–15 percent on the total fare.

TOURS

Generally speaking, the **sightseeing tours** on offer in Toronto are pretty uninspiring – many seem to involve an inordinate amount of time on the bus, and not much in the way of sights. That said, **Gray Line** (℡594-3310; Ⓦ*www.grayline.ca*) operates fairly enjoyable city tours, the most inexpensive of which is a two-hour zip round the main attractions for $27 (two tours daily, April to mid-Nov). They also run ten-hour tours to Niagara Falls (three daily; $110).

Alternatively, the double-decker buses and old streetcars of **Toronto Olde Town Tours** (℡1-800/350-0398, within Toronto ℡614-0999) shuttle around the downtown area from April to mid-October. You can hop on and off as you please (buses appear at regular intervals of one every 30min mid-May to mid-Oct, every 60min April to mid-May; daily 8.30am–4pm), and a full-day's ticket costs $29 (seniors & students $27). The best places to join the tour are the stops beside the CN Tower (Front Street West and John), in the bus parking lot outside Casa Loma, and at the *Delta Chelsea Inn* (Gerrard Street West and Yonge).

There are also a number of speciality companies offering tours of Toronto on bike, foot and even by helicopter. For further details, pick up the annual *Visitor Guide* at either of the city's tourist offices (see p.11).

Downtown Toronto

The skyscrapers etched across **downtown Toronto's** skyline attest to the clout of a city that has shed its dusty provincialism to become the economic and cultural focus of English-speaking Canada. There's no false modesty here, beginning with Toronto's mascot, the **CN Tower**, and continuing with the **SkyDome** and the herd of tower blocks that dominate the nearby **banking district**. Modern behemoths like the **Toronto Dominion Centre** and the gold-coated towers of the **Royal Bank Plaza** are beacons of modern-day prosperity, but the downtown area is also dotted with older skyrises – the **Dominion Bank** and the **Canada Permanent Trust building** for example – whose sumptuous designs (circa 1920) once trumpeted the aspirations of previous generations. Toronto's business elite also funded downtown's two most enjoyable art galleries, the **Toronto Dominion Gallery of Inuit Art** and the superb **Thomson Gallery**, which boasts a connoisseur's collection of Canadian paintings.

At Queen Street, the business district gives way to the main **shopping** area, which revolves around the enormous **Eaton Centre**. Immediately to the west is **City Hall**, another striking example of modern design, and the **Art Gallery of Ontario**, which houses the province's finest collection of paintings and a whole gallery of sculptures by

Henry Moore. Finally, on the western periphery of downtown is **Fort York**, a pleasing reconstruction of the British fort established here in 1793.

Downtown is best explored on **foot**, though the tower blocks can be a bit claustrophobic and local complaints that the city centre lacks a human dimension are legion. To be fair, this sentiment has been taken into account, and although it's a bit late in the day, efforts have been made to make the downtown core more amenable with plazas, pavement cafés and street sculptures.

THE CN TOWER AND METRO CENTRE

Map 3, E6 & F6. 301 Front St West. Jan–April daily 9am–10pm, May–Dec daily 8am–11pm; Observation floor $16, seniors $14, children $11; extra for Skypod ($5.50). Subway Union Station. ⊤868-6937; ⓦ*www.cntower.ca*.

Much to the dismay of many Torontonians, the **CN Tower** has become the city's symbol. It is touted on much of the city's promotional literature, features on thousands of postcards and holiday snaps, and has become the obligatory start to most tourist itineraries. From anywhere in the city you can't miss its slender form poking high above the skyline, reminding some of French novelist Guy de Maupassant's quip about another famous tower: "I like to lunch at the Eiffel Tower because that's the only place in Paris I can't see it."

Unlikely as it may seem, the celebrity status of the CN Tower was entirely unforeseen, and its origins were plain and utilitarian. In the Sixties, the Canadian Broadcasting Company (CBC) teamed up with Canadian National (CN), the railway conglomerate, to propose the construction of a bigger and better transmission antenna. CBC eventually withdrew, but CN, who owned the land and saw a chance for profit, forged ahead. Much to their surprise, they found that the project stirred intense public interest –

so much so that long before the tower was completed in April 1975, it was clear that its potential as a tourist sight would be huge: broadcasting only accounts for about twenty percent of the tower's income these days, and the rest of the revenue is provided by the two million tourists who throng here annually. Come early (especially on school holidays) to avoid the crowds.

Only die-hard critics could deny the sleek elegance of the CN Tower, which tapers to a minaret-thin point 553.33m above the city centre just off Front Street West. To get there, follow the signs at the corner of Front and John streets, which direct you up the stairs and over the ramp spanning the rail lines to the main entrance. The tower is the tallest structure in the world, and details of its construction are provided in a series of touch-screen displays near the entrance on the **Mezzanine Level**. The background information is helpful – especially tidbits revealing that the tower is hit by lightning between sixty and eighty times a year – but the nearby "Daredevil Thrills" film simulations (extra charge) of bungee jumping, tightrope walking and the like are eminently missable.

From the foot of the tower, leg-liquefying glass-fronted **elevators** whisk you up the outside of the building to the indoor and outdoor **Lookout Level** galleries at 346m. These circular galleries provide views over the whole of the city, which lies flattened and without much perspective, though markers help by signalling the most conspicuous sights. This is also where you'll find the *360 Restaurant* (which slowly revolves around the tower, taking 72 minutes to make one revolution) and the vertigo shock of the reinforced **glass floor** – a thrill that more than justifies the tower's fee. You're still 100m from the top of the tower, however, and a separate set of lifts carry visitors up to the **Sky Pod** – though this confined little gallery doesn't justify the extra expense.

Recently revamped and enlarged, the **Metro Convention Centre**, adjacent to the CN Tower, looks pretty dowdy from its back entrance on Front Street West. But the main entrance, on Bremner Boulevard, is chic and smart, with acres of glass and steel, and a foyer with a delightful mosaic of frogs, spawn and turtles – *The Turtle Pond*. Similarly engaging is the sculpture of two giant woodpeckers pecking away at a steel tree outside the main entrance.

THE SKYDOME

Map 3, D6 & E6. 1 Blue Jays Way, off Front Street West. Frequent guided tours depending on event schedules; telephone for latest timetable; $10.50. Subway Union Station. Ⓣ341-2770; Ⓦ*www .skydome.com*.

Next door to the CN Tower is the **SkyDome**, home to two major Toronto sports teams – the Blue Jays baseball team and the Argonauts of Canadian football fame. The stadium seats 53,000 and is also used for special events and concerts, sometimes within the **SkyTent**, which encloses a part of the stadium to create a more intimate arena.

Opened in 1989, the SkyDome was the first stadium in the world to have a fully retractable roof – it only takes twenty minutes to cover the stadium's eight acres of turf and terrace. It was an extraordinary feat of engineering (four gigantic roof panels mounted on rail tracks), and one that was much touted by the city. Unfortunately, the end result was pretty ugly and remains so despite the best efforts of artist Michael Snow, who added a pair of giant cartoon sculptures to the exterior – *The Audience Part 1* and *Part 2* – in an effort to beef up its aesthetic appeal. The sculptures are endearing, but when the roof is closed the SkyDome still looks like a giant armadillo.

Michael Snow's work is also featured
at the Eaton Centre; see p.39.

Guided tours, worth it only if you're sticking around for a sporting event, last an hour and begin with a fifteen-minute film about the stadium's construction. The ensuing walking tour takes in the media centre, a dressing room and a stroll on the field.

For information on the Blue Jays and the Argonauts see "Sports", p.248. Toronto's other leading sports teams are the Maple Leafs of the National Hockey League and the Raptors of the National Basketball Association. Both play in the Air Canada Centre, 40 Bay Street, a short walk from Union Station. Again, see "Sports", p.248, for further details.

UNION STATION

Map 3, G6 & H6. Subway Union Station.

From the Convention Centre, the **Skywalk** is a sheltered walkway that leads to **Union Station**, at Front Street West and Bay Street, a distinguished Beaux Arts structure designed in 1907 and finally completed in 1927. The exterior is imposing, with its long serenade of Neoclassical columns, but its interior is the real highlight, the vast **main hall** boasting a coffered and tiled ceiling of graceful design. Like other North American railway stations of the period, Union Station has the flavour of a medieval cathedral, with muffled sounds echoing through its stone cloisters and daylight filtering through the high arched windows. Its grandiose quality was quite deliberate. In the days when the steam train was the most popular form of transport, architects were keen to glorify the train station, and, in this case, to conjure up images of Canada's vastness: a frieze bearing the names of all the Canadian cities that could be reached by rail runs round the hall.

THE ROYAL YORK HOTEL

Map 3, G5. Subway Union Station.

Directly opposite the railway station, the **Royal York Hotel**, at 100 Front St West, was the largest and tallest building in the British Empire when it opened in 1929. It, too, was designed in the Beaux Arts style by Montreal architects Ross and Macdonald. Instead of the formal symmetries of Union Station, however, the *Royal York* has a cascading, irregular facade with stylistic flourishes reminiscent of a French château. It was built to impress – the hotel had its own concert hall, mini-hospital, a 12,000-book library, and each of the hotel's one thousand rooms had a radio, private shower and bath – and soon became a byword for luxury, where every well-heeled visitor in the city stayed. Over the years its pre-eminent position has been usurped by other newer hotels, but a recent refurbishment has restored it as a favourite with visiting big shots; see p.129 for full details on what it costs to stay here.

THE BANKING DISTRICT

Map 3, G4 through I5.

Union Station and the *Royal York Hotel* mark the southern boundary of the **banking district**, home to many of the city's most impressive buildings, from flamboyant 1920s high-rises to dynamic, modernistic skyscrapers sheathed in glass and steel. It's also a district of bizarre juxtapositions: old, low buildings packed tight alongside their mighty, modern neighbours.

ECCENTRIC ZONING LAWS

In one of the city's stranger ordinances, Toronto's buildings were decreed to have a "notional maximum altitude". Owners of historic properties were not allowed to extend their buildings upwards, but they were permitted to sell the empty space between their roofs and the notional maximum to builders of new structures. Consequently, developers literally bought empty space and added it on to the maximum height they were already allowed for their buildings, thus creating the sky-scrapers that the original ordinance seemed to forbid.

The arrangement enhanced neither the old nor the new, and was quickly followed up by an even stranger agreement. By the late 1980s, preservationists had convinced the city that no more of the city's old buildings should be demolished. Developers, however, still wanted to build new buildings down-town, and several deals emerged where a new complex would incorporate or literally engulf the old – the most extreme exam-ple being BCE Place at the corner of Yonge and Front streets; see p.235.

Royal Bank Plaza and the Toronto Dominion Centre

Map 3, H5.

Opposite Union Station, the two massive towers of the **Royal Bank Plaza**, 200 Bay St, were designed by local architect Boris Zerafa during the architectural boom of the mid-1970s. Each is completely coated with a thin layer of gold, and despite Zerafa's assertion that the gold simply added texture to his creation, it's hard not to believe that the Royal Bank wanted to show off a bit, too.

In between the *Royal York Hotel* and the Royal Bank, a narrow stone stairway climbs up from Front Street West to a tiny plaza overseen by a phalanx of skyscrapers. It is decorated by Catherine Widgery's *City People* (1989), a folksy set of life-size, metal figures attached to the stairway's walls. The walkway continues down to Wellington Street West, just a few metres from the southern (IBM) tower of the **Toronto Dominion Centre**, whose four reflective black blocks straddle Wellington Street between Bay and York. Arguably the most appealing of the city's modern skyscrapers, the four towers are shorn of decoration, but as an ensemble they achieve an austere beauty that can't help but impress.

The Toronto Dominion Gallery of Inuit Art

Map 3, H5. IBM Tower, Toronto Dominion Centre, 79 Wellington St West at Bay. Mon–Fri 8am–6pm, Sat & Sun 10am–4pm; free. Subway King.

The **Toronto Dominion Gallery of Inuit Art** boasts an outstanding collection of over a hundred pieces of Inuit sculpture. The collection, spread over two levels, is owned by the Dominion Bank, who commissioned a panel of experts to celebrate Canada's Centennial in 1965 by collecting the best of post-war Inuit art. The gallery contains examples of all the favourite themes of Inuit sculpture, primarily animal and human studies supplemented by a smattering of metamorphic figures: a hunter might transform into a man-bear, and the shaman (priest) might become a bird to assist with a spiritual journey. Other sculptures depict deities, particularly Nuliayuk (or Sedna) the sea goddess. Inuit religious belief was short on theology, but its encyclopedic animism populated the Arctic with spirits and gods, the subject of all manner of Inuit folk tales. Christianity destroyed this traditional faith, but the legends survived and continue to feature prominently in Inuit art. Most of the sculptures are in **soapstone**, a greyish-blue

THE BANKING DISTRICT

stone that is easy to carve, though there are bone, ivory and caribou-antler creations, too.

In the foyer, beside the revolving doors, the gallery begins with Johnny Inukpuk's raw, elemental *Mother Feeding Child* of 1962, an exquisite piece in which a woman holds her child in an all-encompassing embrace. Hailing from Port Harrison, on the eastern shores of Hudson Bay, Inukpuk was one of the first Inuit sculptors to establish a reputation in the south, and his work has been collected since the late Fifties. There's another of his soapstone sculptures in the foyer: *Tattooed Woman*, a fine almost fierce portrayal of a woman in traditional attire whose eyes stare out into the distance.

Upstairs, distributed among a dozen glass cabinets, is a superb selection of soapstones. In the first cabinet are two striking representations of Sedna, one by Saggiak, the other by Kenojuak Ashevak, both carved in Cape Dorset in 1965. Half-woman, half-seal, **Sedna**, the goddess of the sea and sometimes of life itself, is one of the key figures of Inuit mythology. Her story is a sad one. She was deceived by a young man who posed as a hunter but was in fact a powerful shaman. Sedna married him and he promptly spirited her away from her family. Sedna's father gave chase and rescued his daughter, but on the return journey they were assailed by a violent storm conjured by the shaman. Petrified, the father threw his daughter overboard, and when she repeatedly attempted to get back into the boat, he chopped off her fingers and then her hands. These bits and pieces became whales, seals, walruses and fish, but she herself sank to the depths of the ocean, where she remains.

Other striking works to look out for include Joe Talirunili's *Migration*, a dynamic stone and antler carving depicting a traditional *umiak* (boat) crowded with migrating Inuit, and a magnificent *Bear* by Cape Dorset's Pauta Saila. The bear is crudely carved, but the jaws are all that's needed to convey the animal's ferocity, and the blurring of the trunk and the legs gives the appearance of great strength.

There's more top-quality Inuit art at the Art Gallery of Ontario (see p.45).

St Andrew's Presbyterian Church and around

Map 3, H5. Subway St Andrew.

Crossing over Wellington Street, and walking between the other three towers of the Toronto Dominion Centre, you will pass Joe Fafard's herd of grazing cows – seven extraordinarily realistic bronze **statues**. From here, it's a short detour west along King Street to **St Andrew's Presbyterian Church**, 75 Simcoe St (daily 9am–4pm; free). Marooned among the city's skyscrapers, this handsome sandstone church is a reminder of an older Toronto, and its Romanesque Revival towers and gables have a distinctly Norman appearance. Built in 1876 for a predominantly Scottish congregation, the church has a delightful interior. Its cherrywood pews and balcony slope down towards the chancel, and dappled light streams through the stained-glass windows. Most importantly, St Andrew's has an admirable history of social action. Since the earliest days of the city's settlement, this and many other Toronto churches have played a leading role in the campaign against poverty and homelessness. It is perhaps a bit surprising, therefore, that the church basement has been turned into the **48th Highlanders' Museum** (Wed & Thurs 10am–3pm; donation), honouring the regiment that has attracted Scottish Canadians to its colours since its formation in 1891. The museum displays uniforms and weaponry alongside an intriguing collection of old photographs,

THE BANKING DISTRICT

27

tracking through the regiment's involvement in the Boer and both world wars.

Across the street, **Roy Thompson Hall** (see p.206) is the home of the Toronto Symphony Orchestra. It was completed in 1982 to a design by Canada's Arthur Erickson, and although it looks like an upturned soup bowl by day, at night its glass-panelled walls transform its appearance with a skein of filtered light. Next door, **Metro Hall**'s trio of glass-and-steel office blocks is set around an attractive plaza of water fountains and lawns. Built in the early Nineties, the complex represents a break from the brash, harshly designed buildings of previous decades (like the unappealing **Canadian Broadcasting Company** just to the south, across Wellington Street), and a move toward more fluid, people-friendly designs.

From Roy Thompson Hall, it's a twenty-minute stroll to Fort York (see p.32) – or take the King Street streetcar (#508 or 504) to Bathurst and walk from there.

The Design Exchange and the CIBC buildings

Map 3, H5.

The old **Toronto Stock Exchange**, at 234 Bay St and King Street West, has been mutilated by its incorporation within a skyrise that imitates – but doesn't match – the sober blocks of the adjacent Toronto Dominion Centre (see p.24). Nevertheless, the facade has survived, and its stone lintel is decorated with muscular, Art Deco carvings of men at work. The frieze was given a political twist with the inclusion of a top-hatted figure – the capitalist – who dips his hand into a worker's pocket, a subversive subtext by an unknown stonemason that seems to have gone unnoticed

THE BANKING DISTRICT

by the stockbrokers. Inside, the ground floor is routinely modern, but the trading floor upstairs has been preserved in all its Art Deco pomp, its geometric panelling decorated with a series of delightful ribbon murals celebrating industry. On the ground floor, the Stock Exchange now accommodates the temporary exhibitions of the **Design Exchange** (Tues–Fri 10am–6pm, Sat & Sun noon–5pm; admission charged for some exhibitions), or "DX", whose purpose is to foster innovative design. Recent displays have covered everything from local furniture design to prototype plans for making the city more environmentally conscious.

Across the street, the formidable **Canadian Imperial Bank of Commerce**, 243 Bay St, is a stainless-steel behemoth erected in the 1970s to a design by world-renowned architect I.M. Pei, famed for his sleek modern designs, like Boston's John Hancock Tower and the glass pyramids at the Louvre museum in Paris. Pei's CIBC tower, with its sheer, overweening size and severe angles, is a sharp departure from the design used for the former **CIBC building**, next door to the north at 25 King St West. This structure went up just after the stock market crash of 1929, and its exterior is relatively severe except at the main entrance, where the cathedral-like doors are draped with carved reliefs that beckon you into a lavish interior of magnificent chandeliers, gilt-coffered ceilings, and sinuous marble tracery.

The Bay-Adelaide development

Map 3, H4.

Walking north from King Street West on Bay Street, turn right on Temperance Street for a glimpse of the **Bay-Adelaide** development, the city's biggest real estate fiasco. The big wheels of the business community decided to plonk a mammoth office complex right here in the mid-1980s, when property speculation was at a fever pitch.

Millions of dollars were invested, but in 1988 the bottom fell out of the office rental market just as construction work began. In near panic, the developers cancelled further work on the project, leaving a scattering of foundations and a rough, concrete block six storeys high that was intended to be the core of the main skyscraper and now stands forlorn here on Temperance Street. Many Torontonians delighted in the collapse of the project, chuckling at the concrete stump, which was nicknamed the "Magnificent Hulk" by a *Toronto Star* columnist. What will happen to the site now is anybody's guess, but further development seems unlikely.

The Dominion, Royal and Trader's banks

Map 3, I5.

At the east end of Temperance Street, turn right along Yonge Street and you soon reach the handsome, sturdy stonework of the **Dominion Bank**, at 1 King St West (Mon–Thurs 9.30am–4pm, Fri 9.30am–5pm; free). Inside, a luxurious marble stairway curves up to the main banking hall, a spacious room framed by fluted marble columns and graced by brass grills.

On the opposite side of Yonge Street, at 2 King St East, the **Royal Bank** was designed by Ross and Macdonald, who also created Union Station and the *Royal York Hotel* (see 23). Clumsily modernised, the ground floor is less than inspired, but the austere symmetries of the building as a whole still impress and so do the classical motifs that were gracefully worked into the main frieze.

A quick step to the south, **Trader's Bank**, 67 Yonge St at King (no public access), was Toronto's first skyscraper, a fifteen-storey structure completed in 1906. The owners were apprehensive that the size of the building might prompt accusations of vanity, so they insisted on overhanging eaves and stumpy classical columns in an effort to make it look shorter. They need not have bothered: as soon as it was finished the bank was thronged by visitors and the top floor was turned into an observation deck. Newer skyscrapers now dwarf the bank and the once unhindered view is long gone.

On the stairway of the Dominion Bank, look out for the portrait of James Austin, who was the bank's first president and the owner of Spadina House (see p.70).

THE HOCKEY HALL OF FAME

Map 3, I5. 30 Yonge St at Front Street West. Sept to mid-June Mon–Fri 10am–5pm, Sat 9.30am–6pm, Sun 10.30am–5pm; mid-June to Aug Mon–Sat 9.30am–6pm, Sun 10am–6pm; $12, children under 13 $7. Subway Union Station. ⓣ360-7735; ⓦ*www.hhof.com*. From Trader's Bank, it's a short haul south to the **Hockey Hall of Fame**, a highly commercialised, ultra-modern tribute to Canada's national sport – though you wouldn't think so from outside. The only part of the complex visible from the street is the old **Bank of Montreal** building, a Neoclassical edifice dating back to 1885. The bank is actually one of Toronto's finer structures – its intricately carved stonework is adorned by a dainty sequence of pediments and pilasters – but its incorporation into the Hall of Fame is awkward. The bank's entrance has been blocked off and the interior bowdlerised to house a collection of hockey trophies.

The **entrance** to the Hall of Fame is below ground in the adjacent BCE Place (see p.235), a glitzy retail complex on the west side of Yonge Street between Front and Wellington streets. Inside the museum are a series of exhibition areas, with particularly enjoyable sections on the evolution of the goalie's mask and a replica of the Montreal

THE HOCKEY HALL OF FAME

Canadiens' locker room. Other areas, including endless bio-graphical displays on the sport's great names and details of the various National Hockey League (NHL) teams, are geared to the most rabid of fans, but there's plenty to keep the less-obsessed entertained as well. Highlights include the mini ice-rink where visitors can blast away at hockey pucks and a small theatre showing films of hockey's most celebrat-ed games. The film of the 1972 "World Summit Series" between the USSR and Canada is filled with Cold War res-onance and is gripping stuff even for the non-enthusiast. Finally, the **trophy room**, located inside the old bank, contains the very first **Stanley Cup**. The trophy was origi-nally donated by Lord Stanley, the Governor General of Canada, in 1893. An English aristocrat, Stanley was con-vinced that sports raised the mettle of the men of the British Empire. Concerned that Canadian ice hockey lacked a trophy of any stature, he inaugurated the Stanley Cup, which has become the defining emblem of the sport.

- -
For more on ice hockey, see "Sports" on p.248.
- -

FORT YORK

Map 3, A6. Garrison Road, off Fleet Street. Late May to Aug daily 10am–5pm; Sept to late May Mon–Fri 10am–4pm, Sat & Sun 10am–5pm; $5. Bathurst streetcar (#511). ⊤392-6907.

Modern-day Toronto traces its origins to **Fort York**, built on the shores of Lake Ontario to bolster British control of the Great Lakes in 1793. It was, however, never properly fortified (partly because of a lack of funds and partly because it was too remote to command much attention), and even though the township of York had become the capital of Upper Canada, within ten years the stockade was in a state of disrepair. In 1811 the deterioration in Anglo-American relations put the fort back on active duty. Its main military achievement during this time, though, was entirely accidental: forced to evacuate the fort in 1813, the British blew up the gunpowder magazine, but underestimated the force of the explosion. They killed ten of their own men, but also 250 of the advancing enemy, including American general Zebulon Pike. After the war, Fort York was refurbished and its garrison made a considerable contribution to the development of Toronto, as York was renamed in 1834. The British army moved out in 1870 and their Canadian replacements stayed for another sixty years, by which time landfill had pushed the lakeshore to the south; nowadays the fort is marooned amidst a tatty area in the shadow of the Gardiner Expressway.

Opened as a museum in 1934, the site is staffed by guides who provide informative and free hour-long tours; or you can wander around on your own. The carefully restored **ramparts** are low-lying, thick and constructed in a zigzag pattern, both to mitigate against enemy artillery and to cultivate various lines of fire. They enclose a haphazard sequence of log, stone and brick buildings, notably a couple of well-preserved **blockhouses**, complete with heavy timbers and snipers' loopholes, the **Officers' Quarters** and a stone **powder magazine**, built with two-metre-thick walls and spark-proof copper and brass fixtures. Also here, the **Blue Barracks**, or junior officers' quarters, have an absorbing exhibition on the various military crises that afflicted Canada from 1792 to 1967, including the War of 1812 and the curious affair of the Fenian Raids (see overleaf). The displays in the Blue Barracks are supplemented, in **Blockhouse No. 2**, with exhibits focusing on the history of Fort York and the various bits and pieces archaeologists have found here – buckles, brooches, tunic buttons and so forth.

It takes about twenty minutes to walk to the fort from Union Station. Follow Front Street West to its end, turn

FORT YORK

THE FENIAN RAIDS

During the American Civil War the British continued to trade with the Confederacy, much to the chagrin of the Union army in the North. After the war, the **Fenian Brotherhood**, formed by Irish exiles in New York in 1859, believed that the US should turn its military might north and seize Canada. Their tactics were simple: they organised a series of cross-border raids, hoping that if they provoked a military retaliation from the British, Washington would be forced to invade. The most serious Fenian raid crossed the border in 1866 with 1000 men. The British drove the Fenians out, but Congress didn't take the bait.

left down Bathurst Street and, after crossing the railway bridge, take the signposted footpath on the right that leads to the fort's rear entrance. To reach the front entrance, take either the Bathurst streetcar (#511) or streetcar #509 from Union Station, and get off at the foot of Garrison Road, from where it's a ten-minute walk.

CITY HALL AND NATHAN PHILLIPS SQUARE

Map 3, H2 & H3. Subway Queen.

Nathan Phillips Square, one of Toronto's most distinctive landmarks, lies on Queen Street, just north of the banking district. Laid out by the Finnish architect Viljo Revell, the square is framed by an elevated walkway and focuses on a reflecting pool, which becomes a skating rink in winter. The square is overlooked by Toronto's **City Hall**, whose curved glass and concrete towers are fronted by *The Archer*, a Henry Moore sculpture that resembles a giant propeller. Surprising as it seems today, when such designs are comparatively commonplace, Revell won all sorts of awards for this project, which was the last word in dynamism in the 1960s, but, with its rain-stained piers, has since become a rather jaded symbol of urban planning.

The imperial connection is recalled by the statue of Winston Churchill located in the southwest corner of Nathan Phillips Square. Inscribed upon it is a quotation from one of his most famous wartime speeches, given to the Canadian House of Commons on December 30, 1941: "(The French) generals advised France's divided cabinet 'In three weeks, the English will have their necks wrung like a chicken'. Some chicken! Some neck!"

In its creation, however, the square became a catalyst for change in Toronto. Named after its sponsor, Nathan Phillips, Toronto's first Jewish mayor, the space suddenly provided the kind of public gathering place the city so sorely lacked, kick-starting the process by which the private Toronto of the 1950s became the extrovert metropolis of today.

Had Revell's grand scheme been carried out fully, the city would have bulldozed the **Old City Hall**, a flamboyant pseudo-Romanesque building on the east side of the square. Completed in 1899, it was designed by Edward J. Lennox, who developed a fractious relationship with his paymasters on the city council. They had a point: the original cost of the building had been estimated at $1.77 million, but Lennox spent an extra $750,000 and took all of eight years to finish the project. Nevertheless, Lennox had the last laugh, carving gargoyle-like representations of the city's fathers on the arches at the top of the front steps and placing his name on each side of the building – something the city council had expressly forbidden him to do.

Edward J. Lennox was also responsible for the
construction of Casa Loma; see p.68.

THE THOMSON GALLERY

Map 3, I3. The Bay department store, 9th Floor, 176 Yonge St at Queen Street. Mon–Sat 11am–5pm; $2.50. Subway Queen.

Across the street from the Old City Hall, on the 9th Floor of The Bay department store (see p.234), you'll find the **Thomson Gallery**, which offers an outstanding introduction to many of Canada's finest artists, especially the Group of Seven (see p.48). Well organised and labelled, highlights include an impressive selection of paintings by Lawren Harris, like his surreal *Lake Superior* of 1923, and, amongst a fine sample of canvases by J.E.H. MacDonald, both his superb *Rowan Berries*, painted in 1922, and the startling sweep of *October Shower Gleam*. Tom Thomson is well represented by over thirty preparatory sketches of lakes and canyons, waterfalls and forests, each small panel displaying the vibrant, blotchy colours that characterise his work. Larger Thomson paintings include the sticky dabs of colour of *Maple Springs* and his *Autumn's Garland*, an oil on panel finished the year before he died. Arthur Lismer weighs in with the dappled oranges and yellows of *Sumach and Maple*, while the talents of A.J. Casson are perhaps best recalled by the jumble of snow-covered roofs of his *House Tops in the Ward*. Emily Carr, a contemporary – but not a member – of the Group has several characteristic works here too, including a dark and haunting *Thunderbird* of 1930.

The gallery's assortment of works by early and mid-nineteenth century Canadians is less distinguished than the Group of Seven paintings, but there are still some fascinating canvases, namely the curiously unflattering *Portrait of*

CORNELIUS KRIEGHOFF

A prolific artist, **Cornelius Krieghoff** (1815–72) had a roller-coaster life. Born to a German father and Dutch mother, he emigrated to New York in 1836 and promptly joined the US army, serving in the Second Seminole War in Florida. Discharged in 1840, Krieghoff immediately re-enlisted, claimed three months' advance pay and deserted, hot-footing it to Montreal with the French-Canadian woman he had met and married in New York. Montreal was a disaster – no-one would buy his paintings – but when he moved to Quebec City in 1852, he found a ready market for his work among the British officers who were garrisoned here, along with their well-heeled friends. This was the start of Krieghoff's most productive period, and in the next eight years he churned out dozens of souvenir pictures – finely detailed, anecdotal scenes of French Canadian life that are his best work. In the early 1860s, however – and for reasons that remain obscure – he temporarily packed in painting, returning to Europe for five years before another stint in Quebec City, though this time – with the officer corps gone – he failed to sell his work. In 1871, he went to live with his daughter in Chicago and died there the following year, a defeated man.

Joseph Brant by William Berczy, and a number of winter scenes by Cornelius Krieghoff (see above). In particular, look out for Krieghoff's *The Portage*, whose autumnal colours surround a tiny figure struggling with a canoe, and the light-hearted humour of his *Toll Gate*.

Don't leave the museum without observing the intriguing work of **Paul Kane** (1810–71). Like many early Canadian artists, Kane's paintings often displayed a conflict in subject and style: the subject was North American but the style was European (it wasn't until the Group of Seven

CHRISTMAS DINNER: BUFFALO HUMP

In 1859 **Paul Kane** published *Wanderings of an Artist among the Indian Tribes of North America*, the story of his epic journey (see below). It includes this account of Christmas dinner at Fort Edmonton: "At the head, before Mr Harriett, was a large dish of boiled buffalo hump; at the foot smoked a boiled buffalo calf... one of the most esteemed dishes among the epicures of the interior. My pleasing duty was to help a dish of mouffle, or dried moose nose [while] the worthy priest helped the buffalo tongue and Mr Randall cut up the beaver's tails. The centre of the table was graced with piles of potatoes, turnips and bread conveniently placed, so that each could help himself without interrupting the labours of his companions. Such was our jolly Christmas dinner at Edmonton."

that a true Canadian style emerged). The perfect example is Kane's *Landscape in the Foothills with Buffalo Resting*, where bison are pictured in what looks more like a placid German valley than a North American prairie.

Born in Ireland, Kane first emigrated to Toronto in the early 1820s. He returned to Europe at the age of thirty, where, ironically enough, he was so impressed by a touring exhibition of paintings on the American Indian that he promptly decided to move back to Canada. In 1846, he wrangled a spot on a westward-bound, fur-trading expedition, and started an epic journey: he travelled from Thunder Bay to Edmonton by canoe, crossed the Rockies by horse, and finally returned to Toronto two years later. During his trip, Kane made some seven hundred sketches, which he then painted onto canvas, paper and cardboard.

THE EATON CENTRE

Map 3, I2 & I3. 220 Yonge St. Mon–Fri 10am–9pm, Sat
9.30am–7pm, Sun 11am–6pm. Subway Queen or Dundas.

A second-floor walkway crosses Queen Street to connect
The Bay with the **Eaton Centre**, a three-storey assortment of shops and restaurants spread out underneath a
glass-and-steel arched roof. By shopping mall standards,
the design is appealing and the flock of fibreglass Canada
geese suspended from the ceiling adds a touch of flair.
Maps of the shopping mall are displayed on every floor,
but the general rule is the higher the floor, the more
expensive the shop.

The centre takes its name from Timothy Eaton, an
Ulster immigrant who opened his first store here in 1869.
His cash-only, fixed-price, money-back-guarantee trading
revolutionised the Canadian market and made him a fortune. Soon a Canadian institution, Eaton kept a grip on
the pioneer settlements in the west through his mail-
order catalogue, known as the "homesteader's bible" – or
the "wish book" among native peoples – whilst Eaton
department stores sprang up in all of Canada's big cities.
In recent years, however, the company has struggled to
maintain its profitability and this branch is now run by
Sears.

About two thirds of the way along the Eaton Centre
from Queen Street, a side exit leads straight to the **Church
of the Holy Trinity**, an appealing nineteenth-century
structure whose yellow brickwork is surmounted by a pair
of sturdy turrets and matching chimneys. It was here, with
the church set against the skyscrapers that crowd in on it,
that Canadian movie director David Cronenberg filmed the
last scene of *Dead Ringers*. The dubious moral content of
the film – the unscrupulous exploits of twin rogue gynecol-
ogists, both played by Jeremy Irons – prompted Cronenberg

THE EATON CENTRE

GLENN GOULD

In the 1970s, anyone passing the Eaton's department store around 9pm on any day of the year might have seen the door unlocked for a distracted-looking figure swaddled in overcoat, scarves, gloves and hat. This character, making his way to a recording studio set up for his exclusive use inside the shop, was perhaps the most famous citizen of Toronto and the most charismatic pianist in the world – **Glenn Gould**.

In 1964, aged just 32, he retired from the concert platform, partly out of a distaste for the accidental qualities of any live performance, partly out of hatred for the cult of the virtuoso. Yet no pianist ever provided more material for the mythologisers. He possessed a memory so prodigious that none of his acquaintances was ever able to find a piece of music he could not instantly play perfectly. He loathed much of the standard piano repertoire, dismissing romantic composers such as Chopin, Liszt and Rachmaninoff as little more than showmen, but was nonetheless an ardent fan of Barbra Streisand – an esteem that was fully reciprocated – and once wrote an essay titled "In Search of Petula Clark". He travelled everywhere with bags full of medicines and would never allow anyone to shake his hand, and even in a heatwave he was always dressed as if

to defend his subject matter thus: "I don't have a moral plan. I'm a Canadian."

The Eaton Centre ends at the corner of Dundas and Yonge streets, once the city's main intersection and now, after years of decay, revamped with the construction of a public piazza – **Dundas Square** – at its southeast corner. Across the road, the AMC Metropolis movie theatre, with its thirty screens and seating for 6000, is scheduled for completion by 2002.

a blizzard were imminent. To many of his colleagues, Gould's eccentricities were maddening, but what mattered was that nobody could play like Glenn Gould. As one exasperated conductor put it, "the nut's a genius".

Gould's first recording, Bach's *Goldberg Variations*, was released in 1956 and became the best-selling classical record of that year. Soon after, he became the first Western musician to play in the Soviet Union, where his reputation spread so quickly that for his final recital more than a thousand people were allowed to stand in the aisles of the Leningrad hall. On his debut in Berlin, the leading German critic described him as "a young man in a strange sort of trance", whose "technical ability borders on the fabulous". The technique always dazzled, but Gould's fiercely wayward intelligence made his interpretations controversial, as can be gauged from the fact that Leonard Bernstein, conducting Gould on one occasion, felt obliged to inform the audience that what they were about to hear was the pianist's responsibility, not his. Most notoriously of all, he had a very low opinion of Mozart's abilities – and went so far as to record the Mozart sonatas in order to demonstrate that Wolfgang Amadeus died too late rather than too soon. Gould himself died suddenly in 1982 at the age of 50 – the age at which he had said he would give up playing the piano entirely.

THE ELGIN THEATRE AND WINTER GARDEN AND THE MACKENZIE HOUSE

Map 3, J2 & I3. Subway Queen or Dundas.

Across from the Eaton Centre, the **Elgin Theatre and Winter Garden**, 189 Yonge St at Queen Street (guided tours only, Thurs 5pm & Sat 11am; 90min; $7; ⊤597-0965), is one of the city's most unusual attractions. The first part of the guided tour covers the Elgin, an old vaudeville theatre which has been restored after years of neglect and is now equipped with ornate furnishings and fittings, all columns, engravings and gilt mirrors. The Elgin was turned into a cinema in the 1930s and, remarkably enough, its accompaniment, the top-floor **Winter Garden**, also a vaudeville theatre, was sealed off. Such double-decker theatres were introduced in the late nineteenth century in New York and soon became popular along the east coast, but only a handful have survived. Even better, when this one was unsealed, its original decor was found to be intact, the ceiling hung with thousands of preserved and painted beech leaves illuminated by coloured lanterns. In the event, much of the décor had to be replaced, but the restoration work was painstakingly thorough and the end result is delightful. Vaudeville was an informal business, with customers coming and going and performances following each other non-stop. Every theatre had a ready supply of **backcloths**, and several were discovered here when the Winter Garden was unsealed; they are now a feature of the tour.

It's hardly an essential visit, but the **Mackenzie House** (Oct–May Sat & Sun noon–5pm, June–Sept Tues–Sun noon–5pm; $3.50, children $2.50), a five-minute walk east of Eaton Centre along Dundas at 82 Bond St, is of some interest as the home of William Lyon Mackenzie. Born in Scotland, Mackenzie moved to Toronto where he scraped together a living publishing *The Colonial Advocate*, a radical anti-Tory newspaper. Frustrated with the politics of the colony's early leaders, Mackenzie was one of the instigators of the Rebellion of 1837, after which he was exiled to the US for twelve years before being pardoned. Mackenzie lived in this house between 1859 and 1861, and it has been restored to an approximation of its appearance at the time, complete with a print shop (circa 1845) whose workings are demonstrated by costumed guides.

OSGOODE HALL, CAMPBELL HOUSE AND QUEEN STREET WEST

Map 3, G3 & F3. Subway Osgoode.

Immediately to the west of Nathan Phillips Square, along Queen Street, stands **Osgoode Hall** (no public access), a Neoclassical pile built for the Law Society of Upper Canada in the nineteenth century. Looking like a cross between a Greek temple and an English country house, it's protected by wrought-iron gates, designed to keep cows and horses off the lawn. Nearby, in the middle of University Avenue, stands a **War Memorial** honouring those Canadians who fought (for the British imperial interest) in the South African – or Boer – War at the turn of the twentieth century. The memorial features two Canadian soldiers of heroic disposition, and the column is engraved with the names of the battles where Canadian regiments fought.

The elegant Georgian mansion on the west side of University Avenue is **Campbell House** (Mon–Fri 9.30am–4.30pm, Sat & Sun late May to early Oct noon–4.30pm; $3.50, students $2.50), originally built on Adelaide Street for Sir William Campbell, Chief Justice and Speaker of the Legislative Assembly. The house was transported to its current location in 1972. There are regular guided tours of the period interior, providing a well-researched overview of early nineteenth-century Toronto, in which Campbell was a surprisingly progressive figure: he eschewed the death penalty whenever feasible and even awarded the radical William Mackenzie (see opposite) damages when his printing press was wrecked by a mob of Tories in 1826.

Beyond the Campbell House, **Queen Street West** between University and Spadina is one of the grooviest parts of the city, its assorted cafés and bars attracting the sharpest of dressers. That said, the alternative crew of students and punks who once hung around here have moved further west, out to what is known as **Queen West West**, between Spadina and Bathurst. In the daytime this whole section of Queen Street is a great place to be – but at night it is even better.

THE CANADA LIFE BUILDING AND THE MUSEUM FOR TEXTILES

Map 3, F3 & G2. Subway Osgoode or St Patrick.

Back behind Campbell House rises the **Canada Life Building**, whose monumental Art Deco lines are capped by a chunky tower-cum-weather beacon – the yellow neon lights flash up or down with the temperature, and the cube on top signifies white for snow, red for rain and green for sun. The Canada Life Building is the first of the bristling tower blocks which flank **University Avenue** as it cuts north from Queen Street West to the Ontario Legislative Assembly Building (see p.54).

Between Queen Street West and Dundas Street West, on the north side of Osgoode Hall, is **Armoury Street**, the site of the old city armoury and the place where the province's soldiers mustered before embarking for the battlefields of both world wars. Just off Armoury Street, the **Museum for Textiles**, 55 Centre Ave (Tues, Thurs, Fri 11am–5pm, Wed 11am–8pm, Sat & Sun noon–5pm, ⊤599-5515; ⊚*www.museumfortextiles.on.ca*; $5, students/seniors $4), occupies two floors of an office block with a rolling programme of temporary exhibitions. International in outlook, the museum has featured everything from contemporary domestic textile pieces to traditional work, such as Oriental rugs and the hooked mats that were once handmade in Newfoundland and Labrador. The displays are often very good and are supplemented by practical demonstrations of different textile techniques.

Just north of here, watch out for the bust of **Mary Pickford** (1893–1979) on the east side of University Avenue just beyond Elm Street (Map 3, G1). Pickford was born in Toronto, but left on a theatrical tour at the tender age of eight. She dropped her original name – Gladys Mary Smith – when she was working as a motion-picture extra in Hollywood in 1909. Renowned as "America's sweetheart", she earned the sobriquet with her cute face and fluffy mop of hair, which enabled her to play little-girl roles in films well into her thirties.

THE ART GALLERY OF ONTARIO

Map 3, E2. 317 Dundas St West. Tues, Thurs & Fri 11am–6pm, Wed 11am–8.30pm, Sat & Sun 10am–5.30pm; recommended donation $6 for permanent collection, but fixed charges for temporary exhibitions. Subway St Patrick. Ⓣ979 6648; Ⓦ www.ago.on.ca.

Just west of University Avenue along Dundas Street West, the **Art Gallery of Ontario** (AGO) is renowned both for its wide-ranging collection of foreign and domestic art and for its excellent temporary exhibitions. The gallery, however, is housed in an oddly discordant and rather confusing building, the result of several different phases of construction, and there is not enough room to exhibit all of the permanent collection at any one time, which means that the exhibits are rotated. The exterior is a stern, modern facade decorated by a scaffold-like tower and a matching pair of Henry Moore sculptures, large and chunky bronzes uninspiringly called *Large Two Forms*. Inside, the AGO's **Street Level** boasts European works, and there is an excellent art shop and café here too. The **Upper Level** holds contemporary art, a superb sample of Canadian paintings and an extensive collection of Henry Moore sculptures. Museum maps are issued free at reception.

Walker Court and the European collection

Just beyond the main entrance, turn right and stroll down a long corridor (S2) lined with marvellous samples of European applied art, including ivory and alabaster pieces, exquisite cameos and fine porcelain, all on permanent loan from Ken Thomson's private collection – the same tycoon who funds the Thomson Gallery (see p.36). At the end of the corridor, the central **Walker Court** is surrounded on three sides by the European art galleries (S3–S9), which cover the Italian Renaissance through to French Impressionism. Early works include some rather pedestrian Italian altarpieces, but Pieter Brueghel the Younger's incident-packed *Peasants Wedding* is a particular highlight. Other Dutch painters represented here include Rembrandt, Van Dyck, Cuyp, Frans Hals, Goyen and Carel Fabritius, whose exquisite *Portrait of a Lady with a Handkerchief* – though the authorship of this painting has been disputed – is one of only a few of his works that survived the powder-magazine explosion that killed the artist at Delft in 1654. **French** painters are much in evidence too, from the seventeenth century onwards; look out in particular for *St Anne with the Christ Child* by Georges de la Tour, and Poussin's *Venus Presenting Arms to Aeneas*. **Impressionist** works here include Degas's archetypal *Woman in the Bath*, Renoir's screaming-pink *Concert*, and Monet's wonderful *Vétheuil in Summer*, with its hundreds of tiny jabs of colour.

The fourth side of Walker Court (S10) is bordered by the Twentieth Century European Art gallery, where pride of place goes to Picasso's classically cubist *Seated Woman*; Marc Chagall's *Over Vitebsk*, a whimsical celebration of his

Russian birthplace; and Paul Gauguin's evocative *Hina and Fatu*, a wooden stump carved with Polynesian figures. Also exhibited here are Magritte's unnerving *The Birthday*, Barbara Hepworth's *Two Figures*, and Modigliani's *Portrait of Mrs Hastings*, in which you have to assume the subject wasn't seeking flattery.

The Canadian collection

The Upper Level of the AGO holds the outstanding **Canadian Art to 1960** section (U9–20), where the emphasis is on the work of the **Group of Seven** (see box on p.48) and their contemporaries. One of the most distinctive artists of the Group of Seven was **Lawren Harris**, whose *Above Lake Superior* of 1922 is a pivotal work – its clarity of conception, with its bare birch stumps framing a dark mountain beneath Art Deco clouds, quite exceptional. The adjacent *West Wind* by **Tom Thomson** is another seminal work, an iconic rendering of the northern wilderness that is perhaps the most famous of all Canadian paintings. Thomson was the first to approach wilderness landscapes with the determination of an explorer and the sense that they could encapsulate a specifically Canadian identity. Several of his less familiar (but no less powerful) works are here as well, including the moody *A Northern Lake* and the Cubist-influenced preparatory painting, *Autumn Foliage 1915*.

    J.E.H. MacDonald, also one of the Group of Seven, was fond of dynamic, sweeping effects, and his panoramic *Falls, Montreal River* sets turbulent rapids beside hot-coloured hillsides. His friend **F.H. Varley** dabbled in portraiture and chose soft images and subtle colours for his landscapes as exemplified by the sticky-looking brushstrokes he used for *Moonlight after Rain*. A sample of **A.Y. Jackson**'s work includes the characteristically carpet-like

THE GROUP OF SEVEN

In the autumn of 1912, a commercial artist by the name of **Tom Thomson** returned from an extended trip to the Mississauga country, north of Georgian Bay, with a bag full of sketches that were to add a new momentum to Canadian art. His friends, many of them fellow employees of the art firm of Grip Ltd in Toronto, saw Thomson's naturalistic approach to indigenous subject matter as a pointer away from the influence of Europe, declaring the "northland" as the true Canadian "painter's country". World War I and the death of Thomson – who drowned in 1917 – delayed these artists' ambitions, but in 1920 they formed the **Group of Seven**: Franklin H. Carmichael, Lawren Harris, A.Y. Jackson, Arthur Lismer, J.E.H. MacDonald, F.H. Varley and Frank Johnston (later joined by A.J. Casson, L.L. Fitzgerald and Edwin Holgate). Working under the unofficial leadership of Harris, they explored the wilds of Algoma in Northern Ontario in the late 1910s, travelling around in a converted freight car, and later foraged even further afield, from Newfoundland and Baffin Island to British Columbia.

They were immediately successful, staging forty shows in eleven years, a triumph due in large part to Harris's many influential contacts. However, there was also a genuine popular response to the intrepid frontiersman element of their aesthetics. Art was a matter of "taking to the road" and "risking all for the glory of a great adventure", as they wrote in 1922, whilst "nature was the measure of a man's stature", according to Lismer. Symbolic of struggle against the elements, the Group's favourite symbol was the lone pine set against the sky, an image whose authenticity was confirmed by reference to the "manly" poetry of Walt Whitman.

surface of *Algoma Rocks, Autumn*, painted in 1923, while **A.J. Casson**'s bright and rather formal *Old Store at Salem* offers a break from the scenic preoccupations of the rest of the Seven. **Emily Carr**, represented by several works here, was a great admirer of the Seven, but she was never accepted as a member despite her obvious abilities – the deep green foliage of her *Indian Church* and *Western Forest*, both painted in 1929, are good examples of her talent.

The Canadian Art section also features the work of earlier leading artists – most notably Paul Kane (see p.37) and Cornelius Krieghoff (see p.37) – and nearby, beside and above the spiral staircase, there are two small galleries of **Inuit art** (U8). Here, look out for examples of the work of Pauta Saila – *Dancing Bear* – and John Tiktak (1916–81), generally regarded as one of the most talented Inuit sculptors of his generation. The death of Tiktak's mother in 1962 had a profound effect on him, and his *Mother and Child* forcefully expresses this close connection, with the figure of the child carved into the larger figure of the mother. Tiktak's *Owl Man* is another fine piece, an excellent example of the metamorphic figures popular amongst the Inuit, as is Thomas Sivuraq's *Shaman Transformation*. There is also the work of Joe Talirunili, who specialised in migration boat scenes. The *Migration* exhibited here is typical, with the traditional *umiak* (boat) of the Inuit crowded with boisterous, roughly carved figures.

Contemporary art and the Henry Moore Sculpture Gallery

Most of the rest of the Upper Level (U3–U7) is given over to the AGO's collection of **contemporary art**, showcasing works by European, British and American artists. Works are regularly rotated, but watch out for Warhol's *Elvis I* and *II*, Mark Rothko's strident *No.1 White and Red* and Claes Oldenburg's quirky if somewhat frayed *Giant Hamburger*.

The contemporary art exhibits culminate in the **Henry Moore Sculpture Gallery** (U1), the world's largest collection of pieces by Moore, with the emphasis firmly on his plaster casts alongside a selection of his bronzes. Given a whole gallery, Moore's exhibit space is enormous, but it was something of an accident that his work ended up here at all. In the 1960s, Moore had reason to believe that London's Tate Gallery was going to build a special wing for him. When the Tate declined, Moore chose the AGO instead, persuaded to do so by the AGO's British representative, Anthony Blunt, the art expert who was famously uncovered as a Soviet spy in 1979.

More of Henry Moore's sculptures can be found in front of the AGO (see p.45) and in Nathan Phillips Square; see p.34.

The Grange

May–Oct Tues noon–4pm, Wed noon–9pm, Thurs–Sun noon–4pm; Oct–May Wed noon–9pm & Thurs–Sun noon–4pm; no extra charge.

Attached to the back of the AGO is **The Grange**, an early nineteenth century brick mansion with Neoclassical trimmings built by the Boultons, one of the city's most powerful and reactionary families. The last of the line, William Henry – "a privileged, petted man...without principle", according to a local journalist – died in 1874, and his property passed to his widow, Harriette, who promptly married an English expatriate professor named Goldwin Smith. Goldwin enjoyed Toronto immensely, holding court and boasting of his English connections, and when he died in 1910 (after Harriette) he bequeathed the house to the fledgling Art Museum of Toronto, the predecessor of the AGO. The Grange remains part of the AGO and it has been restored to its mid-nineteenth century appearance. Guides dressed in period costume show you around, enthusiastically explaining the ins and outs of life in nineteenth-century Toronto. Several of Harriette's paintings have survived, and while the antique furnishings and fittings are appealing, it's the beautiful wooden staircase that really catches the eye.

CHINATOWN AND KENSINGTON MARKET

Map 3, C1 & D1. Subway St Patrick.

The Art Gallery of Ontario is hemmed in by **Chinatown**, a bustling and immensely appealing neighbourhood cluttered with shops, restaurants and street stalls selling every and any type of Asian delicacy. The boundaries of Chinatown are somewhat blurred, but its focus has been Dundas Street West between Bay Street and Spadina Avenue ever since the Sixties, when the original Chinatown was demolished to make way for the new City Hall. The first Chinese to migrate to Canada arrived in the mid-nineteenth century to work in British Columbia's gold fields. Subsequently, a portion of this population migrated east, and a sizeable Chinese community sprung up in Toronto in the early twentieth century. Several more waves of migration – the last influx following the handing over of Hong Kong to mainland China by the British in 1997 – have greatly increased the number of Toronto's Chinese in recent years, bringing the population to approximately 250,000 (about eight percent of the city's total).

For recommendations of restaurants in Chinatown, see p.151.

Next door to Chinatown, just north of Dundas Street West between Spadina and Augusta avenues, lies Toronto's most ethnically diverse neighbourhood, pocket-sized **Kensington Market**. It was here, at the turn of the twentieth century, that eastern European immigrants squeezed into a patchwork of modest little brick and timber houses that survive to this day. On Kensington Avenue they established the **open-air street market** that has been the main feature of the neighbourhood ever since, a lively, entertaining bazaar whose stall owners stem from many different ethnic backgrounds. The lower half of the market, just off Dundas Street, concentrates on second-hand clothes, while the upper half is crowded with fresh food stalls. Even if you don't want to actually buy anything, it is one of the city's funkiest neighbourhoods, a great place to just hang out.

Uptown Toronto

Beginning north of Gerrard Street, **uptown Toronto** is something of an architectural hodgepodge. The bristling, monochromatic office blocks of University Avenue lead straight to uptown's structural highlight, the **Ontario Legislative Assembly Building**, one of the city's finest Victorian structures. The building also marks the start of a small museum district, made up of the **Gardiner Museum of Ceramic Art** and the **Royal Ontario Museum**, the latter of which possesses one of the country's most extensive collections of applied art. Furthermore, the Legislative Assembly Building is located close to the prettiest part of the sprawling **University of Toronto** campus, on and around King's College Circle.

Moving north, Bloor Street West is choked by office blocks and shops, but it's here you'll find the fanciful **Bata Shoe Museum**, as well as the ritzy little neighbourhood of **Yorkville**. From this area, it's a twenty-minute walk – or a short subway ride – up a quiet, residential stretch of Spadina Avenue to the city's two finest historic homes, the neo-baronial **Casa Loma** and the debonair **Spadina House** next door.

The other main north–south corridor, Yonge Street, cuts a lively and gritty route north from Gerrard Street and is lined with bars and shops. At Wellesley Street, it cuts through the edge of the **Gay and Lesbian Village** and then pushes on to emerge amongst the tower blocks of Bloor Street. The only sights hereabouts are, however, further east in **Cabbagetown**, a charming old neighbourhood of leafy streets and terrace houses.

THE ONTARIO LEGISLATIVE ASSEMBLY BUILDING

Map 4, F8. Mon–Fri 8.30am–6.30pm, also late May to Aug Sat & Sun 9am–4.30pm. Free. Also frequent free guided tours lasting 30min from 10am to 4pm when open. Subway Queen's Park. ⓣ416/325-7500; ⓦwww.ontla.on.ca.

Just north of College Street on University Avenue is the pink sandstone mass of the **Ontario Legislative Assembly Building**, which was completed in 1892. Elegant it certainly isn't, but although the building is heavy and solid, its ponderous symmetries do have a certain appeal, with block upon block of roughly dressed stone assembled in the full flourish of the Romanesque Revival style. Close up, the design is even more engaging, its intricacies a pleasant surprise: above the chunky columns of the main entrance is a sinuous filigree of carved stone, with mythological creatures and gargoyle-like faces poking out from every nook and cranny. The main facade also sports a Neoclassical frieze in which the Great Seal of Ontario is flanked by allegorical figures representing art, music, agriculture and so forth.

Inside, the foyer leads to the wide and thickly carpeted Grand Staircase, whose massive timbers are supported by gilded iron pillars. Beyond, among the long corridors and arcaded galleries, is the **Legislative Chamber**, where the formal mahogany and sycamore panels are offset by a series of whimsical little carvings: look for the owl overlooking the doings of the government and the eagle overseeing the opposition benches. Under the Speaker's gallery, righteous inscriptions have been carved into the pillars – which is a bit of a hoot considering the behaviour of the building's architect, Richard Waite. Waite was chairman of the committee responsible for selecting an architect. And as chairman, he selected himself.

A fire burned the building's **west wing** down in 1909, and to avoid a repeat performance, parliament had its replacement built in marble the following year. No expense was spared in the reconstruction, so there was a substantial fuss when one of the MPPs (Members of the Provincial Parliament) noticed what appeared to be blemishes in the stone on several of the pillars. The blotches turned out to be dinosaur fossils, and nowadays they are pointed out on the guided tour. The provincial assembly typically sits from mid-September to June, with breaks at Christmas and Easter, and although guided tours avoid the chamber when it's in session, the **visitors gallery** is open to the public during deliberations.

Back outside, in front of the main entrance, are a pair of Russian **cannons** that were captured during the Crimean War. Queen Victoria gave them to the city in 1859 in honour of those Canadian regiments who had fought alongside the British during the siege of Sevastopol. The cannons are flanked by a series of **statues** of politicians and imperial bigwigs that spread across the manicured lawns of **Queen's Park**. Two of the more interesting are just a few metres to the east of the assembly's main entrance, beginning with Queen Victoria, who sits on her throne with a rather inconclusive crown on her head. Strangely, Victoria looks very male and, as if to compensate, her bust appears much too large for her slender frame. The adjacent statue of John Graves Simcoe (1752–1806) is a much happier affair, with the one-time lieutenant-governor of Upper Canada cutting a dashing figure with a tricorn hat in one hand and a cane, held at a jaunty angle, in the other. On the west side of the

THE ONTARIO LEGISLATIVE ASSEMBLY BUILDING

building stands a bust of anti-Tory radical William Lyon Mackenzie, and close by is a plaque honouring the **Mac-Paps**. Named after the joint leaders of the Rebellion of 1837 – Mackenzie and Louis Joseph Papineau – the Mac-Paps were a 1500-strong Canadian battalion of the International Brigades, who fought Franco in the Spanish Civil War.

For more on William Lyon Mackenzie, see p.42 & p.286. For more on John Graves Simcoe, see p.284.

There's more statuary behind the Legislative Building on the other section of Queen's Park. Here, right in the middle of the greenery, lording it over the pigeons and the squirrels, is a heavyweight equestrian statue of King Edward VII in full-dress uniform. Originally plonked down in Delhi, this imperial leftover looks a bit forlorn – and you can't help but feel the Indians must have been pleased to off-load it.

THE ROYAL ONTARIO MUSEUM

Map 4, F6. 100 Queen's Park. Mon–Thurs 10am–6pm, Fri 10am–9.30pm, Sat 10am–6pm, Sun 11am–6pm; $15, children (5–14) $8; free after 4.30pm on Fri. Subway Museum. ☎586-8000; ⓦwww.rom.on.ca.

From the Legislative Building, it's a brief walk north along Queen's Park Boulevard to the **Royal Ontario Museum**. Known locally as the ROM, this is Canada's largest and most diverse museum, with ambitious collections of fine and applied art from all over the world as well as a first-rate programme of temporary exhibitions. Opened in 1914, the museum occupies a handsome five-storey building whose precise neo-Gothic symmetries were subsequently embellished with Art Deco flourishes. The main doors are

THE DISCOVERY GALLERY

On Floor 2, the ROM's **Discovery Gallery** is one of the best education facilities in Toronto, giving children the opportunity to handle and study museum artefacts. Over a dozen workstations are set up with slides and microscopes, or identification drawers containing butterflies, insects, minerals and prehistoric pottery. Kids can try on virtual reality headsets or seventeenth-century helmets, handle the leg bone of a Stegosaurus dinosaur, and learn how to write in hieroglyphics.

The Gallery keeps the same hours as the main museum (see opposite) but is often closed 10am–noon during school terms. Children under ten must be accompanied by an adult.

imposingly large and above them a complement of muses, astrological symbols and mythological beasts stands guard.

With over forty different galleries and six million objects and artefacts, the ROM can be overwhelming, and there's precious little point in trying to see everything – at least not on one visit. In addition, some departments, notably the Chinese collections, have first-rate displays of international significance; others, like the Greco-Roman and Medieval European galleries, merely give representation to their subject areas and shouldn't be ranked too high on a must-see list. Museum plans are available for free at the entrance.

The ROM makes a cheerful start with a domed and vaulted **entrance hall** whose ceiling is decorated with a brilliant mosaic of imported Venetian glass. Just beyond, bolted into the stairwells, are four colossal Native Canadian Haida and Nisga'a **crest poles** (commonly but erroneously referred to as totem poles). Dating from the 1880s, the striking poles (the tallest is 24.5 metres high) are decorated with stylised carvings representing the supernatural animals and birds, as well as origins and rights, that were associated with particular clans.

Canadian Heritage floor

Occupying Floor 1B (one below street level) the **Canadian Heritage** section puts to rest the notion that Canada is a "new" land by producing evidence of twelve thousand years of human settlement. In particular, the Ontario Archaeology section – in Room 5 – holds a modest collection of prehistoric artefacts, notably a variety of arrow heads and a selection of polished and shaped stones used as tools by Canada's prehistoric peoples. Nearby, the Canadiana room – Room 2 – kicks off with a glass cabinet crammed with late eighteenth- and early nineteenth-century trade silver, an intriguing assortment of silver ornaments – brooches, earrings, crucifixes, medals and the like – which European traders swapped with natives for furs. This is followed by a series of period rooms, the pick of which illustrate the tastes of the early French and British settlers. In one of these rooms is the iconic *Death of Wolfe* by Benjamin West. The British general James Wolfe inflicted a crushing defeat on the French outside Quebec City in 1759, but was killed during the battle. West's painting transformed this grubby colonial conflict into a romantic extravagance with the dying general in a Christ-like pose, a pale figure held tenderly by his subordinates. West presented the first version of his painting to the Royal Academy of Arts in 1771 and it proved so popular that he spent much of the next decade painting copies.

Chinese Art

Back on the museum's street level and straight back from the main entrance is the **Bishop White Gallery of**

Chinese Temple Art, one of the ROM's most significant collections. It features three Daoist and Buddhist wall paintings dating from around 1300 AD, including a matching pair of Yuan Dynasty murals depicting the lords of the Northern and Southern Dipper, each of whom leads an astrological procession of star spirits. The murals are complimented by an exquisite sample of Buddhist sculpture, temple figures dating from the twelfth to the fourteenth centuries.

Close by, the **T.T. Tsui Galleries of Chinese Art** contain artefacts spanning six millennia, from 4500 BC to 1900 AD. Among the most important pieces is a remarkable collection of toy-sized tomb figurines – a couple of hundred ceramic pieces representing funerary processions of soldiers, musicians, carts and attendants. Dating from the early sixth to the late seventh century, they recreate the habits of early China – how people dressed, how horses were groomed and shod, changes in armoury, and so forth. There is also a fabulous collection of snuff bottles, some carved from glass and rock crystal, others from more exotic materials – amber, ivory, bamboo and even tangerine skin. Europeans introduced tobacco to China in the late sixteenth century and although smoking did not become popular in China until recent times, snuff went down a storm and anyone who was anybody at court was snorting the stuff by the middle of the seventeenth century. Perhaps the most popular component of the Chinese galleries, however, is the **Ming Tomb**, just beyond the T.T. Tsui Galleries. The aristocracy of the Ming Dynasty (1368–1644 AD) evolved an elaborate style of monumental funerary sculpture and architecture, and this is the only example outside of China – though it is actually a composite tomb drawn from several sources rather than an homogeneous whole. Central to the Ming burial conception was a Spirit Way, a central avenue with large-scale carved figures of guards, attendants and

THE ROYAL ONTARIO MUSEUM

animals placed on either side. At the end of the alley was the tumulus, or burial mound – in this case the tomb-house of a seventeenth-century Chinese general by the name of Zu Dashou.

Life Sciences

The focal point of the second-floor Life Sciences exhibits is the **Dinosaur Gallery**. Dioramas and simulations have made this one of the most informative parts of the museum and also one of the most visited. Among the assorted fossil-skeletons, the most dramatic are those retrieved from the Alberta Badlands, the richest source of dinosaur, fossils in the world. Millions of years ago, the Badlands were lush lowlands attractive to many types of dinosaur and their remains accumulated in the region's sediments, which were then, over hundreds of thousands of years, turned to stone. Over 300 complete skeletons have been unearthed in the Badlands, which lie near Calgary, and many have been dispatched to museums across the world including the ROM. Altogether, the Alberta Badlands have produced 35 dinosaur species – ten percent of all those known – with the first fossilised skeleton, that of the aptly named Albertosaurus, being stumbled upon by the palaeontologist Joseph Tyrrell in 1884. The ROM has a superb collection of these fossils, including several Albertosaurus, but it is the rampant herd of Allosaurus – a Jurassic-period carnivore of large proportions and ferocious appearance – that commands your attention. Other popular sections on this floor are the replica **bat cave** and a large display on the country's **insects** – and a fearsome-looking bunch they are too, including the No-see-um, which drives caribou to distraction by burrowing into their nostrils.

The Mediterranean World and Europe

The third floor holds four rooms devoted to **Europe** – including a series of period rooms and collections of metalwork, ceramics and glass – and eight rooms dedicated to the **Mediterranean World**, where the highlight is the **Ancient Egypt Gallery**. There are several finely preserved mummies here, including the richly decorated sarcophagus of Djedmaatesankh, a court musician who died somewhere around 850 BC. Even more unusual is the assortment of mummified animals, including a crocodile, a hawk and a weird-looking cat. The same gallery also has the **Punt Wall**, a plaster cast dating from 1905 of the original in Queen Hatshepsut's temple in Deir el-Bahri, Egypt. The events depicted on the wall occurred in the year 1482 BC, and represent a military expedition to Punt, which lay south of Egypt near present-day Somalia.

THE GEORGE R. GARDINER MUSEUM OF CERAMIC ART

Map 4, F6. 111 Queen's Park. Mon, Wed, Thurs & Fri 10am–6pm, Tues 10am–8pm, Sat 10am–5pm, Sun 11am–5pm; $5, students $3, but free the first Tues of every month. Subway Museum. ⊤586-8080; Ⓦ*www.gardinermuseum.on.ca*.

Named after its wealthy patron, the **George R. Gardiner Museum of Ceramic Art**, just across the street from the ROM, holds a superb connoisseur's collection of ceramics. Spread over two small floors, the museum's exhibits are beautifully presented and key pieces are well labelled and explained. An audioguide is also available.

Downstairs, the **Pre-Columbian** section is especially fine, composed of over three hundred pieces from regions stretching from Mexico to Peru. One of the most comprehensive collections of its kind in North America, it provides an intriguing insight into the lifestyles and beliefs of the Mayan, Incan, and Aztec peoples. The sculptures are all the more remarkable for the fact that the potter's wheel was unknown in pre-Columbian America, and thus everything on display was necessarily hand-modelled. While some of the pieces feature everyday activities, it is the religious sculptures that mostly catch the eye, from wonderfully intricate Mexican incense burners and lurid Mayan plates and cylindrical vases to the fantastical zoomorphic gods of the Zapotecs. Also downstairs is an exquisite sample of fifteenth- and sixteenth-century tin-glazed **Italian majolica**, mostly dishes, plates and jars depicting classical and Biblical themes designed by Renaissance artists. The early pieces are comparatively plain, limited to green and purple, but the later examples are brightly coloured, for in the second half of the fifteenth century Italian potters learnt how to glaze blue and yellow – and ochre was added later. The most superb pieces are perhaps those from the city – and pottery centre – of Urbino, including two wonderful plates portraying the fall of Jericho and the exploits of Hannibal.

The upstairs level is devoted to eighteenth-century **European porcelain**, with fine examples of hard-paste wares (fired at very high temperatures) from Meissen, Germany, and an interesting sample of Chinese-style blue and white porcelain, long the mainstay of the European ceramic industry. An unusual collection of English ware features both well-known manufacturers, primarily the ornate products of Royal Worcester, and less familiar pieces, notably the demure and modest crockery produced in the village of Pinxton, on the edge of Sherwood Forest in England, in the eighteenth century. On this floor also is a charming collection of Italian *commedia dell'arte* figurines, doll-sized representations of theatrical characters popular across Europe from the middle of the sixteenth to the late eighteenth century. The predecessor of pantomime, the *commedia dell'arte* featured stock characters in improvised settings, but with a consistent theme of seduction, age and beauty: the centrepiece was always an elderly, rich merchant and his beautiful young wife.

Finally, the museum **gift shop** also merits special mention as it specialises in contemporary Canadian ceramics and thereby directly supports artists by carrying their works.

UNIVERSITY OF TORONTO

Map 4, D6 through E8.

The sprawling campus of the **University of Toronto**, which extends north–south from College to Bloor and east–west from Bay to Spadina, is dotted with stately college buildings and halls of residence. The best-looking of the lot can be found at the west end of Wellesley Street, beginning on Hart House Circle, where the ivy-covered walls, neo-Gothic interiors and cloistered quadrangles of **Hart House College**, which dates from the early twentieth century, are reminiscent of Oxford and Cambridge – just as they were designed to be.

Hart House is attached to the **Soldiers' Tower**, a neo-Gothic memorial to those students who died in both world wars; it was erected in 1924. The arcaded gallery abutting the tower lists the dead of World War I and is inscribed with Canadian John McCrae's *In Flanders Fields*, arguably the war's best-known poem: "...We are the Dead. Short days ago/We lived, felt dawn, saw sunset glow,/Loved and were loved, and now we lie,/In Flanders fields...".

Hart House Circle leads into the much larger **King's College Circle**, where a large field is flanked by university buildings. On the north side stands **University College**, an imposing Romanesque-style structure. Further around the

JOHN STRACHAN

Toronto's first Anglican bishop was the redoubtable **John Strachan**, a one-time schoolmaster who made a name for himself in the War of 1812. The Americans may have occupied the city easily enough, but Strachan led a spirited civil resistance, bombarding the occupiers with a veritable deluge of requests and demands about everything from inadequate supplies to any lack of respect the Americans showed to private property. Perhaps surprisingly, the Americans treated Strachan's complaints very seriously, though they did get mightily irritated. After the war, Strachan turned his formidable energies to education. All of moneyed Toronto believed in the value of university education, but the problem was agreeing who should provide it, as Canada's various religious denominations all wanted a piece of the educational action.

In 1827, Strachan obtained a royal charter for the foundation of Toronto's first college of higher education, but his plans for an Anglican-controlled institution were resisted so forcibly that King's College, as Strachan's college was called, didn't open its doors until 1843. Even then, Strachan's triumph was short-lived: Anglican control lasted just six years before the provincial government secularised the institution and renamed it the University of Toronto.

Over the ensuing decades the university was brow-beaten by theological colleges that considered a secular university to be immoral. But by the turn of the twentieth century, the University of Toronto had made a name for itself, ultimately becoming one of North America's most prestigious educational institutions. It was here that insulin was discovered in 1921, and later, Marshall McLuhan taught at the university and wrote *The Medium is the Message*.

circle, the rough sandstone masonry of **Knox College**, dating from 1874, sports a set of dinky little chimneys, and beyond that rises the elegant rotunda of **Convocation Hall**.

Backtracking to Hart House Circle, walk through the arch of the Soldiers' Tower, turn right along Hoskin Avenue and – just before you reach the traffic island – watch for the footpath on the left. This is **Philosopher's Walk**, an easy, leafy stroll which leads north, slipping around the back of the ROM (see p.56) on the way to Bloor Street West.

Free guided tours (1–2 daily; ☎978-5000) of the University of Toronto begin at the Nona MacDonald Visitors' Centre, 25 King's College Circle. The entrance to the centre is on the south side of the Knox College building.

YORKVILLE

A couple of minutes' walk north of Bloor Street West, along and around Cumberland Street and Yorkville Avenue, are the bars, shops and restaurants of the well-heeled **Yorkville** neighbourhood. This fashionable district makes for a pleasant stroll (especially if you've got some spare cash), and many of the old timber-terrace houses have been meticulously maintained. Here too, on the corner of Cumberland and Bellair streets, is the **Village of Yorkville Park**, a small, cleverly designed park where a hunk of granite brought from northern Ontario is edged by a variety of neat little gardens, displaying every native habitat from upland conifers to wetlands.

BATA SHOE MUSEUM

Map 4, D5. 327 Bloor St West at St George Street. Tues, Wed, Fri, Sat 10am–5pm, Thurs 10am–8pm, Sun noon–5pm; closed Mon. $6. Subway St George. ☎979-7799; ⓦ*www.batashoemuseum.ca*.

YORKVILLE • BATA SHOE MUSEUM

Within easy walking distance of both the ROM and Yorkville, the **Bata Shoe Museum** was designed by Raymond Moriyama, the much-lauded Vancouver-born architect whose other creations include the Ontario Science Centre (see p.88) and the Scarborough Civic Centre (see p.85). Opened in 1995, the museum was designed to resemble a shoe box – the roof supposedly suggests a lid resting on an open box – and was built for Sonja Bata, of the Bata shoe manufacturing family, to house the extraordinary assortment of footwear she has spent a lifetime collecting.

A leaflet issued at reception steers visitors around the museum, starting with an introductory section entitled "All About Shoes" on Level B1, which presents an overview on the evolution of footwear, beginning with a plaster cast of the oldest human footprint ever discovered, roughly 3,700,000 years old. Among the more interesting exhibits in this section are pointed shoes from medieval Europe, where different social classes were allowed different lengths of toe, and Chinese silk shoes used for binding women's feet. Banned by the Chinese Communists when they came to power in 1949, foot binding was common practice for over one thousand years, and the "ideal" length of a woman's foot was a hobbling three inches. Begun in early childhood, the process effectively crippled women and, in its contraction and bending of the foot, created a U-shaped orifice that was commonly used for sexual penetration by the master of the house. A small adjoining section is devoted to specialist footwear, including French chestnut-crushing clogs from the nineteenth century, inlaid Ottoman platforms designed to keep aristocratic feet well away from the mud, and a pair of US army boots from the Vietnam War with the sole shaped to imitate the sandal prints of the Vietcong.

Moving on, Level G holds a glass cabinet of celebrity footwear. The exhibits are rotated regularly, but look out for

Buddy Holly's loafers, David Bowie's signed trainers, Elvis's blue-and-white patent-leather loafers, Princess Diana's red court shoes and Elton John's ridiculous platforms.

Levels 2 and 3 are used for temporary exhibitions – some of which are very good indeed – and there's also a small section explaining the museum's role in restoring and repairing old footwear.

CABBAGETOWN

Although the precise boundaries of **Cabbagetown** continue to be a matter of dispute between local historians and real estate agents – the former try to narrow the area and the latter try to expand it – this Victorian neighbourhood is roughly bounded by Dundas Street to the south, Parliament Street to the west, Wellesley Street to the north, and the Don River to the east. Cabbagetown got its name from nineteenth-century Irish immigrants who grew cabbages in their yards instead of flowers. Contemporary Cabbagetowners have embraced the vegetable and even have their own flag with a large, leafy cabbage prominently displayed at the centre. In the early twentieth century, the area was pocked by substandard homes and dire living conditions, prompting novelist Hugh Garner to anoint it "the largest Anglo-Saxon slum in North America". Today, most of the houses have been renovated by prosperous owners, and the neighbourhood has become a haven for the city's hip and wealthy. Cabbagetown is also home to **Spruce Court**, on Spruce Street, once a low-income housing project and now Canada's oldest residential co-operative. Built prior to World War I as a tiny arts and crafts village, the co-op continues to thrive, serving as a counter-balance to the all-encroaching gentrification.

Specific sights in Cabbagetown are thin on the ground, but **Winchester Street**, a short walk south of Wellesley, does possess a particularly appealing ensemble of Victorian houses, as does adjoining **Metcalfe Street**. Common architectural features include high-pitched gables, stained glass windows, stone lintels and inviting timber verandas. At the east end of Winchester Street, the entrance to one of the city's oldest cemeteries is marked by a handsome Gothic Revival **chapel** and matching pavilion, whose coloured tiles and soft yellow brickwork date to the middle of the nineteenth century. Inside the **cemetery**, the gravestones are almost universally modest and unassuming, but their straightforward accounts of the lives of the dead give witness to the extraordinary British diaspora that populated much of Victorian Canada.

Cabbagetown is home to the oldest neighbourhood festival in Toronto; see p.270.

CASA LOMA

Map 4, C1. 1 Austin Terrace. Daily 9.30am–5pm; last admission 4pm; $9. Subway Dupont. ⊤923-1171; ⊛*www.casaloma.org.*
A couple of minutes' walk up the slope north from Dupont subway station, along Spadina to Davenport Road, a flight of steps leads to **Casa Loma**. The house, Toronto's most bizarre attraction, is an enormous towered and turreted mansion built to the instructions of Sir Henry Pellatt and his architect Edward J. Lennox between 1911 and 1914. A free diagram of the layout of the house is available at the reception, as are audiocassette tours.

The clearly numbered route around the house begins on the ground floor in the **Great Hall**, a pseudo-Gothic extravaganza with an eighteen-metre-high cross-beamed ceiling, a Wurlitzer organ and enough floor space to accommodate several hundred guests. Hung with flags,

heavy-duty chandeliers and suits of armour, it's a remarkably cheerless place, but in a touch worthy of Errol Flynn,
the hall is overlooked by a balcony at the end of Pellatt's
second-floor bedroom: presumably Sir Henry could, like
some medieval baron, welcome his guests from on high.
Pushing on, the **Library** and then the walnut-panelled
Dining Room lead to the **Conservatory**, an elegant and
spacious room with a marble floor and side-panels set
beneath a handsome Tiffany glass ceiling. Well lit, this is
perhaps the mansion's most appealing room. Its worm-like
network of steam pipes are original, installed by Pellatt to
keep his flowerbeds warm in winter. Close by, the **Study**
was Sir Henry's favourite room, a serious affair engulfed by
mahogany panelling and equipped with two secret passage-
ways, one leading to the wine cellar, the other his wife's
rooms. On the second floor, **Sir Henry's Suite** has oodles
of walnut and mahogany panelling, which is in odd contrast to the 1910s white-marble, high-tech bathroom, featuring an elaborate multi-nozzle shower. Lady Pellatt was-
n't left behind in the ablutions department either – her
bathroom had a bidet, a real novelty in George V's Canada.
Of interest on the third floor are the **Round Room**, with
its curved doors and walls, and the **Windsor Room**,
named after – and built for - the Royal Family in the
rather forlorn hope that they would come and stay here.
Of course they never did – Pellatt was much too parvenu
for their tastes (see box overleaf).

When you've finished exploring the house, you can wander down the long tunnel that leads to the stables and the
carriage room. Spare time also for the terraced **gardens**
(May–Oct daily 9.30am–4pm; no extra charge), which
tumble down the hill behind the house. They are parcelled
up into several different sections including a water garden, a
rhododendron dell and a meadow garden flanked by cool,
green cedars.

CASA LOMA

SIR HENRY PELLATT

Sir Henry Pellatt made a fortune by pioneering the use of hydroelectricity, harnessing the power of Niagara Falls to light Ontario's expanding cities. Determined to become a man of social standing, Pellatt became a major general in the Queen's Own Rifles and managed to get himself knighted. Still, he was much too flashy to be accepted into the old elite – for one thing he was fond of dressing up in a costume that combined a British colonel's uniform with the attire of a Mohawk chief.

In 1911, Pellatt started work on Casa Loma, gathering furnishings from all over the world and even importing Scottish stonemasons to build the wall around his six-acre property, the end result being an eccentric mixture of medieval fantasy and early twentieth-century technology. Pellatt spent more than $3 million fulfilling his dream, but his penchant for reckless business dealings finally caught up with him, forcing him to move out and declare himself bankrupt in 1923. He died penniless sixteen years later, his dramatic fall from grace earning him the nickname "Pellatt the Plunger".

SPADINA HISTORIC HOUSE & GARDENS

Map 4, C1. 285 Spadina Rd. Guided tours only, April–Sept Tues–Sun noon–5pm; $5. Subway Dupont. T392-6910. Ⓦ*www.torontohistory.on.ca.*

What the occupants of **Spadina House** must have thought when Casa Loma went up next door can only be imagined, but there must have been an awful lot of curtain-twitching. The two houses are a study in contrasts: Casa Loma a grandiose pile, and Spadina an elegant Victorian property of genteel appearance dating from 1866. Spadina was built by James Austin, an Irish immigrant from County Armagh, who was a printer's apprentice before becoming a successful businessman and a co-founder of the Toronto Dominion Bank. After his death, Spadina House passed to Albert Austin, who enlarged and modernised his father's home, adding a billiard and laundry room, a garage and a refrigerator room to replace the old ice house. Albert's property eventually passed to his three daughters, who lived in the house until the last of the sisters, Anna Kathleen, moved out in 1983, the year before she died. Anna bequeathed Spadina House to the City of Toronto, which now manages and maintains the place. The Austins' uninterrupted occupation of Spadina House means that the house's furnishings are nearly all genuine family artefacts, and they provide an intriguing insight into the family's changing tastes and interests.

Narrated by enthusiastic volunteers, the **guided tour** is a delight. Particular highlights include the conservatory trap door that allowed the gardeners to come and go unseen by their employers; an assortment of period chairs designed to accommodate the largest of bustles; a couple of canvases by Cornelius Krieghoff; the original gas chandeliers; and the unusual arcaded arches at the top of the first flight of stairs, which were installed in the 1890s. Pride of place, however, is the Billiard Room, where an inventive Art Nouveau decorative frieze, dating from 1898, is complemented by several fine pieces of furniture, including a sturdy oak desk, bentwood chairs and a swivel armchair that imitated the designs of Englishman William Morris.

For more on Cornelius Krieghoff, see p.37.

SPADINA HISTORIC HOUSE & GARDENS

The waterfront and the Toronto Islands

D espite patches of industrial development and the heavy concrete brow of the Gardiner Expressway, there is much to enjoy on the shore of **Lake Ontario**. This is particularly true during Toronto's humid summers, when city-dwellers head for the breezy tranquillity of the **Toronto Islands** – a short ten-minute ferry ride offshore – or enjoy the footpaths and cycling trails that thread along the lakeshore. On the water, there is also the **Harbourfront Centre**, where a constant schedule of activities – music festivals, contemporary art, dance and the like – go on year round, and **Ontario Place**, a leisure complex spread over three man-made islands.

THE WATERFRONT

Map 3, D8 through I8.

Toronto's docks once disfigured the shoreline on the edge of the city centre, a swathe of warehouses and factories that was unattractive and smelly in equal measure. Today it's another story: the port and its facilities have been concentrated further east, beyond the foot of Parliament Street, while the **waterfront** west of Yonge Street has been redeveloped in grand style, sprouting luxury condominium blocks, jogging and cycling trails, offices, shops and marinas. The focus of all this activity is the **Harbourfront Centre**, whose various facilities include an open-air performance area and the **Power Plant Contemporary Art Gallery**. To reach the Harbourfront Centre by public transport, take the streetcar from Union Station and get off at the third stop – Queens Quay Terminal.

The Harbourfront Centre

Map 3, E8–G8. Streetcar #509 or #510 Queens Quay Terminal.
The centrepiece of Toronto's downtown waterfront is the ten-acre **Harbourfront Centre**, an expanse of lakefront property stretching from the foot of York Street in the east to the Molson Place outdoor stage, about five minutes' walk away to the west. This is one of Toronto's most creative quarters, and many of the city's artistic and cultural events are held here, either outside or indoors at one of several venues, principally the du Maurier Theatre Centre (see p.207).

The east end of the Harbourfront Centre is marked by the **Queens Quay Terminal building**, a handsome, glassy structure built as a combined warehouse and shipping depot in 1927. Attractively refurbished, it now holds cafés, offices and smart shops. Close by, the **Power Plant Contemporary Art Gallery** (Tues & Thurs–Sun noon–6pm, Wed noon–8pm; $4, but free on Wed after 5pm; ⓣ973-4934; ⓦ*www.thepowerplant.org*) is housed in an imaginatively converted 1920s power station. The gallery presents about a dozen exhibitions of contemporary art every year and often features emerging Canadian artists. It is mostly cutting-edge stuff, indecipherable to some, exciting

THE WATERFRONT

to others. The gallery shares the power station with the du Maurier Theatre Centre.

Close by, just to the west, another former warehouse has been turned into the **York Quay Centre** with performance areas, meeting spaces and craft galleries. The south entrance of the Centre lets out to a shallow pond that converts into a skating rink during the winter. To the west is **Molson Place**, an outdoor stage with a graceful fan-like roof designed to suggest a ship's deck.

The Pier museum and around

Map 3, B8 through F8.

Cross the footbridge on the west side of the Harbourfront Centre and you're a few metres from **The Pier**, 245 Queens Quay West (July & Aug daily 10am–6pm, late March–June and Sept & Oct daily 10am–4pm; $5; ☏338-7437. Streetcar #509 or #510 to Rees Street), the recent reincarnation of the city's old marine museum, reinvented with two floors of engaging displays and an abiding interest in all things nautical. The emphasis is on Toronto's history as a major inland port, and a detailed section tracks the evolution of the city's waterfront from colonial outpost to industrial power house. There are also interactive displays – including one on nautical communications – and a workshop where a team of shipwrights builds wooden boats along traditional lines.

A short walk away to the west, across Queens Quay Street at the foot of Spadina Street, is the **Harbourfront Antique Market** (☏260-2626; Tues–Sun 10am–6pm), a covered marketplace with a myriad of stalls, booths and stores selling everything from tiny Victorian purses to whopping Empire bedroom suites. Some very good bargains are available, although the dealers are now well established, meaning the days of heavy bartering are well and truly over. A **flea market** operates on the upper level of the market on Saturday and Sunday.

Back on the lakeshore, a slice of old industrial land has been reclaimed and turned into the landscaped **Toronto Music Garden,** essentially a series of rockeries with vague musical allusions that meanders west towards the giant silos of the **Canada Maltings building**. This imposing concrete hulk was erected in 1928 for the storage of barley brought here from the west by the ships which once thronged the St Lawrence Seaway. Closed in 1987, the building is derelict today, but architecturally – as an example of a Modernist industrial structure - it is much too fine a building to be demolished, and Torontonians have been debating its future for years. On its far side is Bathurst Street and the dinky little ferry that shuttles across the narrow Western Channel to the City Centre Airport (see p.9).

ONTARIO PLACE

Map 2, F7. 955 Lakeshore Blvd West. Mid-May–early Sept daily 10am–midnight. An all-day pass covering most attractions in the complex costs $24.50 for visitors up to 54 years old and over 106cm tall, $15 for over-55s and $11 for those under 4 years old and under 106cm. Bathurst streetcar (#511). ⓣ314-9900. ⓦwww.ontarioplace.com.

Ontario Place, a couple of kilometres west of the Harbourfront Centre along Lakeshore Boulevard West, rises out of the lake like a post-Modernist Atlantis. Architect Eberhard Zeidler was given a mandate to create "leisure space in an urban context", and he came up with these three man-made islands, or "pods", covering 95 acres with landscaped parks, lagoons and canals. The attractions here are almost entirely themed around water and hydrodynamics, and rides like the Rush River Raft Ride, the Purple Pipeline and the Pink Twister provide exciting ways to get

ONTARIO PLACE

dizzy and wet. Visitors looking for less frenetic activities, however, can rent **pedal boats** (available at all of the park's various lagoons), two-seater aquatic bicycles used to thrash through the canals that separate the pods.

Both an amusement park and an entertainment complex, Ontario Place was the template for facilities like Florida's EPCOT Center, and is therefore teeming with young families and teenagers during the day. The atmosphere at night tends to be a bit more mature, particularly at the **Molson Amphitheatre**, which puts on a series of summer concerts dominated by headliner rock groups and singers; for information and a schedule of who's playing, call ☎870-8000.

Also at Ontario Place is the **Cinesphere**, whose distinctive geodesic dome, containing a 750-seat theatre with a curved, six-storey screen, was the world's first IMAX film theatre (it opened to the public in 1971). IMAX technology was first developed by the Toronto-based IMAX Corporation in 1967. The frames of the IMAX film are physically larger than in any other processing format, the film runs through a behemoth projector at 24 frames per second, and the screens average 20m (65 feet) in height. The cumulative sensation is one of being immersed in the film, and it has certainly proved a popular formula – there are now IMAX theatres all over the world. To see an IMAX film here, it is a good idea to book ahead, either in person at the Ontario Place Box Office or by calling ☎870-8000.

Symphony of Fire, a spectacular international fireworks competition, overwhelms Ontario Place every June and July. Pyrotechnic teams from around the world congregate at the water's edge and try to win with creative routines and sheer fire power. For full details, see the "Festivals" chapter, p.267.

ONTARIO PLACE

THE TORONTO ISLANDS

Map 2, inset.

Originally a sandbar peninsula, the **Toronto Islands**, arching around the city's harbour, were cut adrift from the mainland by a violent storm in 1858. First used as a summer retreat by the Mississauga Indians, the islands went through various incarnations during the twentieth century: they once hosted a baseball stadium where slugger Babe Ruth hit his first professional home run, and they even served as a World War II training base for the Norwegian Air Force. Today, this archipelago, roughly 6km-long and totalling around 800 acres, is seemingly worlds away from the bustle of downtown, a haven for rest and relaxation – and a place where visitors' motor cars are banned. The city side of the archipelago is broken into a dozen tiny islets dotted with cottages, leisure facilities, neat gardens and clumps of wild woodland. By comparison, the other side of the archipelago is a tad wilder and more windswept, consisting of one long finger of land that is somewhat arbitrarily divided into three "islands". From the east, these are **Ward's Island**, a quiet residential area with parkland and wilderness; **Centre Island**, the busiest and most developed of the three and itself divided into two sections by a narrow waterway; and **Hanlan's Point**, edging Toronto's tiny City Centre Airport and with the best sandy beach. Hanlan's Point is also the location of Toronto's official **nude beach**. As Lake Ontario is generally too polluted for swimming, the only bathing that goes on here is sunbathing.

Practicalities

Three separate **ferries** depart for the Toronto Islands from the mainland ferry terminal, which is located behind the conspicuous *Westin Harbour Castle Hotel*, at the foot of

Yonge and Bay streets. To get to the ferry terminal from Union Station, take the #509 or #510 streetcar and get off at the first stop – Queen's Quay (Ferry Docks). The Ward's Island and Hanlan's Point services run year-round, while the ferry running to Centre Island operates only from spring to early fall. During peak season (May to early Sept), all the ferry lines depart every twenty minutes; at other times of the year they operate at regular intervals, either every half-hour, forty-five minutes or hour. Ferries begin between 6.30am and 9am and end between 9pm and 11.30pm, depending on the service and the season. For schedule details, telephone ☎392-8193. Regardless of the time of year, a return **fare** for adults is $5, $3 for seniors and students.

Cars are not allowed on the Toronto Islands without a special permit, which is only available to island residents. Aside from walking, cycling or rowing, the other means of conveyance is a free but irregular trackless **train** that runs between the ferry docks at Hanlan's Point and Ward's Island; get on the train at any of the three ferry docks. Several hours are needed to cover the islands' trails by bicycle, and a full day can easily be spent meandering about on foot. Rollerblades are permissible on the islands, but must be removed while on board the ferries. **Bicycles** are allowed on the ferries but restrictions may apply on busy weekends.

Ward's Island

Named after the Ward family, who settled on the then-peninsula in 1830, **Ward's Island** possesses a sloping, sandy beach and a pleasant boardwalk, which arches along the Lake Ontario side of the island, lined with cottages, some of which double as artists' studios. The island is home to approximately 700 full-time residents, but remains one of the least developed of the chain – the landscape is still dominated by primeval-looking scrub reed and birches mixed with wild apple trees and grape vines. A network of footpaths explores this terrain and a trio of small footbridges connects the island with its tiny neighbours – Algonquin, Snake Island and Snug Harbour, just to the north.

Centre Island

Centre Island is where most of the action is during the summer season, when ferries arrive at its harbour carrying boatloads of day-trippers. The first building you'll see as the ferry docks is the *Island Paradise Restaurant*, a favourite watering hole for the thirsty sailors of the adjacent **Toronto Island Marina**. A snack bar and information kiosk lie straight ahead, beside the **Hong Kong Lions Club Pavilion**, home to the organisation that hosts a spectacular Dragon Boat Race every June (see p.266).

Walking five minutes east of the docks will lead you to **Centreville** (late May–Aug daily plus Sept weekends 10.30am–7pm; ☎203-0405), a children's amusement park with charmingly old-fashioned rides, from paddle boats shaped as swans to a carousel, a Ferris Wheel and the Lake Monster roller-coaster. Each ride costs a specified number of tickets, from two to board the carousel up to a maximum of six to experience the Lake Monster. Individual tickets are 60¢, or you can lash out on an all-day pass costing $19.95 for adults and anyone over four feet, $13.95 for kids under four feet. At the east end of Centreville is the **Far Enough Farm**, a pint-sized farm and petting zoo popular with very young children.

Just to the south of Centreville, a footbridge spans the narrow waterway that separates the two parts of Centre Island to reach the **Avenue of the Islands**, a wide walkway surrounded by trim gardens. At its southern end, this walkway extends into a forked pier that pokes out beyond the stone breakwater into the lake. At the foot of the pier is one of the island's two **Toronto Island Bicycle Rental** outlets (☎203-0009), which stocks conventional bicycles, tandems, and even quadracycles, which take four cyclists. **Boat rental** is available near the Avenue of the Islands too, and from here you can paddle through the lagoons and explore tiny islands like **Forestry Island**, which is otherwise inaccessible.

Hanlan's Point

Hanlan's Point is named for another old island family who first settled here at Gibraltar Point, on the island's southwestern tip, in 1862. The most famous member of the family was Edward "Ned" Hanlan, who earned Canada's first Olympic gold medal as a champion rower, a skill he honed rowing back and forth to the mainland. The Hanlans built a hotel-resort here and others followed, though none has survived and neither has the old amusement park, which was demolished in the 1930s to make way for what is now the Toronto City Centre Airport.

Ferries arrive on the northeast side of the island close to the airport. The ferry dock is the location of the other **Toronto Island Bicycle Rental** outlet (see above), as well as washrooms, showers and a snack bar. From here, footpaths and bicycle trails run south, passing behind – and just east – of **Hanlan's Point Beach**, a stretch of tawny sand that is more valued as an environmentalist's haven than a swimming area. Indeed, generations of budding biologists have been nurtured at the nearby **Toronto Islands Public and Natural Science School**, which teaches city children about the flora and fauna of both the islands and Lake Ontario. The school is on the south side of the island, and nearby also are both the filtration plant and the limestone

Gibraltar Point Lighthouse, built in 1808 and reputedly haunted by its first keeper. Although it has not functioned as a beacon since 1958, the Gibraltar is open to the public, free of charge.

The suburbs

Toronto's **suburban communities** surround the city in a mixture of parkland, residential neighbourhoods and monotonous stretches of malls, parking lots and high-rises. The discerning eye, however, will see beyond the monochromatic urban sprawl to notice that the ethnic diversity so prevalent downtown extends to the suburbs as well, keeping the city's environs from sinking into the yawning blandness characteristic of many North American city outskirts.

In 1998 Ontario's provincial government decided that the City of Toronto and its suburban municipalities would amalgamate into one huge city. This "Mega City", as it's colloquially known, has a population of over four million people and covers an area of 632 square kilometres. While the consolidation was a major social and political controversy for residents, to outsiders it's of little consequence, and the only potential for confusion might be the continued use of the different suburbs' names by the local population.

Venturing outside the city centre is certainly worth your while, particularly since a fair number of major attractions – like the Metro Zoo, the Ontario Science Centre and Black Creek Pioneer Village – make their homes in the suburbs, especially the Scarborough and North York neighbourhoods. Toronto's extensive transit system takes passengers to the perimeters of Toronto's suburbs for the flat fare of $2 – the same price as a subway ride in the downtown core. It's advisable to rely on public transport rather than a rental car, as the arterial roadways can be scary prospects during rush-hour traffic.

On weekends, suburban bus and train routes run less frequently. Contact the Toronto Transit Commission (TTC) for route information; ☎393-4636.

THE BEACHES

Map 2, I7 & J7.

A century ago, **The Beaches**, located to the east of downtown Toronto, was what the Toronto Islands are today: a summer vacation area used for frolicking about on the shores of Lake Ontario. Today, The Beaches is more a residential than a holiday spot, but its overall atmosphere has retained the look and feel of a turn-of-the-century seaside resort. It has a three-kilometre boardwalk, ample Queen Anne-style houses with generous front porches, and a charming bandshell in Kew Park, which serves as the main stage for the neighbourhood's many festivals; see p.262. The fact that The Beaches has been so successfully preserved is remarkable, especially considering that Toronto's downtown core is only twenty minutes away by streetcar.

In the 1880s the Toronto Street Railway Company (the predecessor to the Toronto Transit Commission) installed a streetcar line that ran east along Queen Street and led to the sparsely settled Beaches. Initially, the church-going city was scandalised by the TSR's idea to run its trams on Sundays, so that the city's working people could get out in the fresh air and visit the amusement parks that were springing up in the area. But commerce and recreation triumphed, and the line – which continues to this day – spurred the growth of The Beaches community. In 1903 the city began a thirty-year project to acquire the private parks clustered along the waterfront. The consolidation of the private parks led to the opening of the public **Beaches Park**, whose tennis courts, parklands, boardwalks and unspoiled beaches offer unparalleled rest and relaxation to the city's masses.

While those from Toronto proper often refer to this area as "The Beach", local residents prefer "The Beaches". There are two main sections to the community, **Kew Beach** and **Balmy Beach**, and neither wants to be thought of as subordinate to the other – hence the insistence on pluralisation. Kew Beach, however, is probably the most popular. Here, **Kew Beach Park**, situated just below Queen Street, is a picture-perfect park with rolling, grassy hills and a sandy beachfront that is delightful even on a packed Sunday afternoon. Balmy Beach is separated from Kew Beach by a tiny inlet at the foot of Silverbirch Avenue, but, contrary to local belief, there's very little distinction between the two – Balmy's beach and parklands are just as nice as Kew's. Slightly west of Kew Beach is **Cherry Beach**, a favourite among hikers, bird watchers and cyclists; it begins at **Ashbridges Bay Park**, which is at the corner of Lakeshore Boulevard East and Coxwell Avenue. Signs inside the park point out the **Martin Goodman Trail**, a hiking route that spans the entire Toronto waterfront.

One of the strangest and most intriguing sights in The Beaches is the **RC Harris Water Filtration Plant**, built during the Great Depression and located at 2701 Queen St East (☎392-3566). Commissioner Harris, whose career achievements are referred to in Michael Ondaatje's novel *In the Skin of the Lion* (see p.303), decided that a project as grand as turning the water of Lake Ontario into safe, clean drinking water for the people of Toronto demanded a magnificent building, complete with a palatial, Byzantine-style edifice; it looks like something a multi-millionaire would have built for himself. Instead, it's Toronto's temple to public health. There are free tours (Sat 10am, 11.30am and 1pm) of the filtration complex, which reveal the inner workings of the mammoth architecture and monstrous machines – a must for fans of architectural exotica.

SCARBOROUGH

Map 2, J3 through N5.

Scarborough, unjustly, is best known for its dreary strip malls and doughnut shops; it was stuck with the unfortunate nickname "Scarberia" by other Torontonians. The area, however, does have a couple of notable attractions – as well as native son Mike Myers, whose parody of growing up in this suburb was repackaged as the American midwest and released as the motion picture *Wayne's World*.

Toronto Zoo

Map 2, N3. Meadowvale Road, north of Hwy-401 exit 389. March–Sept 9am–7.30pm, Oct–Feb 9.30am–5.30pm, closed Dec 25; $12, children $7; Ⓣ 392-5900.

Set on the hilly edge of the Rouge Valley in Scarborough, the **Toronto Zoo** (about fifty minutes from downtown on public transport) encompasses a 710-acre site that does its best to place animals in their own environments. To this end, seven **pavilions** representing different geographic regions are filled with indigenous plants and more than five thousand animals. Hardy species live outside in large paddocks, and an open train, the **Zoomobile** ($3), zips around the vast site for those opposed to hiking between enclosures. In addition to polar bears, musk oxen, Siberian tigers and camels, a variety of wildlife – raccoons, chipmunks and foxes – drop in from the wooded land surrounding the zoo for frequent visits.

Some of the most popular attractions include the **Underwater Exhibits**, featuring South African fur seals, beavers and the ever-popular otters; and **Edge of Night**, an extension of the Australasian Pavilion, which simulates night-time in the Australian outback. The zoo also has an extensive breeding programme, which has helped reintroduce a variety of threatened species back into the wild, most notably the Puerto Rican crested toad, the wood bison and the black-footed ferret. When new zoo babies are born – occasions that are often trumpeted with considerable media fanfare – the zoo goes on red-alert to accommodate the influx in visitor attendance.

Arriving by **car**, take Hwy-401 to Scarborough (exit 389) and drive north on Meadowvale Road, following the signs for the zoo. Via **public transport**, catch the Sheppard East #85B bus from the Sheppard subway station. **Eating** at the zoo is dominated by McDonald's, which has a monopoly on the hot food concessions. There are, however, pleasant picnic areas if you bring your own lunch.

SCARBOROUGH BLUFFS

Map 2, K6 & L6.

When Elizabeth Simcoe, the wife of Upper Canada's first lieutenant-governor, sailed past these bluffs, she remarked how they reminded her of the Scarborough cliffs in England, and hence the most easterly part of Toronto got its name. The **Scarborough Bluffs** are indeed a beautiful and significant geological feature, and they have been preserved from rampant development by the Metropolitan Toronto and Region Conservation Authority, which has created three parks: **Bluffer's Park**, which features a public marina, **Scarborough Heights**, the smallest and least spectacular of the three, and **Cathedral Bluffs Park**, which has dramatic spires of eroded sandstone cliffs rising more than 90m above Lake Ontario. All are within a short walk of the Kingston Road (#12) bus stop on Kingston Road. For more information about these or any of Toronto's parks call ☏392-8186.

Another scenic stop along the bluffs is **Guildwood Park** and the **Guild Inn** (☏261-3331), accessible either by turning south onto Guildwood Parkway from Kingston Road, or by taking the Morningside #116 bus, which departs from the Kennedy subway station and heads east into the park. Although a succession of people have owned the property since the eighteenth century, its name and reputation were established in 1932, when Spencer and Rosa Clark decided to turn their 36-acre estate into a "Guild of all arts", and established a rent-free colony for artists and craftspeople. They also collected over seventy architectural ornaments from several of the historic Toronto buildings that were torn down to make way for the skyscrapers that dominate the skyline today. Huge keystones and fanciful arches and doorways (minus their buildings) dot the Guild Inn grounds, while the main part of the Art Deco house at the centre of the park is now an attractive restaurant, serving moderate to expensive family-style meals. The real reason to eat here isn't the food, however, but the stunning view of Lake Ontario from the dining room.

Finally, tucked in behind the Guild Inn estate is an early nineteenth-century **log cabin**, similar in style to the late eighteenth-century homes built by Upper Canada's earliest settlers. The cabin and its site, which are part of an ongoing archaeological excavation, are open to the public free of charge during the summer months.

SCARBOROUGH BLUFFS

NORTH YORK

Map 2, E2 through I3.

By far the best reason to visit North York is the **Ontario Science Centre**, a sprawling testament to the notion that science and technology can be fun. To reach North York from downtown, take the Yonge subway line north to the North York Centre stop.

The Ontario Science Centre

Map 2, I5. 770 Don Mills Rd. Daily 10am–5pm, closed Dec 25; $7.50; ☎696-3191.

The 800-plus exhibits on science and technology here are so captivating that visitors often forget they're supposed to be learning something in the process. Although children are the primary audience, adults shouldn't deprive themselves of the pleasure of exploring interactive displays on subjects like genetics and electromagnetics. One of the most popular exhibits is **The Human Body**, where visitors can discern the inner workings of human biology through life-sized three-dimensional displays and various quizzes and games. There's also information on complex medical advances like bioengineering, DNA fingerprinting and immunology, all presented in mediums and manners comfortable to the layman.

One of the biggest draws at the Science Centre is the new **OMNIMAX Theatre** (call ☎696-1000 for show schedules). The 320 (reclining) seat theatre features a 24-metre-high wraparound screen with digital sound that creates an enveloping cinematic experience.

To reach the Science Centre by **car** from downtown Toronto, take the Don Valley Parkway and follow the signs from the Don Mills Road North exit. By **public transport**, take the Yonge Street subway line north to

Eglinton station and transfer to the Eglington East bus; get off at Don Mills Road. The trip should take about thirty minutes from the vicinity of downtown's Union Station.

BLACK CREEK PIONEER VILLAGE

Map 2, D2 & E2. Jane Street and Steels Avenue, Yorkville.
May–June Mon–Fri 9.30am–4pm, Sat & Sun 10am–5pm; July–Sept daily 10am–5pm; Oct–Dec Mon–Fri 9.30am–4pm, Sat & Sun 10am–4.30pm; $9, children $4.

A distant second in popularity to the Ontario Science Centre, North York's **Black Creek Pioneer Village** is nonetheless worth a visit. Like the Fort York "living history" site in Toronto proper (see p.32), Pioneer Village is staffed by guides dressed in period attire. Here visitors are immersed in an Upper Canadian village dating from the 1860s, and learn about the everyday activities of the early settlers. The site has over 35 authentically restored buildings, heritage gardens and a host of working pioneers: gunsmiths make muskets, smiths work the forge, and women perform various domestic chores like churning butter, carding and spinning wool, and weaving cloth. On the whole, the Village presents a pleasing but somewhat sentimentalised view of the past and pioneer self-sufficiency. And in that sense, it has more to do with nostalgia than it does with history. The details are all there, but it lacks an authentic spirit.

Arriving by **car**, travel north on Hwy-400 and exit on Steels Avenue East. From here, turn west on Murray Ross Parkway, which is one block east of Jane Street, to find the Village's parking lot. Via **public transport** (about forty minutes from downtown), take the Yonge subway line to Finch station and board the Steels bus (#60 B, D or E).

PARAMOUNT CANADA'S WONDERLAND

Map 2, D1. Hwy-400 (Rutherford exit). May–Aug daily, Sept & Oct 2–4 days weekly; opening and closing times vary – call ☎905/832-7000 for latest details. One-day pass covering all rides $41; children 3–6 years $20; grounds only $26; parking $6.50.

Paramount Canada's Wonderland is Toronto's Disney World. A theme park featuring over fifty different rides, it is spread over a large chunk of land about 30km north of downtown in the suburb of **Vaughan**, whose only worthwhile attraction is the park. Among the many attractions here are roller-coasters, a twenty-acre water park with sixteen water slides, souped-up go-karts, mini-golf and roaming cartoon and TV characters – everything from Fred Flintstone to Star Trek "Klingons". The roller-coaster rides are enough to make the strongest stomachs churn, if the kitsch of the place doesn't do it first. By public transport, catch the Wonderland Express GO bus from the Yorkdale or York Mills subway stations; buses leave every hour and take forty minutes.

THE MCMICHAEL CANADIAN ART COLLECTION

Map 2, B2. Hwy-400 (Rutherford exit). May–Oct daily 10am–5pm; Nov–April Tues–Sat 10am–4pm, Sun 10am–5pm; $7.

The **McMichael Canadian Art Collection** is situated in the nondescript commuter township of **Kleinburg**, roughly 40km north of downtown. The collection, housed in a series of handsome log and stone buildings in the wooded Humber River valley, was put together by Robert and Signe McMichael, devoted followers of the Group of Seven (see p.48), and given to the province in 1965. On the **Lower Level**, a series of small galleries focuses on various aspects of the Group of Seven's work. Gallery Two, for example, begins with the artistic friends and contemporaries who influenced the Group's early style, while Gallery Three zeroes in on the Group's founder, Tom Thomson. The galleries boast fine paintings here by Group of Seven luminaries like J.E.H. MacDonald, Lawren Harris, Edwin Holgate, F.H. Varley and L.L. Fitzgerald, as well as works by their talented contemporary Emily Carr.

The museum's **Upper Level** is devoted primarily to modern First Nations Art and Inuit soapstone carvings and lithographs. Rotating temporary exhibitions appear on the Upper Level as well, but they are often of dubious quality.

When you've finished with the paintings, allow a little time to stroll the footpaths that lattice the **woods** surrounding the McMichael. Maps are provided free at reception, and as you wander around you'll bump into various pieces of sculpture as well as Tom Thomson's old wooden shack, moved here from Rosedale in 1962.

HIGH PARK

Map 2, D6 & D7. Subway Dundas West.

There have been Poles in Toronto since the middle of the nineteenth century, but the first major influx came in the 1890s when their homeland was wracked by famine. These early immigrants were reinforced on several subsequent occasions, most notably during and immediately after World War II, when the Germans and then the Russians occupied Poland, driving thousands into exile. In the 1950s, the Poles, along with other Slavic speakers from Eastern Europe, gravitated to the **High Park** district of Toronto, about 5km west of Yonge Street. It's not a particularly attractive neighbourhood, consisting for the most part of a low tangle of undistinguished brick buildings, but the long main street – **Roncesvalles Avenue** – is lined with eastern European eateries and shops.

On Roncesvalles' western edge is the hilly expanse of **High Park**, a rectangle of greenery running north from the Gardiner Expressway to Bloor Street West. The park traces its origins to John George Howard, an Englishman who bought the land hereabouts shortly after his arrival in Toronto in 1832. The Howard family later bequeathed their estate to the city, but the old family home, **Colborne Lodge** (guided tours only; Tues–Fri noon–4pm, Sat–Sun noon–5pm; $3.50), has survived, tucked away among the wooded ravines on the southern edge of the park. The lodge looks pretty dreary from the outside, but the interior has been delightfully restored to its appearance in the middle of the nineteenth century. John Howard was a keen watercolourist, painting dozens of early Toronto scenes. A regularly rotated selection of his work is displayed at the lodge, and although he was hardly an outstanding artist, his watercolours are enjoyable, especially in the eccentric way he manages to squeeze a jubilant animal (or two) into each and every one of his paintings. John and his wife, Jemima Francis, were buried a short stroll north of the lodge beneath the large **stone cairn**.

The flatter, northern half of the park is prime picnic territory, with primly mown lawns and a scattering of sports facilities. The park's southwest corner boasts the charming **Hillside Gardens**, a manicured stretch of gardens that border the wooded slopes above **Grenadier Pond**. The pond was supposedly named after the British grenadiers who paraded here on the winter ice, though there are more lurid theories: the most widely believed has a young skater spotting a grinning grenadier frozen under the ice. Unfortunately, the pond – really a mini-lake – is currently in a bit of a mess, its ecosystem unbalanced by a surfeit of phosphorus. Efforts are being made to rectify matters and revive the bass and pike population, but it will take years.

The north side of the park is a short walk from the High Park subway station; the south and east sections are readily reached on bus #80, which leaves Keele subway station and travels down the eastern edge of the park along Parkside Drive.

Day-trips

The most popular day-trip destination from Toronto is without a doubt **Niagara Falls**, a vast arc of water crashing over a 52-metre cliff. One of the most celebrated sights in North America, the Falls are just 130km south of Toronto, along and around the heavily industrialised Lake Ontario shoreline. They adjoin the uninspiring town of Niagara Falls, which bills itself as the "Honeymoon Capital of the World" – and its hotels and motels have the heart-shaped double beds to prove it. The Falls are the most conspicuous feature of the **Niagara River**, which links lakes Erie and Ontario. The other prime attraction hereabouts is the delightful little town of **Niagara-on-the-Lake**, whose colonial villas abut Lake Ontario 26km downstream from the Falls.

Less familiar to visitors is the **Lake Huron shoreline**, 210km west of Toronto across a thick band of fertile farmland. The lakeshore is dotted with pretty little country towns, especially **Goderich** and **Bayfield**; the first is coveted for its rustic atmosphere and intriguing Huron Historic Gaol, the second for its old-fashioned graces and leafy streets adorned by elegant clapboard villas – a far cry from the fast-food joints and neon billboards that disfigure many Canadian towns.

Finally, there's **Severn Sound**, a couple of hours north of Toronto by car. This is the southeastern inlet of Georgian Bay, an area of bare, glacier-shaved rocks, myriad lakes and spindly pines immortalised by the Group of Seven painters (see p.48). Severn Sound is one of the most beautiful parts of southern Ontario, and although the region is dotted with country cottages, pristine landscapes have been conserved in the **Georgian Bay Islands National Park**, accessible by water taxi from the tiny resort of **Honey Harbour**. Also on Severn Sound are the region's two outstanding historical reconstructions: the seventeenth-century Jesuit complex of **Sainte-Marie among the Hurons** and the British naval base at **Discovery Harbour**, founded outside Penetanguishene in 1817.

With the exception of Niagara Falls – which is easily reached from Toronto by train or bus – **public transportation** to destinations outside the city is limited and for the smaller towns a car is pretty much essential.

Theatre enthusiasts will want to explore the town of Stratford, which puts on North America's largest classical theatre festival every year from May to November. For complete details, see "Performing Arts and Film", p.202.

Niagara Falls

Map 1, E6.

In 1860, thousands watched as Charles Blondin walked a tightrope across **NIAGARA FALLS**. Midway, he paused to cook an omelette on a portable grill and then had a marksman shoot a hole through his hat from the *Maid of the Mist* boat, fifty metres below. As attested by Blondin's antics, and by the millions of waterlogged tourists who jam the tour boats and observation points, Niagara Falls is a dramatic attraction. Still, the stupendous first impression doesn't last long, and to prevent each year's crop of visitors from becoming bored, Niagarans have created an infinite number of vantage points: you can ogle the 52-metre shoot from boats, viewing towers, helicopters, cable cars and even tunnels in the rock face behind the cascade. Of the options, the **tunnels** and **boats** best capture the extraordinary force of the waterfall, a perpetual white-crested thundering pile-up that had Austrian composer Gustav Mahler bawling "At last, fortissimo!" over the din.

Available from mid-May to mid-October, the Explorer's Passport Plus is a combined ticket for three of the Falls' main attractions – the Journey Behind the Falls tunnel tour, the Great Gorge Adventure and the Butterfly Conservatory (see pp.97–100 for descriptions) – along with all-day transportation on Niagara Parks' People Mover buses. It costs $20 for adults, $10 for children (6–12 years old). The Explorer's Passport is the same deal without the bus – price is $16 ($8 for children). Alternatively, the Natural Wonderpassport Plus replaces the Butterfly Conservatory with the Spanish Aero Car and costs $18 ($9 for children). Tickets are available at the Table Rock Information Centre. Incidentally, tickets for the highly sought-after "Maid of the Mist" boat tour must be purchased separately, and cost $10.65. The Niagara Parks Web site is Ⓦ *www.niagaraparks.com*.

From Toronto, **trains** and **buses** serve the town of Niagara Falls, 3km north of the waterfall. The most straightforward way to get here is to take the Toronto–Niagara Falls train, which runs six times daily, takes two hours and costs $26 each way. If you're travelling by **car** you'll have more than enough time to squeeze in a visit to delightful **Niagara-on-the-Lake** (see p.103), 26km downstream. If you decide to seek accommodation in the region, look here, skipping the crassly commercialised town of Niagara Falls – but note that room availability is extremely tight during the summer high season, when it's essential to book a few days in advance.

THE FALLS AND ENVIRONS

Map 1, E6; inset, p.98.

Though you can hear the growl of the **Falls** miles away, nothing quite prepares you for your first glimpse – a fearsome white arc shrouded in clouds of dense spray, with the riverboats struggling far below. There are actually two cataracts as tiny Goat Island – which must be one of the wettest and bleakest places on earth – divides the accelerating water into two channels: on the American side, the river slips over the precipice of the **American Falls**, 320m wide but still only half the width of **Horseshoe Falls** on the Canadian side. The spectacle is even more amazing in winter, when snow-covered trees edge a jagged armoury of freezing mist and heaped ice blocks. It all looks like a scene of untrammelled nature, but it isn't. Since the early twentieth century, hydroelectric schemes have greatly reduced the water flow, and all sorts of tinkering has spread what's left of the Niagara River more evenly across the Fall's crest line. As a result, the process of erosion – which has moved the Falls some 11km upstream in twelve thousand years – has slowed from one metre a year to just 30cm. This obviously has advantages for the tourist industry, but the environmental consequences of harnessing the river are still unclear.

Beside Horseshoe Falls, **Table Rock House** has a small, free observation platform and elevators that travel to the base of the cliff, where **tunnels** (open daily from 9am; $6.50), grandly named the Journey Behind the Falls, lead to points directly behind the waterfall. For a more panoramic view, a small **Incline Railway** ($1) takes visitors up the hill behind Table Rock House to the **Minolta Tower**, 6732 Oakes Drive ($7), which has observation decks, though the

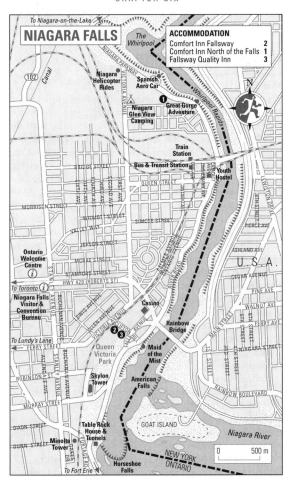

NIAGARA FALLS

To Niagara-on-the-Lake

The Whirlpool

ACCOMMODATION

Comfort Inn Fallsway	2
Comfort Inn North of the Falls	1
Fallsway Quality Inn	3

N

(102)

NIAGARA PARKWAY

Canal

VICTORIA AVENUE

Niagara Helicopter Rides

Spanish Aero Car

Niagara Glen View Camping

1

Great Gorge Adventure

Whirlpool Rapids

LEWISTON DRIVE

Train Station

Bus & Transit Station

Youth Hostel

QUEEN STREET

BRIDGE STREET

FIRST AVENUE

SECOND AVENUE

THIRD AVENUE

FOURTH AVENUE

MORRISON STREET

PIERCE AVE

WILMOT STREET

SIMCOE STREET

ASHLAND AVE

VALLEY WAY

JEPSON STREET

U.S.A.

MCRAE STREET

Ontario Welcome Centre ℹ

STAMFORD STREET

HURON AVENUE

CEDAR AVENUE

To Toronto ℹ

HWY 420 (ROBERTS ST)

PINE AVE

Niagara Falls Visitor & Convention Bureau

LEWIS AVENUE

WALNUT AVE

BUCHANAN AVENUE

Casino

MAIN STREET

To Lundy's Lane

STANLEY AVENUE

VICTORIA AVENUE

FALLS AVENUE

2 **3**

FERRY STREET

Rainbow Bridge

FERRY AVE

NIAGARA STREET

Queen Victoria Park

CLIFTON HILL

Maid of the Mist

ROBINSON ST

THIRD STREET

Skylon Tower

American Falls

RAINBOW BOULEVARD

MURRAY STREET

DIXON STREET

GOAT ISLAND

Niagara River

Table Rock House & Tunnels

DUNN STREET

Minolta Tower

PORTAGE RD

NEW YORK

ONTARIO

0	500 m

Horseshoe Falls

To Fort Erie

NIAGARA FALLS

views are better from the Skylon Tower (see p.99).

From Table Rock House, a wide and crowded path leads north along the cliffs, with the manicured lawns of Queen Victoria Park to the left and views of American Falls to the right. After a few minutes' march, turn left up Murray Street to the **Skylon Tower** ($7.95), whose observation deck is high above the Falls, or continue along the path to the foot of Clifton Hill, where **Maid of the Mist boats** edge out into the river and push up towards the Falls, an exhilarating (and extremely damp) trip (April–June & Sept–Oct Mon–Fri 10am–5pm, Sat & Sun 10am–6pm; July–Aug daily 9am–8pm; boats leave every 15min in high season, otherwise every 30min; they cost $10.65 per person, including waterproofs).

Clifton Hill itself is a tawdry collection of fast-food joints and bizarre attractions like the eminently missable Believe It or Not Museum, where you can see a dog with human teeth and a Chinese chap with two pupils in each eye. If you stick to the river's edge, though, you can avoid both this unattractive side of Niagara and the area's second-biggest crowd puller – the 24-hr, bristlingly new **casino**, near the Rainbow Bridge that connects to the United States.

DOWNSTREAM FROM THE FALLS

The **Niagara River Recreation Trail** is a combined bicycle and walking track that travels the entire length of the Niagara River from Lake Ontario to Lake Erie, running parallel to the main road – the Niagara Parkway. Downstream from the Falls, the trail cuts across the foot of Clifton Hill (see above) before continuing north for a further 3km to the **Great Gorge Adventure** (May–Oct; $5), which – despite the grand title – is no more than an elevator and then a tunnel leading to a boardwalk that oversees the Whirlpool Rapids, where the river seethes and fizzes as it makes an abrupt turn to the east. From here, it's a further 1km to the brightly painted **Spanish Aero Car** (April–Dec daily from 9am; $5.50), a cable-car ride across the gorge that's as close as you'll come to emulating Blondin's tightrope trick, and another 1.5km to **Niagara Helicopter Rides**, 3731 Victoria Ave (℡905/357-5672), which offers a nine-minute excursion over the Falls for $85 per person, $300 for four. You don't need to book ahead, as the helicopters whiz in and out with unnerving frequency from 9am to sunset, weather permitting. Pushing on, the trail soon reaches the **Niagara Glen Nature Area**, where paths lead down from the cliff top to the bottom of the gorge (a hot and sticky trek in the height of the summer). Nearby, about 800m further downstream, lie the spick-and-span **Niagara Parks Botanical Gardens** (free), whose splendid **Butterfly Conservatory** (daily; May–Sept 9am–9pm, Oct–April 9am–6pm; $8; ℡905/356-0025 or 1-877/642-7275) attracts visitors in their droves.

About 3km further on, the main road begins a curving descent down to the pretty little village of **Queenston**, once an important transit centre when goods had to be carted round the Falls. In the village, on Partition Street, the **Laura Secord Homestead** (May–Aug daily 10am–5pm; $1.75) is a reconstruction of the house of Massachusetts-born Laura Ingersoll Secord, whose dedication to the Imperial interest was such that she ran 30km through the woods to warn the British army of a surprise attack planned by the Americans in the War of 1812.

PRACTICALITIES

The **VIA train station** in Niagara Falls is located in the less touristy part of town, about 3km north of the Falls. The **bus station** is across the street, 420 Bridge St at Erie Avenue. Next door to the bus station, **Niagara Transit**

(☎905/356 1179) operates the **Falls Shuttle** bus service (March–Nov daily 9am–1am; single ticket $2.75, all-day pass $5). This service runs across town, stopping – amongst many places – at the foot of Clifton Hill and beside the Skylon Tower; buses run every thirty minutes during peak periods, otherwise hourly. The Shuttle connects to the Niagara Parks' **People Mover** system (April to mid-June & Sept to late Oct daily 10am–6pm, often later; mid-June to Aug daily 9am–11pm), which traditionally operates from April to late October, though in the future the buses may well run all year. These People Movers travel 30km along the riverbank between Queenston Heights Park, north of the Falls, and the Rapids' View car park to the south, passing all the major attractions on the way. People Movers appear at twenty-minute intervals and an **all-day pass** costs $5.

As for **information**, steer clear of the gaggles of privately run tourist centres that dot the area, and head instead for the official **tourist information centre** (☎905/371-0254 or 1-877/NIA-PARK) at the Table Rock complex beside the Horseshoe Falls. Alternatively, if you're after information on the town of Niagara Falls, check out the **Niagara Falls Visitor and Convention Bureau**, just off Hwy-420 as you head into town from the QEW, at 5515 Stanley Ave (May–Aug daily 8am–8pm; Sept–April Mon–Fri 8am–6pm, Sat 10am–6pm & Sun 10am–4pm; ☎905/356-6061 or 1-800/563-2557; ⊛*www.niagarafallstourism.com*). Finally, the **Ontario Welcome Centre** (June–Aug daily 8am–8pm; May & Sept Mon–Thurs & Sun 8.30am–6pm, Fri & Sat 8am–8pm; Oct–April daily 8.30am–4.30pm; ☎905/358-3221) is well stocked with literature on the whole of the province; it is located beside Hwy-420 at the Stanley Avenue intersection.

- -
For accommodation price codes, see p.126.
- -

NIAGARA FALLS

ACCOMMODATION

Comfort Inn Fallsway
4960 Clifton Hill
ⓣ905/358-3293
or 1-800/263-2557;
ⓕ905/358-3818;
ⓦ*www.comfortniagara.com*.
Nothing extraordinary perhaps, but this chain motel has
entirely adequate rooms decorated in brisk, modern style
and is handily located near
the Falls. ❹.

Comfort Inn North
of the Falls
4009 River Rd
ⓣ905/356-0131

or 1-800/565-0035;
ⓕ905/356-1800.
Similar to the *Comfort Inn*
listed above, but with a more
attractive location, flanked by
parkland near the Spanish
Aero Car (see p.100). ❺.

Fallsway Quality Inn
4946 Clifton Hill
ⓣ905/358-3601
or 1-800/263-7137;
ⓕ905/358-3818;
ⓦ*www.fallsresort.com*.
Comfortable, pleasantly furnished motel-style rooms in a
300-room inn on its own
grounds (or rather car park)
on Clifton Hill. ❹.

EATING AND DRINKING

- -
For restaurant price codes, see p.143.
- -

Big Anthony's
5677 Victoria Ave.
ⓣ905/354-9844. Inexpensive.
Tasty Italian food at this
small, family-run place
owned by a well-known ex-
professional wrestler, pictures of whom decorate the

windows. Close to Clifton
Hill.

Golden Griddle
At the Fallsway Quality Inn,
4946 Clifton Hill.
ⓣ905/358-3601. Inexpensive.
A good family-style restaurant

NIAGARA FALLS

with a basic menu and main courses from around $9.

Ponderosa Steak House
5329 Ferry St. Inexpensive.

Budget steak house that serves up decent cuts of meat along with an all-you-can-eat salad bar, all at reasonable prices.

Niagara-on-the-Lake

Map 1, E6.

One of the prettiest places in Ontario, **NIAGARA-ON-THE-LAKE**, 26km downstream from the Falls, boasts elegant clapboard houses and well-kept gardens, all spread along tree-lined streets. The town, much of which dates from the early nineteenth century, was originally known as Newark and became the first capital of Upper Canada in 1792. Four years later it lost this distinction to York (Toronto) because it was deemed too close to the American frontier, and therefore vulnerable to attack. The US army did, in fact, cross the river in 1813, destroying the town. It was quickly rebuilt (and renamed), and has managed to avoid all but the most sympathetic of modifications ever since. The town attracts a few too many day-trippers for its own good, but the crowds are rarely oppressive, except on weekends in July and August.

THE TOWN

It is the general flavour of Niagara-on-the-Lake that appeals rather than any specific sight, but **Queen Street**, the main drag, does hold the **Apothecary** (mid-May–Aug daily noon–6pm; free), which is worth a look for its beautifully carved walnut and butternut cabinets and porcelain jars.

There is also the **Niagara Historical Museum**, at 43 Castlereagh St and Davy (Jan–Feb Sat–Sun 1–5pm; March, April, Nov & Dec daily 1–5pm; May–Oct daily 10am–5pm; $3), whose accumulated artefacts track through the early history of the town and include mementoes of the Laura Secord family (see p.100). More diverting still is the British military post of **Fort George** (May–Oct daily 10am–5pm; $6), 700m southeast of town via Picton Street. In the early nineteenth century, so many of its soldiers were hightailing it off to the States that the British had to garrison the fort with the Royal Canadian Rifle Regiment, a troop of primarily married men approaching retirement who were unlikely to forfeit their pensions by deserting. If they did try and were caught, they were branded on the chest with the letter "D" (for "Deserter"), and were either lashed or transported to a penal colony – except in wartime, when they were shot.

The fort was destroyed during the War of 1812, but today's site is a splendid reconstruction. The palisaded **compound** holds ten buildings, among them three pine blockhouses and the powder magazine, its inside finished in wood and copper to reduce the chances of an accidental explosion – and the soldiers working in here wore shoes with no metal fastenings. There are also lantern-light **ghost tours** of the fort – good fun with or without an apparition (May–June Sun at 8.30pm; July–Aug Mon, Thurs & Sun at 8.30pm; $5). Tours leave from the parking lot in front of the fort; tickets can be purchased either in advance at the fort's gift shop, or from the guide at the beginning of the tour.

Niagara-on-the-Lake is the location of one of Canada's most acclaimed theatre festivals, the Shaw Festival. See p.204 for details.

PRACTICALITIES

The easiest way to reach Niagara-on-the-Lake via public transport is on the **Shuttle bus** (℡905/357-4000; $16 return) from Niagara Falls. From May to October there are three services daily in each direction, and usually one daily in winter. Pick-up points include the Minolta Tower and the *Sheraton Fallsview Hotel*, 6755 Oakes Drive. In Niagara-on-the-Lake, the Shuttle bus stops right in the centre at the intersection of Queen and Gate streets. The Niagara-on-the-Lake **tourist office**, 153 King St at Prideaux Street (Jan & Feb Mon–Fri 9am–5pm; March–Dec Mon–Fri 9am–5pm, Sat–Sun 10am–5pm; ℡905/468-4263; Ⓦ*www.niagaraonthelake.com*) issues town maps and operates a free **room reservation service**. This is invaluable, as the town's hotels and B&Bs, of which there are dozens, are frequently booked up months in advance. Bed-and-breakfast rates range from $60 to $100. It only takes a few minutes to stroll from one end of town to the other, but to venture further afield – especially to the Falls – you might consider renting a **bicycle** from Niagara Wine Tours International, 92 Picton St (℡905/468-1300), whose main business is running cycle tours to local wineries.

For accommodation price codes, see p.126.

ACCOMMODATION

Adam Lockhart's Storrington House

289 Simcoe St ℡905/468-8254; Ⓕ905/468-9023. Niagara-on-the-Lake boasts dozens of charming B&Bs, but this is one of the best, with each of the guest bedrooms of this 1817 house decked out in impeccable style. Breakfasts are a treat too, and it's an easy stroll from here to the town centre. ❺.

Moffat Inn

60 Picton St ⓣ905/468-4116.
This modest hotel is located
in a modernised building
close to the centre of town.
The rooms are pleasant but
undistinguished, which means
that its prices are lower than
most of its rivals and there is
sometimes space here when
everyone else is full. ❹.

Oban Inn

160 Front St
ⓣ905/468-2165
or 1-888/669 5566;
ⓕ905/468-4165.
A delightful and luxurious
hotel across from the lake and
within easy walking distance
of the town centre. The original *Oban* burnt to the
ground in 1992, but its
replacement was built in true
colonial style, with an elegant
wooden veranda. The gardens
are beautiful and the breakfasts are first rate too. ❼.

EATING AND DRINKING

The Angel Inn

224 Regent St. Inexpensive.
Decked out in the style of a
British pub, this lively spot
offers filling bar snacks and is
a good place for a drink. Just
off Queen Street.

Buttery Restaurant

19 Queen St. Moderate.
A pleasant and popular
restaurant with tasty homemade pies on its imaginative
and reasonably priced menu.

Shaw Café and Wine Bar

92 Queen St. Inexpensive.
A smart café-bar serving a
wide range of salads, sandwiches and pasta dishes at
affordable prices. Arguably
the best place in town.

NIAGARA-ON-THE-LAKE

ONTARIO WINES

Until the 1980s Canadian wine was something of a joke. The industry's most popular product was a sticky, fizzy concoction called "Baby Duck", and other varieties were commonly called "block-and-tackle" wines after a widely reported witticism of a member of the Ontario legislature: "If you drink a bottle and walk a block, you can tackle anyone." This state of affairs has, however, been transformed by the **Vintners Quality Alliance** (VQA), who have, since 1989, come to exercise tight control over wine production in Ontario, which produces eighty percent of the country's wine. Still, as you might expect from a developing wine area, quality is rather inconsistent. Of the varieties produced in Ontario, the Rieslings – a refreshingly crisp white wine with a mellow, warming aftertaste – are perhaps the best of the present range, white or red.

More than twenty **wineries** are clustered in the vicinity of Niagara-on-the-Lake, and most are very willing to show visitors around. Local tourist offices carry a full list with opening times, but one of the most interesting is **Inniskillin**, Line 3 (Service Road 66), just off the Niagara Parkway, about 5km south of Niagara-on-the-Lake (daily: May–Oct 10am–6pm, Nov–April 10am–5pm; ⓣ905/468-3554; ⓦ*www.inniskillin. com*). Here you can follow a twenty-step self-guided tour that introduces visitors to the winemaking process. This is also one of the few Canadian wineries to produce **ice wine**, a sweet dessert wine made from grapes that are left on the vine until December or January, when they are handpicked at night when frozen. The picking and the crushing of the frozen grapes is a time-consuming business and this is reflected in the price – about $50 per 375ml bottle.

Goderich and Bayfield

A popular summer resort area, the southern section of the
Lake Huron shoreline is trimmed by sandy beaches and a
steep bluff that's interrupted by the occasional river valley.
The water is much less polluted than Lake Ontario, the
sunsets are beautiful, and in **Goderich** and neighbouring
Bayfield, the lakeshore possesses two of the most appealing
places in the whole of the province. It's about 210km – a
good three hours by car – from Toronto, which makes a
day-trip just about feasible, though it's better to stay the
night (Bayfield has the choicer accommodation). There's no
public transport to either destination.

GODERICH

Map 1, A6.

Perched on the edge of Lake Huron, **GODERICH** is a
delightful country town of eight thousand inhabitants. It
began life in 1825 when, amid rumours of bribery and cor-
ruption, the British-owned Canada Company bought two
and a half million acres of fertile southern Ontario – the so-
called Huron Tract – from the government for logging and
then selling off for settlement at the ridiculously low rate of
twelve cents an acre. Today, the wide tree-lined avenues of
Goderich radiate from a grand octagonal **circus**, which is
dominated by a white stone courthouse. From here, the
four main streets follow the points of the compass, with
North Street leading to the compendious **Huron County
Museum** (May–Aug Mon–Sat 10am–4.30pm, Sun
1–4.30pm, closed Sat & Sun Sept–April; $4), which con-
centrates on the exploits of the district's pioneers.
Highlights include a fantastic array of farm implements,
from simple hand tools to gigantic, clumsy machines like a

steam-driven thresher. There's also a beautifully restored Canadian Pacific steam engine, as well as exhibition areas featuring furniture and military memorabilia.

From the County Museum, it's a ten-minute walk to the high stone walls of the **Huron Historic Gaol**, at 181 Victoria St (mid-May to early Sept Mon–Sat 10am–4.30pm, Sun 1–4.30pm; April to mid-May & mid-Sept to Oct daily 1–4.30pm; $4): to get there, walk up to the far end of North Street, turn right along Gloucester Terrace and it's at the end of the street on the right. This joint courthouse and jail was constructed between 1839 and 1842, but the design was most unpopular with local judges, who felt threatened by the proximity of those they were sentencing. The other problem was the smell: several judges refused to conduct proceedings because of the terrible odour coming from the privies in the exercise yard below. In 1856 the administration gave in and built a new courthouse in the town centre. Don't miss the original jailer's apartment and a string of well-preserved prison cells, which reflect various changes in design between 1841 and 1972, when the prison was finally closed. The worst is the leg-iron cell for "troublesome" prisoners, where unfortunates were chained to the wall with neither bed nor blanket.

Back in the centre, West Street leads the 1km through a cutting in the bluffs to the harbour and salt workings on the Lake Huron shoreline. From here, a footpath trails north round the harbourside silos to the **Menesetung Bridge**, a former railway bridge that is now a pedestrian walkway spanning the Maitland River. On the north side of the river, you can pick up the **Maitland Trail**, which wanders down the north bank of the river as far as the marina. In the opposite direction, the shoreline has been tidied up to create a picnic area, and although the sunsets are spectacular the beach is a tad scrawny.

GODERICH

Practicalities

Goderich's **tourist information office** (May–Aug Mon–Sat 9am–7pm, Sun 10am–7pm; Sept–Oct Mon–Fri 9am–4pm; ⊤519/524-6600) is at Nelson and Hamilton streets, beside Hwy-21 and a couple of minutes' walk northeast of the central circus. They have details of the town's bed-and-breakfasts, which average about $60 for a double.

Accommodation

Bedford

92 The Square
⊤519/524-7337;
Ⓕ519/524-2913.
Right on the central circus, this hotel is certainly distinctive. Built in 1896, the *Bedford* has a grandiose wooden staircase just like a saloon in a John Ford movie – though the unimaginatively modernised rooms at the top are a bit of a disappointment. ❸.

Colborne Bed & Breakfast

72 Colborne St
⊤519/524-7400;
Ⓕ519/524-4943.

In a plain brick building dating from the early twentieth century, this bed-and-breakfast is a short walk from the central circus. There are four air-conditioned rooms with en-suite facilities available, and gourmet breakfasts are provided. ❸.

Copper Beech Bed & Breakfast

148 Victoria St North
⊤ & Ⓕ 519/524-8522.
This straightforward B&B contains just three rooms with shared baths. It has air conditioning and pleasant gardens and a full breakfast is served daily. ❷.

GODERICH

- -
For accommodation price codes, see p.126.
- -

Eating and drinking

Big Daddy's Pizza & Grill
42 West St
☎519/524-7777. Inexpensive.
Big pizzas and steaks served
up in an inexpensive café-
diner.

Park House
168 West St. Inexpensive.
The liveliest bar in town,
with views of the lake and
filling pub food.

Robindale's
80 Hamilton St
☎519/524-4171. Moderate.
Situated in a lavishly restored
Victorian house across from
the tourist office, this restaurant has an imaginative menu
featuring tasty seafood.
Closed Mon.

BAYFIELD

Map 1, A6.

Just 20km south of Goderich, pocket-sized **BAYFIELD** is
a wealthy town with handsome timber villas nestled
beneath a canopy of ancient trees. The townsfolk have kept
modern development at arm's length – there's barely a neon
sign in sight, never mind a concrete apartment block – and
almost every house has been beautifully maintained.
Historical plaques give the low-down on the older buildings that line Bayfield's short **Main Street**, and pint-sized
Pioneer Park, on the bluff overlooking the lake, is a fine
spot to take in the sunset. It is primarily a place to relax and
unwind, but you can also venture down to the harbour on
the north side of the village, where, in season, you can pick
wild mushrooms and fiddleheads along the banks of the
Bayfield River.

Practicalities

Bayfield **tourist office** (May–Sept Wed, Thurs, Sat–Sun
10am–6pm, Fri noon–8pm; ☎519/565-2021), in the village

BAYFIELD

hall beside the green at the end of Main Street, will help you find **accommodation**, though their assistance is only necessary in July and August when most places are fully booked.

For accommodation price codes, see p.126.

Accommodation

Albion

Main St ⓣ519/565-2641.
Bang in the middle of Bayfield, this old and pleasant inn has four en-suite bedrooms, the more pleasant of which overlook Main Street. ❹.

Clair on the Square

12 The Square ⓣ519/565-2135.
Occupying a charming Victorian villa, this first-rate bed-and-breakfast is right in the town centre. It offers attractive, comfortable double rooms, all en suite. ❸.

Little Inn of Bayfield

Main St
ⓣ519/565-2611
or 1-800/565-1832;
ⓕ519/565-5474;
ⓦ*www.littleinn.com.*
The best hotel for miles around, the *Little Inn* inhabits a modernised nineteenth-century timber-and-brick building with a lovely second-floor veranda and delightfully furnished rooms, most of which have whirlpool baths. A wonderful spot. ❺.

Eating and drinking

Albion Hotel

Main St ⓣ519/565-2641.
Inexpensive.
A casual dining room offering tasty bar food and a good range of beers at reasonable prices in this early twentieth-century inn.

Little Inn of Bayfield
Main St ⊕519/565-2611.
Expensive.
A superb restaurant whose speciality is fresh fish from Lake Huron – perch, pickerel or steelhead. Smashing bar too.

Red Pump
Main Street ⊕519/565-2576.
Moderate.
Smart, popular and polished restaurant in the heart of Bayfield. The seafood is especially good here.

Severn Sound

Some 150km north of Toronto along Hwy-400, **Severn Sound** is one of the most beguiling parts of Ontario. Its sheltered southern shore is lined with tiny ports, and its deep-blue waters are studded by thousands of rocky little islands. There's enough here for several day-trips, beginning with two of the province's finest historical reconstructions, **Discovery Harbour**, a British naval base, and **Sainte-Marie among the Hurons**, a Jesuit mission. Be sure, also, to spare some time for the wonderful scenery of the **Georgian Bay Islands National Park**, whose glacier-smoothed rocks and wispy pines were so marvellously celebrated by the Group of Seven painters (see p.48).

There are three **buses** daily from Toronto to the regional towns of **Penetanguishene** and **Midland**. Beyond that, however, local bus services are very patchy, and your best bet is to rent a car in Toronto.

SEVERN SOUND

PENETANGUISHENE

The westernmost town on Severn Sound is homely **Penetanguishene** ("place of the rolling white sands"), the site of one of Ontario's first European settlements, a Jesuit mission founded in 1639 then abandoned a decade later. Europeans established a trading station here in the eighteenth century, but the settlement remained insignificant until after the War of 1812, when the British built a naval dockyard that attracted both French- and British-speaking shopkeepers and suppliers. Today, Penetanguishene is one of the few places in southern Ontario to maintain a bilingual (French-English) tradition.

The town's primary thoroughfare, **Main Street**, is a pleasant place for a stroll, its shops and cafés installed behind sturdy red-brick facades, which slope down towards the waterfront. Take a peek also at the **Centennial Museum**, 13 Burke St (May–Sept Mon–Sat 9.30am–4.30pm & Sun 12.30–4.30pm, Oct–April Mon–Fri 12.30–4.30pm; $2.50), a couple of minutes' walk east of Main Street along the waterfront Beck Boulevard. The museum occupies the old general store and offices of the Beck lumber company, whose yards once stretched right along the town's lakeshore. The company was founded in 1865 by Charles Beck, a German immigrant who made himself immensely unpopular by paying his men half their wages in tokens that were only redeemable at his stores. The museum has examples of these "Beck dollars" as well as a fascinating selection of old photographs featuring locals at work and play in the town and its forested surroundings.

From the jetty at the north end of Main Street, there are enjoyable, three-hour **cruises** of the southern stretches of Georgian Bay and its myriad islands – known collectively as the Thirty Thousand Islands (mid-June to Aug, 1–2 cruises daily; May, early June, Sept & early Oct occasional sailings;

$15, teens $10, children $6; ⓣ705/549-7795 or 1-800/363-7447; ⓦ*www.georgianbaycruises.com*). Comparable cruises leave from **Midland**, a small town just a few kilometres to the east. These are operated by PMCL (May–October 1–4 daily; $15; ⓣ705/526-0161). Both cruise lines recommend advance reservations, and although it's usually easy to reserve a same-day spot, it is worth your while to call a day ahead of time.

Practicalities

Penetanguishene's tiny **bus depot** is at Main Street and Robert, a five- to ten-minute walk from the harbour, where the **tourist office** (Mon–Fri 9am–5pm plus summer weekends 9am–5pm; ⓣ705/549-2232) has details of local hotels and bed-and-breakfasts. If needed, Union Taxi (ⓣ705/549-7666) is located next door to the bus station.

For accommodation price codes, see p.126.

Accommodation

Chesham Grove

72 Church St ⓣ705/549-3740, ⓕ705/549-5075.
This attractive stone bungalow sits on a wooded ridge with views out across the bay, not far from the centre of Penetanguishene. The rooms here are comfortable and unassuming, with shared bathroom. ❷.

No. 1 Jury Drive

1 Jury Dr ⓣ & ⓕ705/549-6851.
A pleasant little bed-and-breakfast in a modern house and a leafy suburban setting near Discovery Harbour (see below). ❸.

SEVERN SOUND

Eating

- -

For restaurant price codes, see p.143.

- -

Blue Sky Family Restaurant

48 Main St. Inexpensive.
A most agreeable small-town diner offering good-quality snacks and meals at very affordable prices. Great place for a gossip too.

Memories Restaurant

32 Main St. Inexpensive.
This dinky place has an excellent café menu featuring traditional dishes – hamburgers, apple pie and the like.

DISCOVERY HARBOUR

Map 1, C1. 93 Jury Dr. Late May to June Mon–Fri 10am–5pm; July to early Sept daily 10am–5pm; $5.50. ⓣ705/549-8064.
ⓦ*www.discoveryharbour.on.ca*

About 5km north along the bay from Penetanguishene's town centre is **Discovery Harbour**, an ambitious reconstruction of the important British naval base that was established here in 1817. The purpose of the base was primarily to keep an eye on American movements on the Great Lakes, and between 1820 and 1834 up to twenty Royal Navy vessels were stationed here. Lieutenant Henry Bayfield, who undertook the monumental task of surveying and charting the Great Lakes, used the base as his winter quarters, informing his superiors of his determination "to render this work so correct that it shall not be easy to render it more so". He lived up to his word, and his charts remained in use for decades. The naval station, unfortunately, was more short-lived. By 1834, relations with the US were sufficiently cordial for the navy to withdraw, and

SEVERN SOUND

the base was turned over to the army, who maintained a small garrison here until 1856.

Staffed by enthusiastic costumed guides, the sprawling site spreads along a hillside above a tranquil inlet, its green slopes scattered with accurate reconstructions of everything from a sailors' barracks to several period houses, the prettiest of which is the **Keating House**, named after the base's longest-serving adjutant, Frank Keating. Only one of the original buildings survives, the dour limestone **Officers' Quarters**, which dates from the 1840s, but the place's pride and joy is the working harbour-cum-dockyard. Here, a brace of fully rigged **sailing ships**, the *HMS Bee* and *HMS Tecumseth*, have been rebuilt to their original nine-teenth-century specifications. Both schooners take on volunteers as members of their crews. Sailing times are only definite in July and August, when the ships set out on three- to four-hour treks three times a week for $22–26 per person. Call for times and reservations.

SAINTE-MARIE AMONG THE HURONS

Map 1, C1. Box 160, Huronia Historical Parks, Midland. Late May to mid-Oct daily 10am–5pm; $9.75, students $6.25. ☎705/526-7838.

One of Ontario's most arresting historical attractions is the reconstructed mission **Sainte-Marie among the Hurons**, located 8km southeast of Penetanguishene off Hwy-12. There are no buses, but a taxi from Penetanguishene only costs about $15.

In 1608, the French explorer **Samuel de Champlain** returned to Canada convinced that the only way to make the fur trade profitable was by developing partnerships with native hunters. Three years later, he formed an alliance with the **Huron** tribe of southwest Ontario, cementing the agreement with a formal exchange of presents. However, his decision to champion one tribe over another – and particularly the fact that he gave firearms to the Hurons, who promptly turned them on the rival Iroquois – destroyed the balance of power among the native societies of the St Lawrence and Great Lakes areas – and this was to have dire consequences.

Social cohesion within the Huron community itself was undermined after 1639, when the **Jesuits** established their centre of operations here at Sainte-Marie, where they succeeded in converting a substantial minority of the native people, by then enfeebled by three European sicknesses: measles, smallpox and influenza. In 1648 the Dutch, copying Champlain, began to sell firearms to the Hurons' rival, the **Iroquois**, who were eager to take their revenge against the Huron. In March 1649, the Iroquois launched a full-scale invasion of Huron territory – Huronia – slaughtering their enemies as they moved in on Sainte-Marie. Fearing for their lives, the Jesuits of Sainte-Marie burned their settlement and fled. Eight thousand Hurons went with them; most starved to death on Georgian Bay, but a few made it to Quebec. During the campaign, two Jesuit priests, fathers Brébeuf and Lalemant, were captured at the outpost of Saint-Louis (near present-day Victoria Harbour), where they were bound to the stake and tortured – as per standard Iroquois practice. Despite the suffering brought upon the Hurons, it was the image of Catholic bravery and Iroquois cruelty that long lingered in the minds of French Canadians.

The Mission and around

A visit to Sainte-Marie starts in the impressive **reception centre**. An audio-visual show provides some background information, ending with the screen lifting dramatically away to reveal the painstakingly restored **Mission** site. The twenty-odd wooden buildings are divided into two sections: the Jesuit area with its watchtowers, chapel, forge and farm buildings; and the native area, including a hospital and a pair of bark-covered long houses – one for Christian converts, the other for heathens. Fairly spick-and-span today, it takes some imagination to see the long houses as they appeared to Father Lalement, who saw "a miniature picture of hell... on every side naked bodies, black and half-roasted, mingled pell-mell with the dogs... you will not reach the end of the cabin before you are completely befouled with soot, filth and dirt".

Costumed guides act out the parts of Hurons and Europeans with great gusto, answering questions and demonstrating crafts and skills, though they show a reluctance to eat the staple food of the region: *sagamite*, a porridge of cornmeal seasoned with rotten fish. The cemetery contains the remains of several Hurons who died here and in the adjacent wooden church of St Joseph is the **grave** where the remains of Brébeuf and Lalement were interred. At the end of the tour, a path leads from the site to the excellent **museum**, which traces the story of early Canada with maps and displays on such subjects as fishing and the fur trade.

Overlooking Sainte-Marie from across Hwy-12, the twin-spired church of the **Martyrs' Shrine** (late May to early Oct daily 9am–9pm; $2) was built in 1926 to commemorate the eight Jesuits who were killed in Huronia between 1642 and 1649. Blessed by Pope John Paul II in 1984 – when he bafflingly remarked that it was "a symbol of unity of faith in a diversity of cultures" – the church is massively popular with pilgrims, who have left a stack of discarded crutches in the transept, in sight of the assorted reliquaries that claim to contain the body parts of the murdered priests. The most conspicuous reliquary is the alleged skull of Brébeuf, which is displayed in the glass cabinet near the transept door.

SEVERN SOUND

GEORGIAN BAY ISLANDS NATIONAL PARK

Map 1, C1.

Georgian Bay Islands National Park consists of a scattering of about sixty islands spread between Severn Sound and Twelve Mile Bay, about 50km to the north. The park's two distinct landscapes – the glacier-scraped rock of the Canadian Shield and the hardwood forests and thicker soils of the south – meet at the northern end of the largest and most scenic island, **Beausoleil**. This beautiful island is a forty-minute boat ride west of **Honey Harbour**, the park's nearest port, which contains little more than a jetty, a couple of shops and a few self-contained hotel resorts.

Beausoleil has eleven short **hiking trails**, including two that start at the Cedar Spring landing stage on the southeastern shore: Treasure Trail (3.8km), which heads north behind the marshes along the edge of the island, and the Christian Trail (1.5km), which cuts through beech and maple stands to balsam and hemlock groves overlooking the rocky beaches of the western shoreline. At the northern end of Beausoleil, the Cambrian (2km) and Fairy trails (2.5km) are two delightful routes through harsher glacier-scraped scenery, while, just to the west, the Dossyonshing Trail (2.5km) tracks through a mixed area of wetland, forest and bare granite that covers the transitional zone between the two main landscapes.

Prospective hikers and campers bound for the Georgian Bay Islands National Park need to come properly equipped – this is very much a wilderness environment. Whatever you do, don't forget the insect repellent.

SEVERN SOUND

Practicalities

Honey Harbour is around 170km north of Toronto – take Hwy-400 and watch for the turn-off onto Route 5 (Exit 156) just beyond Port Severn. There's no public transport, so having your own car is essential. The **national park office** in Honey Harbour (June–Aug Mon–Fri 8am–6pm, Sat 10am–6pm; Sept–May Mon–Fri 8am–4.30pm; ☏705/756-2415) provides a full range of information on walking trails and flora and fauna. In winter, a visit is mandatory, as the wardens will advise on where it's safe to ski across the ice to the islands. Three Honey Harbour operators run **water taxis** to Beausoleil, with a one-way trip costing $30–35 in summer, a few dollars less in spring and fall. Of the three, Honey Harbour Boat Club (☏705/756-2411), about 700m beyond the park office, is probably your best bet. There are no set times, but in summer, boats leave for Beausoleil quite frequently. Fares to several of the park's other islands are negotiable, but make sure you agree on a pick-up time before you go. With less time to spare and spend here, the national park's *Georgian Bay Islands Day Tripper* **boat** leaves from Honey Harbour three times daily from July to early September bound for Beausoleil, where passengers get four hours' hiking time. The round trip fare is $15 – further details and reservations at the national park office (☏705/756-2415).

If you decide to overnight, the park has thirteen small **campgrounds**, eleven on Beausoleil and one each on Island 95B and Centennial Island. The charge is $11 a night and all operate on a self-registration, first-come, first-served basis with the exception of Cedar Spring, on Beausoleil, where the Cedar Spring visitor centre near the main boat dock (☏705/756-5909) takes reservations for an additional $10. Less arduously, Honey Harbour has one good **hotel**, the seasonal, lakeshore *Delawana Inn Resort* (☏705/756-2424 or 1-

888/335-2926, ⓕ705/756-1659, ⓦ*www.delawana.com*; ❻),
which has spacious chalet cabins dotted round its extensive,
pine-forested grounds. Guests also have use of the resort's
canoes, kayaks and windsurfing equipment. A more economical option is the *Rawley Lodge* (ⓣ705/538-2272, or 1-
800/263-7538; ❹), a pleasantly old-fashioned, 1920s timber
hotel located on the water's edge in the hamlet of **Port
Severn**, some fifteen kilometres from Honey Harbour, just
off Hwy-400 (Exit 153 or 156). **Restaurants** hereabouts are
few and far between – your best bet is to eat in Port Severn
at *The Inn at Christie's Mill* (ⓣ705/538-2354), where the
brisk modern and reasonably priced restaurant offers tasty
steaks and seafood; reservations are advised.

ALGONQUIN PARK

Too far for a day-trip, but worth considering for a longer excursion, is **Algonquin Park**, 260km north of Toronto. Make your
way to Huntsville on Hwy-11 and then continue 45km along
Hwy-60 to the park's west gate, where there is a visitor centre
(ⓣ1-888/668-7275). Algonquin Park is a great slab of untamed
wilderness boasting dense hardwood and pine forests,
canyons, rapids, scores of lakes and all manner of classic
Canadian wildlife: loons, beavers, moose, timber wolves and
black bears to name but five. Canoeing and hiking are the big
deals here, and several Toronto companies offer all-inclusive
wilderness packages, including meals, permits, guides, equipment and transport to and from Toronto. The pick of the bunch
is Call of the Wild, 23 Edward St, Markham, Ontario
(ⓣ905/471-9453 or 1-800/776-9453; ⓕ905/472-9453;
ⓦwww.callofthewild.ca), which runs a varied programme that
includes three-day ($340) and five-day ($540) canoeing trips
deep into the park.

LISTINGS

LISTINGS

Accommodation

As Toronto's popularity as a tourist destination has increased, the availability of hotel **accommodation**, especially in the mid-price range, has shrunk. During peak season (late June–Aug), and especially around summer events like Caribana (see p.268), it is essential to book well in advance. Prices tend to fluctuate depending on when and for how long you stay, but in general, a clean, centrally located hotel room starts at $80–100. **Bed and breakfast** accommodations tend to be slightly cheaper – even with breakfast thrown in. While most are not as central as the city's hotels, B&Bs take you off the beaten path and into Toronto's quainter, leafy neighbourhoods. Budget-conscious travellers might want to consider Toronto's average **hostels**, but the best deal in town is the **summer residences** at local universities. You'll get bare essentials here, but the rooms are much cheerier than the hostels, and prices start at about $40.

When dialling any of the phone numbers listed in the *Guide*, the prefix ⓣ 416 must be dialled first.
See p.276 for more details.

ACCOMMODATION PRICES

Throughout this book, **accommodation prices** have been graded with the symbols below, according to the cost of the least expensive double room throughout most of the year. Bear in mind that all prices are quoted before taxes. There is a seven-percent federal Goods and Service Tax (GST) and a Provincial Sales Tax (PST) of five percent on all accommodations.

❶ up to $40	❷ $40–60
❸ $60–80	❹ $80–100
❺ $100–125	❻ $125–175
❼ $175–240	❽ $240+

HOTELS

Downtown is the epicentre of Toronto's **hotel** scene – once outside the downtown core the range is almost entirely dictated by bland chains. Any downtown hotel will be sufficiently close to all the main attractions, and although the bread and butter of most is a constant stream of business travellers, some (like the *Delta Chelsea* in particular; see opposite) offer special features and packages geared toward families.

If you're visiting from outside of Canada be sure to
save your accommodation receipts in order to get
a tax refund; see pp.275–276 for more details.

HOTELS

DOWNTOWN

Bond Place

Map 3, J2. 65 Dundas St W

Ⓣ 362-6061 or 1-800/268-9390;

Ⓕ 360-6406;

Ⓦ www.bondplace
hoteltoronto.com

Subway **Dundas.**

A favourite of the tourist-bus crowds, this establishment is just steps away from the Eaton Centre (see p.39) and has all modern conveniences and reasonable rates. ❹.

Delta Chelsea

Map 4, H9. 33 Gerrard St W

Ⓣ 595-1975;

Ⓕ 585-4366;

Ⓦ www.deltachelsea.com

Subway **Dundas.**

A first-rate hotel, replete with bars, restaurants and facilities like day care and play centres for families with young children. The rooms are extremely comfortable and well appointed. The central location could hardly be more convenient. Highly recommended for quality at reasonable prices. ❺.

Executive Motor Hotel

Map 3, A4. 621 King St W

Ⓣ 504-7441;

Ⓕ 504-4722.

Streetcar **King St (#504).**

A quirky alternative to downtown's mainstay hotels, the *Executive* is one of the last budget options near the lakefront. The neighbourhood, once all warehouses and wholesalers, is now nouveau-chic, filled with art galleries and film and music studios. ❹.

Grand Hotel & Suites Toronto

Map 3, K2. 225 Jarvis St

Ⓣ 863-9000;

Ⓕ 863-1100;

Ⓦ www.grandhoteltoronto.com

Streetcar **Dundas (#505).**

The neighbourhood, in the beginning stages of gentrification, still has the odd wino rumbling around, but the *Grand* is a beautiful, full-service surprise, complete with a rooftop jacuzzi and a third floor of cathedral-windowed suites. All rooms contain kitchenettes and sofa beds. ❼.

HOTELS

127

Hilton Toronto

Map 3, G3. 145 Richmond St W
ⓣ869-3456; ⓕ869-3187.
Streetcar Queen (#501).
A massive refurbishment
spruced up this full-service,
downtown property giving it
the stylistic cachet one would
expect of a hotel on the edge
of the Queen Street West
neighbourhood. ❼.

Holiday Inn on King

Map 3, D4. 370 King St W
ⓣ599-4000 or 1-800/263-6364;
ⓕ599-7394; ⓦwww.hiok.com
Streetcar King St (#504).
Especially popular with
business travellers, this large
hotel is close to theatres, the
SkyDome, Roy Thompson
Hall and many fine restaurants
and nightclubs. ❼.

Hotel Victoria

Map 3, I5. 56 Yonge St
ⓣ363-1666 or 1-800/363-8228;
ⓕ363-7327; ⓦwww.toronto
.com/hotelvictoria.
Subway King.
A small hotel with *pension*
charm located in the heart of
downtown. The rooms, while
clean and crisply furnished,
are fairly cramped. ❺.

Metropolitan

Map 3, G2. 108 Chestnut St
ⓣ599-0555 or 1-800/668-6600;
ⓕ599-3317;
ⓦwww.metropolitan.com
Subway St Patrick.
This small, handsomely
decorated hotel is located
right behind the new City
Hall, and is perfectly located
for a visit to the nearby Art
Gallery of Ontario (see
pp.45–51). ❼.

Novotel Toronto Centre

Map 3, J6. 45 The Esplanade
ⓣ367-8900 or 1-800/668-6835;
ⓕ360-8285;
ⓦwww.novotel.com
Subway Union Station.
An attractive hotel offering
excellent service at budget
prices. Its affordability may be
linked to its noisy location:
the hotel butts up against the
busiest stretch of railway in
Canada. Otherwise, the
location is excellent, close to a
number of shopping districts
as well as the Harbourfront
(see p.73). ❺.

Quality Hotel Downtown

Map 3, J4. 111 Lombard St
ⓣ367-5555; ⓕ367-3470;

@ www.toronto.com/qualityhotel
downtown
Subway King.
Clean and affordable, this
place is located on a quiet
street in an older part of
town, and is a ten-minute
walk from downtown. Book
early; this is a favourite among
cost-conscious travellers. ❻.

Le Royal Meridian King Edward

Map 3, J5. 37 King St E
Ⓣ 863-3131 or 1-800/543-4300;
@ www.lemeridien-hotels.com
Subway King.
This dowager of a hotel was
designed by E.J. Lennox (see
p.35), and a recent facelift has
restored its Beaux Arts
opulence. Polished brass, red-
coated doormen, and top-
notch service contribute to
the premium price. ❼.

Royal York

Map 3, G5. 100 Front St W
Ⓣ 368-2511 or 1-800/441-1414;
Ⓕ 368-2884;
@ www.fairmont.com
Subway Union Station.
As huge, overstuffed and
comfortable as your
grandfather's favourite chair,

the *Royal York* offers luxury-
level services for less than
you'd expect. The lobby is a
sight in itself, opulently
decorated with rich wall
panelling and chandeliers.
The hotel's dependable quality
and central location have kept
it a favourite for generations.
❻.

Sheraton Centre Toronto

Map 3, H3. 123 Queen St W
Ⓣ 361-1000; Ⓕ 947-4854;
@ www.sheratoncentre.com
Subway Queen.
Once past the bland exterior,
the snazzy insides of this hotel
feature a waterfall and islands of
soft leather couches scattered
throughout the lobby. The
Sheraton is connected to the
Underground City (see p.236),
and the clubs, restaurants and
shops on the Queen Street
West strip are also close by. ❻.

SkyDome Hotel

Map 3, D6. 1 Blue Jays Way
Ⓣ 341-7100 or 1-800/441-1414;
Ⓕ 341-5091;
@ www.renaissancehotels.com
Subway Union Station.
This hotel's claim to fame is
its ultra-central location – not

HOTELS

to mention the fact that it overlooks the astro-turfed interior of the SkyDome. The CN Tower is also right next door, as are the shores of Lake Ontario. A favourite among sports-inclined families. .

Strathcona

Map 3, G5. 60 York St
Ⓣ 363-3321 or 1-800/268-8304; Ⓕ 363-4679; Ⓦ *www.toronto .com/strathconahotel*.
Subway Union Station.
A recent refurbishment has totally reinvigorated this downtown hotel, which once had less than savoury patrons. It is about half a block from Union Station, and five minutes from the SkyDome and the CN Tower. .

Toronto Colony

Map 3, G2. 89 Chestnut St
Ⓣ 977-0707 or 1-800/777-1700; Ⓕ 977-1136; Ⓦ *www .toronto-colony.com*
Subway St Patrick.
This large, family-oriented hotel is located behind the new City Hall and is just across the road from the *Metropolitan Hotel* (see p.128). Very popular with Asian

travellers and business people due to its proximity to Chinatown. .

Toronto Marriott Eaton Centre

Map 3, H2. 525 Bay St
Ⓣ 597-9200 or 1-800/228-9290; Ⓕ 597-9211.
Subway Dundas.
If staying in an Eighties glitz hotel attached to one of the largest malls in North America (Eaton Centre; see p.39) is your idea of heaven, search no further. A member of the Marriott chain, the best thing about this establishment is the attentive staff. .

UPTOWN

- -

Best Western Primrose

Map 4, J5. 111 Carlton St
Ⓣ 977-8000 or 1-800/268-8082; Ⓕ 977-6323; Ⓦ *www .torontoprimrosehotel.com*
Subway College.
A short ten-minute walk from downtown, this place has all the basic amenities expected from a large chain hotel, including an outdoor pool. .

HOTELS

Comfort

Map 4, I6. 15 Charles St E
ⓣ924-1222 or 1-800/221-2222;
ⓕ927-1369; ⓦ*www.toronto*
.com/comfortdowntown.
Subway Wellesley.
One of the better budget-range hotel chains, this place is centrally located on a leafy green side street, and close to the bustling intersection of Yonge Street and Bloor West. ❹.

Days Inn Toronto Downtown

Map 4, I9. 30 Carlton St
ⓣ977-6655 or 1-800/DAYS-INN; ⓕ977-0502;
ⓦ*www.daysinn.com*
Subway College.
A good bet for sport fans, this hotel is just up the block from Maple Leaf Gardens, the former home of the Toronto Maple Leafs hockey team (see "Sports and Outdoor Activities", p.248). This chain offers all the basic amenities and a convenient location with all-night eateries and a multiplex cinema close by. ❺.

Four Seasons

Map 4, F5. 21 Avenue Rd
ⓣ964-0411 or 1-800/332-3442;
ⓕ964-2301;
ⓦ*www.fourseasons.com*
Subway Bay.
This well-appointed establishment, situated in the heart of the costly Yorkville neighbourhood, has a reputation for hosting the city's most famous guests. The hotel's restaurants and wine cellar are as stellar as the service, and while the prices here are off the charts, this is *the* place to be if you want to splurge. ❽.

Howard Johnson Yorkville

Map 4, F4. 89 Avenue Rd
ⓣ964-1220 or 1-877/967-5845;
ⓕ964-8692.
Subway Bay.
This small value hotel is tucked into a busy section of Avenue Road, only blocks from the expensive *Four Seasons Hotel*. The helpful staff is always at your beck and call, and the large rooms are tidy and comfortable. ❹.

Inter-Continental

Map 4, E5. 220 Bloor St W
ⓣ 960-5200 or 1-800/327-0200;
ⓕ 960-8269;
ⓦ *www.travelweb.com*
Subway St George.

This place offers its guests all the extras, including fireplaces in a few of the suites. The decor is sleek and classic, and there are frequent celebrity sightings in the lobby. ❼.

Madison Manor Boutique Hotel

Map 4, C5. 20 Madison Ave
ⓣ 922-5579 or 1-877/561-7048;
ⓕ 963-4325;
ⓦ *www.madisonavenuepub.com*
Subway St George.

Located in the heart of the Annex, this neighbourhood inn has 22 comfortable, non-smoking rooms, some with fireplaces and all with en-suite bathrooms as well as the mod-cons (hair dryers, internet access) that you would expect in luxury hotels. A great find. ❺.

Park Hyatt

Map 4, F5. 4 Avenue Rd
ⓣ 924-5471 or 1-800/977-4197;
ⓕ 924-4933; ⓦ *www.hyatt.com*

Subway Museum or Bay.

The rooftop cocktail bar here offers spectacular views of the city, and guests appreciate the central location at the edge of the posh Yorkville neighbourhood. The recently refurbished rooms offer the ultimate in comfort, albeit at a premium price. ❼.

Ramada Hotel & Suites

Map 4, J9. 300 Jarvis St
ⓣ 977-4823 or 1-800/567-2233;
ⓕ 977-4830; ⓦ *www.toronto*
.com/ramadadowntown.
Streetcar Carlton (#506).

A comfortable, convenient high-rise hotel on busy Jarvis street. The facilities are good (indoor swimming pool, sauna, and the like), and Yonge St is just a five-minute walk away. ❻.

Sutton Place

Map 4, H7. 955 Bay St ⓣ 924-9221 or 1-800/268-3790;
ⓕ 924-1778;
ⓦ *www.suttonplace.com*
Subway Wellesley.

A recent renovation has edged this already attractive hotel closer to the high-end market. The rooms are comfortable and plush, and the on-site restaurant is well renowned. Nicely situated for all the downtown sights, it's also a five-minute walk from the Gay and Lesbian Village (see "Gay Toronto", p.215). ❼.

Toronto Marriott Bloor-Yorkville
Map 4, I5. 90 Bloor St E
ⓣ 961-8000 or 1-800/264-6116; ⓕ 961-4635; ⓦ *www.marriott .com*
Subway Yonge-Bloor.
The bunker-like exterior is a bit of a turn-off, but this establishment has one of the best prices for its ultra-central location. The service is professional, and there's plenty of shopping, restaurants and cinemas nearby. ❻.

Town Inn Suites
Map 4, I6. 620 Church St
ⓣ 964-3311 or 1-800/387-2755; ⓕ 924-9466;
ⓦ *www.towninn.com*
Subway Wellesley.
One of the best bargains in the city, this centrally located

hotel offers budget suites equipped with kitchens, and is an excellent option for longer stays, as weekly and monthly rates are available. Very popular with savvy travellers, so book early for the summer months. ❹.

THE HARBOURFRONT
- - - - - - - - - - - - - - - - - - - -

Radisson Plaza Hotel Admiral Toronto Harbourfront
Map 3, E8. 249 Queens Quay W ⓣ 203-3333 or 1-800/333-3333; ⓕ 203-3100; ⓦ *www.radisson .com/toronto.ca_admiral*.
Subway York Quay.
Located right on the waterfront, this full-service chain hotel divides its attention between families and conventioneers. While not as central as other comparable hotels, it's still just ten minutes from downtown by cab. ❻.

Westin Harbour Castle
Map 3, I8. 1 Harbour Square
ⓣ 869-1600 or 1-800/228-3000; ⓕ 869-0573; ⓦ *www.westin.com*

York Quay stop on the LRT from Union Station.

A massive hotel of nearly a thousand rooms, this is a terrific base for forays to the Toronto Islands – ferries dock at the plaza out in front. The *Westin Harbour* makes up for its lack of intimate charm by catering to its guests' every whim, and by the fact that many of the nicely furnished rooms come with splendid views of either Lake Ontario or downtown's skyscrapers. ❹.

BED AND BREAKFASTS

Often cheaper – and certainly more intimate – than the city's hotels, **bed and breakfasts** may be the best bet for a quality stay. While you might not get access to a swimming pool or room service, you will get a realistic sense of what it's like to live in Toronto. Many B&Bs require a tram or subway ride to reach downtown, but Toronto's transit system (see pp.14–16) is efficient, and none of the addresses listed below is more than twenty minutes from the city centre. If there is a particular area you wish to stay in, or if you have special needs as a traveller, contact the **Federation of Ontario Bed and Breakfast Accommodation** (☎613/515-1293, ℻613/475-5267, ⓦ*www.fobba.com*); or **Bed and Breakfast Homes of Toronto** (☎363-6362, ⓦ*www.bbcanada.com/toronto2.html*).

Admiral St George
Map 4, D4. 305 St George St
☎921-1899.
Subway St George.
There are just two rooms in this Edwardian annex home, so reserve well in advance.

Five minutes from the subway, it's a short walk to the University of Toronto and attractions like the Bata Shoe Museum (see p.65) and the Royal Ontario Museum (see p.56). ❹.

Annex House

Map 4, C3. 147 Madison Ave
ⓣ920-3922.
Subway Dupont.
This substantial antebellum-style house has four rooms, each with private baths and air conditioning. Close to the University of Toronto and the restaurants, shops and theatres of the quirky Bloor-Spadina neighbourhood. ❹.

Beaches

Map 2, I7. 174 Waverly Rd
ⓣ699-0818; ⓕ699-2246;
ⓦ*www.memberstripod.com /beachesbb*.
Streetcar Queen (#501).
The Beaches (see p.83) is one of Toronto's more bucolic areas, a pocket of suburban bliss located on the shores of Lake Ontario. As befits the neighbourhood, this B&B accepts pets and offers family-friendly services like baby-sitting. ❹.

Beverly Place

Map 4, D9. 235 Beverly St
ⓣ977-0077; ⓕ599-2242.
Subway St Patrick.
Of the six rooms available in this centrally located

Victorian house, three have private bathrooms and four have fireplaces. Close to the University of Toronto, the Art Gallery of Ontario, and Queen Street West. Non-smoking adults only (children and pets are not allowed). ❹.

Bonnevue Manor

Map 2, E7. 33 Beaty Ave
ⓣ536-1455; ⓕ533-2644;
ⓦ*www.toronto.com /bonnevuemanor*.
Streetcar King (#504).
This large Victorian home has six rooms (three with private bathrooms) and a self-contained family suite. Close to Ontario Place and the quirky shops, cinemas and restaurants of its surrounding neighbourhood, which has a distinctive eastern European feel. ❹.

Casa Loma Inn

Map 4, C5. 21 Walmer Rd
ⓣ924-4540; ⓕ975-5485;
ⓦ*www.toronto.com/casalomainn*.
Subway Spadina.
Located in a residential area, this huge Victorian guest house has 23 nicely decorated

BED AND BREAKFASTS

135

rooms. Close to Casa Loma and Spadina House (see pp.68 & 70). Non-smokers only. ❹.

Dundonald House

Map 4, I7. 35 Dundonald St
Ⓣ 961-9888 or 1-800/260-7227;
Ⓕ 961-2120; Ⓦ *www .dundonaldhouse.com*
Subway **Wellesley**.

This establishment offers handy extras like bicycles and a work-out room. There are five rooms available, all with shared baths. Close to the Gay and Lesbian Village and the theatres and restaurants on Yonge Street. ❹.

High Park

Map 2, E6. 4 High Park Blvd
Ⓣ 531-7963; Ⓕ 531-0060;
Ⓦ *www.bbcanada.com*
Subway **Dundas West**.

This ample home has three rooms, two of which share a bath. The largest room has its own balcony, which overlooks the leafy confines of the surrounding Victorian neighbourhood. The breakfasts here are wonderful, and the service is friendly. ❸.

Jarvis House

Map 4, J9. 344 Jarvis St
Ⓣ 975-3838; Ⓕ 975-9808;
Ⓦ *www.jarvishouse.com*
Subway **College**.

Once upon a time, Jarvis Street was where all the fashionable millionaires lived, and this house is a relic of bygone days. All twelve rooms have private baths, and the location is close to popular sights like Maple Leaf Gardens and Cabbagetown (see p.67). ❺.

Mulberry Tree

Map 4, J6. 122 Isabella St
Ⓣ 960-5249; Ⓕ 960-3853;
Ⓔ *multree@istar.ca*
Subway **Sherbourne**.

This delightful B&B, one of Toronto's most agreeable, occupies a stylishly decorated heritage home close to the city centre. Each of the guest rooms is comfortable and relaxing – indeed the whole atmosphere of the place is just right, combining efficiency and friendliness. Highly recommended. ❹.

Palmerston Inn

Map 2, F6. 322 Palmerston Blvd ⓣ920-7842; ⓕ960-9529; ⓦ*www.toronto.com /palmerstoninn*. Streetcar **College (#506).** This oak-panelled mansion, situated on the edge of the trendy College Strip, has eight rooms decked out in varying degrees of comfort with features such as fireplaces, fresh flowers and bathrobes. Extras include afternoon sherry and a daily maid service. ❹.

Terrace House

Map 4, C1. 52 Austin Terrace ⓣ535-1493; ⓕ535-9616; ⓔ*terracehouseband @sympatico.ca* Subway St Clair West. This pre-World War I, mock-Tudor house is perched high on a hill overlooking the city. The neighbourhood includes noteworthy piles like Casa Loma and Spadina House (see pp.68 & 70), and is close to some of the most exclusive residential neighbourhoods in the city. There are three rooms (two with fireplaces, one with a private bath), all decked out with antiques and North African rugs. It's only a five-minute walk from the Dupont subway station, but it's all uphill. ❹.

UNIVERSITY RESIDENCES AND HOSTELS

Toronto has two large downtown **universities**: the University of Toronto and Ryerson Polytechnic University. From the second week in May to the end of August there is an abundance of student residences available to budget-wise tourists of all ages on a daily, weekly or monthly basis. Quite often this is the best bargain for clean, affordable and relatively private accommodation. Most residences require a night's or week's deposit, depending on the length of your stay.

Toronto's **hostels** are a less inviting option. Some offer private as well as dormitory accommodation, and we've listed three hostels below (including the *YWCA Woodlawn Residence*) – but you're much better off checking into a university residence when in season.

Global Village Backbackers

Map 3, C4. 460 King St W
ⓣ 703-8540 or 1-888/844-7875.
Streetcar King (#504).
The best of Toronto's hostel options, this former hotel (once famed for its freewheeling, Art Deco tap room) has only four private/family rooms; everything else is dormitory-style with bunk beds and no private bathrooms. Apart from the excellent location near sights like the CN tower, theatres, restaurants and clubs, above-standard facilities like a laundry room, kitchen, and games room make this the hostel of choice. The staff rates a special quality mention. ❶-❷.

Hostelling International-Toronto

Map 3, J4. 223 Church St
ⓣ 971-4440 or 1-800/668-4487.
Streetcar Dundas (#505)
Affiliated with the Hostelling International organisation, the single greatest drawback to this hostel is its location. It is in a dodgy part of town with aggressive panhandlers and dreary brick buildings. Otherwise the hostel itself, which only has dormitories, is a middle-of-the-road specimen of its type. It is clean and has kitchen facilities in the basement. ❶.

At the university residences, students with valid
IDs can often get a discount of around ten
percent; inquire at reception.

Ryerson Neill-Wycik College

Map 4, J9. 96 Gerrard St E
ⓣ 977-2320; ⓕ 977-2809;
ⓦ *www.neill-wycik.com*
Subway Dundas.

All available accommodations (singles, doubles and quads) are apartment suites with shared kitchens. There are telephones in all rooms, laundry facilities and limited on-site parking. The campus itself is scenic and quiet, but the youth-magnet intersection of Yonge and Dundas is only a short walk away – which could be good or bad depending on how you like your Saturday nights. Daily, weekly and monthly rates available on all units. ❶.

University of Toronto, Innis College

Map 4, D6. 111 St George St
ⓣ 978-2553; ⓕ 971-2464;
ⓦ *www.utoronto.ca/innis /residence/summer.*
Subway St George.

This recently built residence has air conditioning and a daily maid service. Daily and weekly rentals, however, are restricted to the single rooms. Doubles are only available for long-term stays. ❶.

University of Toronto, Loretto College

Map 4, G6. 70 St Mary's St
ⓣ 925-2833; ⓕ 925-4058.
Subway Wellesley.

Singles and doubles are available here, and some of the singles have private baths. Daily rates include breakfast, and weekly rates include three meals a day. ❶.

University of Toronto, Massey College

Map 4, E6. 4 Devonshire Place
ⓣ 978-2892; ⓕ 978-1759;
ⓦ *www.utoronto.ca/massey.*
Subway St George.

In addition to being the one-time stomping grounds of author Robertson Davies, this beautiful college reportedly boasts the presence of at least one ghost. Singles and doubles are available with breakfast included on weekdays May-July; rates are lower in August, when breakfast is no longer served. ❶.

UNIVERSITY RESIDENCES AND HOSTELS

University of Toronto, St Michael's College

Map 4, G6. 81 St Mary's St
ⓣ 926-7141; ⓕ 926-7139.
Subway **Museum**.
This is the college where Marshall McLuhan taught for his professional life. Singles and doubles available on a weekly rate with weekly maid service. ❶.

University of Toronto, Victoria College

Map 4, F6. 140 Charles St W
ⓣ 585-4524; ⓕ 585-4530;
ⓦ *http://vicu.utoronto.ca /conference.htm*.
Subway **Museum**.
This huge campus site includes accommodation in Annesley Hall, Burwash Hall, Law House and Margaret Addison Hall. The daily rates for doubles and singles include a full breakfast. ❷.

YWCA Woodlawn Residence

Map 2, G6. 80 Woodlawn Ave
ⓣ 923-8454; ⓕ 923-1950;
ⓦ *www.ywcator.org*.
Subway **Summerhill**.
Tucked away in a cul-de-sac in the pretty Summerhill neighbourhood, this women-only residence offers dormitory, single and double rooms at daily and monthly rates, and includes a continental breakfast. There are laundry facilities and vending machines on site, and a good selection of cafés and restaurants close by. ❶.

Restaurants

Eating is one of Toronto's most pleasurable experiences. The city is the gastronomic capital of Canada, and its restaurant scene is fraught with competition, meaning that finding good food, a nice ambience and reasonable prices is never difficult. Eating places blanket the city, but your best bet if you're looking for several options is to try the concentrations of quality restaurants on **Baldwin Street** between Beverly and McCaul streets, **Queen Street** west of McCaul Street, and **College Street** between Euclid and Grace streets.

Toronto's thriving **cafés** are the seam in the city's social fabric – especially in the summer when many places open their terraces for open-air carousing and relaxation. Analogous to the pub scene in London, Torontonians use cafés as places for quick meals, a morning latte, an evening drink, or as a place to meet one's friends. Much less formal – and generally less expensive – than restaurants, cafés are nonetheless excellent places to search out a full meal, especially at lunchtime. Like other cities large and small, a certain Seattle coffee chain is making its presence felt in the **coffee bar** scene, and there are Canadian versions of the same, namely *Timothy's* and *Second Cup*. While these chains give independent establishments a run for their money, they are unable to offer the character, good cooking and sense of place the indies do.

As for **restaurants**, there are more than five thousand in Toronto, representing more than eighty different ethnic cultures. With so much choice, there's little reason to frequent garish tourist traps or hotel coffee shops, which generally serve indifferent food at inflated prices. Many of the city's renown restaurants are in the **downtown core**, but make it a point to explore some of Toronto's **ethnic enclaves** (see pp.5–7), where unassuming eateries offer some of the city's best – and most authentic – menus.

Competition in the restaurant trade is tremendous here, meaning that most restaurants will do somersaults to keep you and their business well fed. For the up-to-the-minute scoop on where to dine, consult either the free weekly paper *NOW* or the glossy *Toronto Life* magazine. A good trick for sampling the food at pricier establishments is to take advantage of lunch menus, offered 11.30am–3pm at roughly two-thirds to half of the cost of dinner menus.

Hours of business and peak flows vary from restaurant to restaurant, so it is a good idea to call ahead to avoid disappointment.

When dialling any of the phone numbers listed in the *Guide*, the prefix ⊤ 416 must be dialled first. See p.276 for more details.

RESTAURANT PRICES

Restaurant listings are price-coded into five categories: **cheap** (under $10), **inexpensive** ($10–15), **moderate** ($15–25), **expensive** ($25–40) and **very expensive** (over $40). This assumes a three-course meal for one person, not including drinks, tax or tip.

RESTAURANTS

CANADIAN CUISINE

There are a number of restaurants springing up which list their menus as "Canadian", a novel and evolving development. Restaurants which define themselves as Canadian are driven more by regional ingredients than by methods of preparation – the opposite, say, of Japanese cuisine. Fiddlehead ferns, caribou, arctic char, and dried cranberries are popular "Canadian" foodstuffs. Regional dishes, such as *tortier* (a rich, savoury meat pie) from Quebec, "three sisters" (corn, squash and beans) stews from the Iroquoian peoples of Ontario, and a bounty of Maritime seafood will also make it onto most menus in a Canadian-style restaurant. Also keep your eyes out for these restaurants' variations on traditional Canadian desserts, especially maple ice cream and the syrupy butter tart.

DOWNTOWN

CAFÉS AND COFFEE HOUSES

Bonjour Brioche
Map 2, H7. 812 Queen St E
Ⓣ 406-1250. Moderate.
Streetcar **Queen** (#501).
This patisserie/café draws hordes from all over the city to sample its jewel-like fruit tarts, buttery croissants, puffy brioche and its delectable *pissaladiere*, a variation on pizza from Provence. There's always a line for Sunday brunch, and almost everything is eaten by 2pm.

Café Bernate
Map 2, F7. 1024 Queen St W
Ⓣ 535-2835. Inexpensive.
Streetcar **Queen** (#501).
The steam machine is in full swing at this neighbourhood spot where the walls are hung with local artists' work. The menu offers a wide variety of plump sandwiches for all tastes, and the regular coffee comes with free refills.

Café la Gaffe

Map 4, E9. 24 Baldwin St
Ⓣ 596-2397. Moderate.
Streetcar College (#506).
Cosy, exposed-brick walls, a
well-stocked, Art Deco bar
and an open kitchen combine
to create a convivial
atmosphere in this neighbourhood bistro. The menu is
heavily Italian (pastas, pizzas,
salads) with some Asian
touches (steamed dumplings in
a bamboo basket, stir-fries).

Epicure Café

Map 3, B3. 512 Queen St W
Ⓣ 504-8942. Moderate.
Streetcar Queen (#501).
Unpretentious, funky and
comfortable, the *Epicure* serves
up a strong selection of tasty
fare. Polenta makes a nice
change from pasta, and crispy-
skinned duck confit with
chutney is a creative
alternative to chicken. There's
also a good selection of local
micro brews and a full wine
list.

Hello Toast

Map 2, H7. 993 Queen St E
Ⓣ 778-7299. Moderate.
Streetcar Queen (#501).

The flea market chic
furnishings are your first clue
that *Hello Toast* positions itself
on the lighter side of serious.
It is famous for its Sunday
brunch, which features the
house specialities, French toast
and Belgian waffles.

Java House

Map 3, A3. 537 Queen St W
Ⓣ 504-3025. Inexpensive.
Streetcar Queen (#501).
The exterior of this popular
local hangout is painted like a
hut from some fabulist
Nubian village, while inside it
is all café, steamy and busy
serving up light meals and
gallons of caffeinated
beverages of all descriptions.

Kensington Café

Map 4, B9. 73 Kensington Ave
Ⓣ 971-5632. Inexpensive.
Streetcar Spadina (#510).
An international soup-and-
sandwich menu with a nod
towards the Middle East. A
small, cosy place to slip in to
if the hectic pace of
Kensington Market gets to be
too much.

DOWNTOWN

Last Temptation

Map 4, B9. 12 Kensington Ave
Ⓣ 599-2551. Inexpensive.
Streetcar **Spadina** (#510).
A locals' kind of place where
gossip and pool are the main
sources of entertainment. The
terrace caters to people
watching, and the menu
features a good selection of
appetisers, as well as basic
sandwiches, stir-fries and
pastas; don't miss the on-tap
microbrews.

Little York Books and Café

Map 3, K4. 187 King St E.
Ⓣ 364-6544. Inexpensive.
Streetcar **King** (#504).
A lovely café that is the
antithesis of *Starbucks*,
Chapters and all their big-box
imitators. Its proprietors sell
beautiful books (specialising in
literature, arts and design),
coffee and light snacks in a
cosy, early Victorian building.
Little York even has its own
literary magazine, the *Little
York Review*, which is available
at the cash counter.

Peter Pan

Map 3, D3. 373 Queen St W
Ⓣ 593-0917.
Moderate/Expensive.
Streetcar **Queen** (#501).
This long, thin Queen West
icon was ground zero for the
metamorphosis of the strip
from a dreary stretch of bargain
stores to hipster heaven. It
wears its age and reputation
well, keeping one eye out for
emerging trends (Asian,
seafood) while also sticking
with old standards (burgers,
pastas), especially with regards
to the dessert menu.

The Rivoli

Map 3, D3. 332 Queen St W
Ⓣ 504-1320. Moderate/Expensive.
Streetcar **Queen** (#501).
High-backed booths line
either side of Queen Street
West's venerable temple to
fusion cooking. Italian panini,
Asian noodle soups, and a
global selection of appetisers
are some of the offerings on
the ever-changing menu.
There is a long bar beside the
dining room, a cabaret space
in the back, and a pool-and-
billiards room upstairs.

DOWNTOWN

Swan Restaurant

Map 2, F7. 892 Queen St W
Ⓣ 532-0452. Moderate.
Streetcar Queen (#501).

Once an ugly duckling lunch
counter, this little eatery is
easy to miss on the westerly
reaches of the Queen West
strip, but once inside its
warm, wood-panelled interior
you'll be happy with your
choice. The meal-sized salads,
creamy risottos, and numerous
oyster dishes, like Angels on
Horseback (oysters wrapped
in bacon), are served by a
youthful, friendly staff.

Tango Palace Coffee Co

Map 2, H7. 1156 Queen St E
Ⓣ 465-8085. Inexpensive.
Streetcar Queen (#501).

Tango Palace is the envy of
neighbourhoods throughout
Toronto. Ensconced in an
Edwardian storefront amongst
a row of antique stores, the
crew here serves up huge cups
and bowls of café au lait,
cappuccinos and just plain
coffee along with a
bewildering variety of sweets,
all to the strains of jitterbug
and doowop tunes.

Tequila Bookworm

Map 3, C3. 490 Queen St W
Ⓣ 504-7335. Cheap.
Streetcar Queen (#501).

The exposed-brick walls in
the front of this café are lined
with magazines for sale,
while the back section is
filled with floor-to-ceiling
bookshelves stuffed with old
textbooks, romance novels
and the odd Penguin classic.
Garage sale armchairs and
coffee tables await patrons
willing to make a serious
time commitment. Espresso
drinks and simple desserts are
served with no fussy
embellishments.

Vienna Home Bakery

Map 3, C3. 626 Queen St W
Ⓣ 703-7278. Cheap.
Streetcar Queen (#501).

Part of the original, pre-cool
Queen West landscape, the
Vienna Bakery has been
providing starving artist types
with caffeine and sugar rushes
for decades. This earnest slice
of central Europe is a
wonderful antidote to
ludicrously named coffee
drinks and low-cal snacks.

ASIAN FUSION

Mata Hari
Map 4, E9. 39 Baldwin St
Ⓣ 596-2832. Moderate.
Streetcar College (#506).
The fusion here is Chinese
and Malay (known as *nyonya*).
Curry, rice and noodle dishes
are the stars, with a tempting
range of desserts. Vegetarian
dishes available.

Monsoon
Map 3, F4. 100 Simcoe St
Ⓣ 979-7172. Expensive.
Subway St Andrew.
The award-interior here
reflects the Asian influence on
the menu. Starters are served
on delicate *rakku* dishes, and
the light, assured cooking
boasts imaginative
combinations (seared tofu in
green-tea marinade, maple-
ginger grouper). An excellent
place to mark a special
occasion.

Queen Mother Café
Map 3, E3. 208 Queen St W
Ⓣ 598-4719.
Moderate/Expensive.
Streetcar Queen (#501).

Neither the name nor the
cosy wood-panelled interior
gives a hint about the menu:
Asian specialities like pad thai,
crispy spring rolls, and lots of
chicken-and-shrimp entrees.
Vegetarians take heart: the
house veggie burger is a local
tradition.

Tiger Lily
Map 3, E3. 257 Queen St W
Ⓣ 977-5499. Moderate.
Streetcar Queen (#501).
One of the best bargains on
the Queen West strip. There
are a wide variety of noodle
and soup dishes, as well as
fresh spring rolls and
innovative deserts.

CANADIAN AND AMERICAN

Canoe
Map 3, G5. Toronto-Dominion
Tower, 66 Wellington St W
Ⓣ 364-0054. Expensive.
Subway King or St Andrew.
Way up on the 54th floor of
an office tower, this elegant
address serves up highly
imaginative Canadian cuisine
(Yukon caribou, feral greens,

DOWNTOWN

wild berries) alongside one of the best wine lists in the city.

Eureka Continuum

Map 3, F3. 205 Richmond St W
Ⓣ 593-8427.
Moderate/Expensive.
Streetcar **Queen** (#501).

Tucked in amid the dance clubs and lounges that line Richmond St West is this novel addition to Toronto's theme-cuisine restaurants. The fare here is billed as "Aboriginal fusion", which would appear to be code for game. The menu includes such exotic items as smoked caribou sausages or a bison steak. Vegetarian options exist primarily in the "Three Sisters" (corn, beans and squashes) food groups, and there is a well-stocked bar. Service is friendly and informative.

Gypsy Co-op

Map 2, F7. 817 Queen St W
Ⓣ 703-5069.
Moderate/Expensive.
Streetcar **Queen** (#501).

An eclectic mix of old-time candy store and traditional Muskoka lodge, the dining space's windows roll up like a garage door in the summer. Alternately, patrons can sit on rotating stools at a long chrome bar and during the chilly depths of winter can park in front of a stone fireplace in comfy club chairs. The creative menu caters to everyone, from rare-steak eaters to vegans, and the atmosphere is agelessly cool and poseur-free.

Indian Motorcycle Café & Lounge

Map 3, C4. 355 King St W
Ⓣ 593-6996.
Moderate/Expensive.
Streetcar **King** (#504).

Few restaurants are named after a motorcycle, and it is safe to assume that the food is a secondary reason for attending after standing round and looking good in the dramatically designed, two-storey interior. Serves upscale pizzas, sandwiches, and vegetarian-options like Asian pastas and stir-fries. The meaty bits are straightforward steak and ribs.

Montreal Restaurant Bistro and Jazz Club

Map 3, L4. 65 Sherborne St
ⓣ 363-0179.
Moderate/Expensive.
Streetcar King (#504).

Like Montreal itself, the menu is a mish-mash of Quebecois, French, Italian and American influences, meaning that you can have split pea soup with your burgers and fries. The real draw of the place is the top jazz acts it books, which attract enthusiastic crowds out for a night on *le ville*. Cover charges usually apply and it is a good idea to call ahead.

Le Papillon

Map 3, J5. 16 Church St
ⓣ 363-0838. Moderate.
Subway Union Station.

Large Breton crepes served sweet or savoury with a Quebecois flair are the house specialities, although the menu also includes *tortier* (a Quebec meat pie) and bistro standards like onion soup and steak *frites*. Convivial, solicitous service in a casually trendy environment.

Red Devil Barbecue & Tavern

Map 3, F4. 14 Duncan St
ⓣ 598-5209. Moderate.
Subway St Andrew.

A youthful, amusing establishment whose strongest suit is enthusiasm. Many of the items on the menu, including salmon steaks, spit-roasted chickens and barbecued ribs, are prepared on the wood-burning grill, and any choice can be washed down with a wide selection of cocktails and beer.

Tundra

Map 3, G3. 145 Richmond St W
ⓣ 869-3456. Expensive.
Streetcar Queen (#501).

As the name suggests, this sleekly turned out dining room – its rich woods, granite embellishments, glass-topped bar and canvas-wrapped pillars all suggest the elements – is intended to be as Canadian as the Great White North. In this case "Canadian" means the ingredients (flash-broiled Arctic char, seared venison tenderloin, Malpeque oysters), prepared with a bracing minimalism by Chef Andre Walker.

DOWNTOWN

Zoom

Map 3, I4. 18 King St E
Ⓣ 861-9872. Expensive.
Subway King.

A midtown eatery popular
with CEOs and corporate
types during lunch. The steel
and glass interior seems
designed to give diners clear
sight lines of all the other
tables, and the food – which
is a light mix of Asian fusion
and nouvelle cuisine – is
given an over-the-top
presentation to make it all
seem special. The least
American characteristic is the
size of the portions, which are
on the smallish side.

CARIBBEAN

Ali's West Indian Roti Shop

Map 2, E7. 1446 Queen St W
Ⓣ 532-7701. Cheap.
Streetcar Queen (#501).

Rotis have become one of
Toronto's most popular
snacks. *Ali's* is one of the best,
featuring succulent *dhalpoori*,
sada and *paratha* roti stuffed
with your choice of meat,
seafood or vegetarian options.

Stews and full dinners are also
available. Island juices and a
homemade soursop ice cream
are on hand to cool spice-
excited palates.

Bacchus

Map 2, E7. 1376 Queen St W
Ⓣ 532-8191. Cheap.
Streetcar Queen (#501).

This tiny restaurant offers a
Guyanese version of rotis,
filled with a selection of
stuffings such as curried goat,
squash, spinach or conch, to
name but a few. Feather-light
dumplings and fritters, peanut
butter cakes and fried
plantains can be accompanied
by a wide selection of tropical
fruit drinks and ginger beers.

The Real Jerk

Map 2, H7. 709 Queen St E
Ⓣ 463-6055. Moderate.
Streetcar Queen (#501).

Jamaican standards like red
beans and rice, rotis, and
banana fritters mingle with
such Toronto inventions as
Rasta Pasta – a linguine dish
with tropical vegetables in a
coconut sauce. Quench your
thirst with bottles of imported
Red Stripe beer.

Roti Factory

Map 4, B9. 177 Baldwin St.
☎ 340-9540. Cheap.
Streetcar Spadina (#510).
This wee Kensington Market outlet is the Trinidadian gold standard for the Indo-Caribbean precursor to the wrap sandwich. In addition to the varieties of stuffings one can order (potato, canna, plantain, oxtail) are the eye-watering variety of hot sauces available.

CHINESE

Grand Yatt Dynasty

Map 3, H8. One Harbour Square
☎ 869-3663. Expensive.
Streetcar from Union Stn: (#510).
The sophisticated, downtown version of the popular suburban outlet, this big-time Chinese eatery is famed for its lunchtime dim sum and won ton soup in particular, but the mains are both beautifully presented and tastefully prepared.

Happy Seven

Map 3, C2. 358 Spadina Ave
☎ 971-9820. Inexpensive.

Streetcar Dundas (#505).
Predominantly Cantonese-style cooking with a few spicy Szechwan dishes, tanks of soon-to-be seafood, and large, attractively presented servings. Bright and spotless, this establishment is always filled with satisfied customers. Open until 5am.

Lai Wah Heen

Map 3, G1. Metropolitan Hotel, 108 Chestnut St
☎ 977-9899. Expensive.
Streetcar Dundas (#505).
The name means "elegant meeting place", which it most certainly is. The complex menu is Hong Kong *moderne*, with dishes like Lustrous Peacock (a salad of barbecued duck, chicken and jellyfish on slivered melons garnished with eggs). Also serves arguably the best dim sum in the city.

Lee Garden

Map 3, C1. 331 Spadina Ave
☎ 593-9524. Inexpensive.
Streetcar Dundas (#505).
An oasis of calm greenery on the frenetic Spadina strip. Locals esteem *Lee's* for the boneless chicken with black

DOWNTOWN

bean sauce and the large selection of fresh fish dishes. The cuisine is mostly Cantonese with plenty of daily specials that may demand your waiter's translation.

Lucky Dragon

Map 3, C1. 418 Spadina Ave
Ⓣ 598-7823. Inexpensive.
Streetcar Spadina (#510).
The extensive Szechwan menu features over 200 items, making the *Lucky Dragon* a prime spot for anyone craving spicy, garlicky food. The noodle dishes contain some delicate surprises, like a fine noodle dressed simply in green onion and ginger. There is a wide variety of soups, hearty hot-pots, and lots of pork and seafood dishes with plenty of vegetarian options available to those who ask. Delicious and authentic.

FRENCH
- - - - - - - - - - - - - - - - - - - -

Le Select

Map 3, D3. 328 Queen St W
Ⓣ 596-6406. Moderate.
Streetcar Queen (#506).
Rib-sticking Gallic favourites are served in a bistro atmosphere, with embellishments like a genuine Parisian zinc bar and little baskets of bread raised and lowered at each table by a Rube Goldberg-like pully system. Use Sunday brunch as an excuse to sample one of the establishment's cloud-like omelettes served with the best *frites* in town. If your main intent is to lounge on the enclosed patio and people watch, the beer and wine list is sterling, and the service is consistently excellent.

Verveine

Map 2, I7. 1097 Queen St E
Moderate/Expensive.
Streetcar Queen (#501).
When prettily decorated establishments serving contemporary takes on bistro classics (steamed mussels bathed in mango butter, fat sandwiches served with crispy *pomme frites*) pop up in formerly proletarian sections of town, locals cluck their tongues at the gentrification of yet another neighbourhood – and then line up to sample the menu. All the above is

true of *Verveine* which, despite its name and lovely green interior, has few herbaceous items on its menu.

INDIAN

Babur

Map 3, E3. 237 Queen St W
☎ 599-7720. Moderate/Expensive.
Streetcar **Queen (#501).**
Rich, buttery sauces, delicately spiced stews and fluffy *naan* and *pori* breads, all delivered to your linen-cloth table by a helpful wait staff.

Bombay Palace

Map 3, K4. 71 Jarvis St
☎ 368-8048.
Moderate/Expensive.
Streetcar **King (#504).**
Mostly northern-style cooking with a nod towards Delhi. Crispy *pakoras* and *samosas* are good bets for starters. Main courses of mulligatawny soup and a full range of fish, meat and vegetable dishes are served with flourish in a serene, attractive dining room.

ITALIAN

La Fenice

Map 3, E4. 319 King St W
☎ 585-2377. Expensive.
Streetcar **King (#504).**
The consistently high standards of this long-time favourite are one reason its clientele keep coming back. Another is the deliberate unfashionability of the antipasti, pastas, risottos, and fish dishes. Tradition reigns in the upstairs dining room. The downstairs pasta bar is another matter: stark, high-design modernity reigns in that environment, which offers pasta dishes to a younger and more budget-conscious crowd

John's Italian Café

Map 3, E1. 27 Baldwin
☎ 596-8848. Moderate.
Streetcar **College (#506).**
This is a particularly pleasant, unpretentious little café. It specialises in pizzas and pastas with Italian *dolce* to round out the meal, although regulars also treasure it as a wonderful place to chat with friends over bowls of coffee or carafes of wine.

DOWNTOWN

Kit Kat

Map 3, E4. 297 King St W
ⓣ 977-4461. Moderate.
Streetcar **King** (#504).
Excellent pastas, steaks and seafood dominate the uncomplicated menu. While typically busy, the atmosphere is friendly and the service is attentive. First-timers are invited to pat the tree growing in the middle of the kitchen for good luck.

Pizzabilities 'R' Endless

Map 4, B9. 69 Kensington Ave
ⓣ 971-5521. Cheap.
Streetcar **Spadina** (#510).
This tiny storefront in the middle of Kensington Market produces delicious and original pizzas. Square slices of daily specials such as paper-thin Yukon gold potatoes on a béchamel sauce topped with rosemary and olive oil, or asparagus, peppers, onion and five cheeses ensure a dedicated clientele. Sometimes there are panini or stuffed pastas available for lunch (take away or sit at one of the little tables outside), but the pizzas rule here.

Terroni

Map 2, F7. 720 Queen St W
ⓣ 504-0320. Moderate.
Streetcar **Queen** (#501).
Cognoscenti squash themselves into this narrow, unobtrusive hideaway for thin and crispy pizzas, which can be ordered with a dazzling variety of toppings. The panini are particularly well built and tasty and can be made to specifications. Italian beer, wine and sodas are available, along with the usual espresso drinks.

JAPANESE

Hiro Sushi

Map 3, K4. 171 King St E
ⓣ 304-0550. Expensive.
Streetcar **King** (#504).
Hiro-san raised the bar in Toronto's sushi establishments when he opened this sliver of a restaurant. It offers unparalleled subtlety in all respects: decor, presentation and of course the food itself. Considered to be the best in town by many.

Nami

Map 3, J4. 55 Adelaide St E
ⓣ 362-7373. Expensive.
Streetcar King (#504).

A very fine Japanese restaurant with a dark, elegant interior lined with discrete private booths. The sushi bar is the standard fare, but the *robata* counter (grilled seafood prepared in front of you) is the main draw.

Sushi Bistro

Map 3, E3. 204 Queen St W
ⓣ 971-5315. Moderate.
Streetcar Queen (#501).

Its colourful clientele matches the variety of its sushi menu and bento boxes. Entrees come with soup, salad, tea and rice and there is an impressive sake selection. If you tire of watching the sushi chef or your fellow diners there is a karaoke bar upstairs.

LATIN AMERICAN AND SPANISH

– – – – – – – – – – – – – – – – – – –

Xango

Map 3, E4. 106 John St
ⓣ 323-9651. Expensive.
Streetcar King (#504).

The menu here calls up a continent's worth of ingredients – empanadas, ceviches, lobster *chupe* – and presents them with verve and style. Try sharing a tiered platter of sample-sized items to get a feel for the kitchen. Dancing and live entertainment in the Mambo Lounge on weekends make for a full night out.

SEAFOOD

– – – – – – – – – – – – – – – – – – –

Filet of Sole

Map 3, F4. 11 Duncan St
ⓣ 598-3256.
Moderate/Expensive.
Streetcar Queen (#501).

Extensive range of fairly straightforward seafood (lobsters, scallops, trout and salmon) served in lively warehouse-style surroundings with a bit more emphasis on quantity than quality. Very popular with the office crowd so reservations are advisable.

DOWNTOWN

Rodney's Oyster House

Map 3, K4. 209 Adelaide St E
ⓣ363-8105. Expensive.
Streetcar King (#504).
Toronto's favourite oyster bar serves up oysters, oysters and more oysters, along with scallops, mussels and shrimp. The only non-crustaceous seafood available is the smoked salmon. The wine and dessert menus are short but the selection of beer and scotch is impressive.

Whistling Oyster

Map 3, F3. 207 11 Duncan St
ⓣ598-7707. Moderate.
Streetcar King (#504).
This youthful, amicable establishment doesn't take itself too seriously. A large, circular bar makes people watching and neighbour chatting easy and is particularly crowded before shows at the nearby Royal Alexandra or Princess of Wales theatres. Oysters, mussels, and scallops are the stars here, but Asian flourishes like chicken satay are available as a seafood alternative.

STEAKHOUSES

Barberian's

Map 3, I1. 7 Elm St
ⓣ597-0335. Expensive.
Subway Dundas.
Barberian's hasn't changed much since it opened its doors in 1959, which appeals to both young Rat Pack wannabes and those who were actually there. It offers no-nonsense dining geared towards carnivores in a comfy, clubby environment. The wine list is excellent.

The Senator

Map 3, J2. 253 Victoria St
ⓣ364-7517.
Moderate/Expensive.
Subway Queen.
A Fifties motif dominates the decor in what is arguably the best steakhouse in Toronto. Superb steaks, legendary burgers and fries and fifties cocktail icons like crab cakes hark back to a simpler time. The legendary jazz club (see p.192) is upstairs.

DOWNTOWN

THAI

Bangkok Garden
Map 3, I1. 18 Elm St
☎ 977-6748.
Moderate/Expensive.
Subway Dundas.
Set in one of Elm Street's beautiful old brownstones, *Bangkok Garden* is set up like a fine dining room with Southeast Asian embellishments, soft lighting and plenty of nooks. The heat on the curries is turned down a notch to accommodate all tastes. Specialities include interesting treatments of fresh lake fish, and a nice selection of salads, noodles and curries.

Golden Thai
Map 3, J4. 105 Church St
☎ 868-6668. Moderate.
Streetcar King (#504).
It is almost worth visiting *Golden Thai* for the space alone: huge, Neoclassical fan windows, high ceilings and a cavernous interior make the space an island of calm. Fortunately the food lives up to the decor. There is an emphasis on freshness and

allowing the taste of the ingredients to come through, fire-hot spices and all. The lemon shrimp soup is recommended, and vegetarians have a good range of choice.

Salad King
Map 3, I2. 335 Yonge St
☎ 971-7041. Cheap.
Subway Dundas.
This Thai fast-food counter for take out or sit down shows its stuff with punchy spicing (beware the Evil Jungle Prince, a fiery vegetable stir-fry), plenty of vegetarian options amid the many varieties of chicken dishes, and imported Thai beer. The Thai basil soup is a meal in itself.

Vanipha Fine Cuisine
Map 4, B9. 193 Augusta Ave
☎ 340-0491.
Streetcar Dundas (#505).
This walk-down restaurant offers the best and most original examples of Lao-Thai cuisine in the city. The menu offers subtle and sophisticated versions of dishes that may be familiar by name (lemon grass,

DOWNTOWN

shrimp soup, fresh spring rolls), but which usually receive a heavy hand. Here, peppers, ginger, coriander, coconut and lemon grass are used with care, not abandon. Vegetarians will be pleased with the number of options available.

VEGETARIAN

Bo De Duyen
Map 3, C3. 254 Spadina Ave
Ⓣ 703-1247. Moderate.
Streetcar Spadina (#510).
This popular walk-up greets guests with puffs of incense and an ancestral shrine half-way up the stairs. It offers Chinese-Vietnamese cooking for vegetarians. The utter absence of any animal by-products means that even the strictest vegan can eat here with a clear conscience. Pages and pages of selections, including "mock" meat and seafood items.

Fressen Herbacious Cuisine
Map 3, B3. 478 Queen St W
Ⓣ 504-5127. Moderate.
Streetcar Queen (#501).

This restaurant is too cool to bill itself as being vegetarian per se. The tag line here is "herbacious cuisine", but veggie it is, replete with vegan options. Regulars pass over the pastas and pizzas for the innovative entrees. A full meal can also be made of the appetisers, the kitchen's main claim to fame, and the juice/smoothie list is extensive.

Juice for Life
Map 3, C3. 521 Bloor St W
Ⓣ 531-2635. Inexpensive.
Streetcar Queen (#501).
Vegan purists hit the roof when this hipster gourmet juice bar, eating counter and bakery started to serve dairy and alcohol, but the range of options for vegans remains one of Toronto's best. Of course regular vegetarians are delighted to be able to order a veggie cheeseburger and a beer and watch the Queen Street West parade go by.

King's Café Vegetarian Coffee Shop
Map 4, B9. 192 Augusta Ave
Ⓣ 591-1340. Cheap.
Streetcar College (#506).

If Kensington Market is a microcosm of Toronto's mind-boggling mix of cultures and sub-cultures, *King's Café* is a microcosm of Kensington. Broadly speaking, the menu could be described as Chinese vegetarian, but Portuguese ladies come here for coffee and cream-filled puff pastries, ravers pop in all-day breakfasts (which start at $2.99), and pan-generational members of Toronto's different Asian communities drop by for a vegetarian version of their indigenous cuisine. The light blond wood and brushed steel interior is fresh and contemporary, and the large patio out front is a popular summer meeting spot. A highly recommended experience.

Le Commensal

Map 3, G9. 655 Bay St (entrance off Elm Street) ⊤596-9364. Moderate. Subway Dundas.

The cafeteria-style set-up of this large and airy restaurant is its only drawback. Otherwise the variety of offerings is excellent. Soups, great salads, hearty pot-pies, stews, casseroles and baked goods are clearly marked for vegans or lacto-ovo vegetarians. A large dessert counter tempts with delectables like maple sugar pie, fruit cobblers, and sweet pastries. Take-out is also available.

Lotus Garden

Map 3, E2. 393 Dundas St W ⊤598-1883. Inexpensive. Streetcar Dundas (#505).

Right across the street from the Art Gallery of Ontario, this little Vietnamese-Buddhist eatery is the only vegetarian Vietnamese restaurant in Toronto. Ignore the "mock" beef, pork and seafood dishes and go straight to the soups, noodle dishes, or stuffed vegetables. The Vietnamese crepes are particularly tasty, and the iced coffee is habit-forming in the extreme.

VIETNAMESE

Pho 88 Restaurant

Map 3, C2. 270 Spadina Ave ⊤971-8899. Cheap. Streetcar Spadina (#510).

The speciality here is *pho*, a spicy noodle soup with beef and vegetables that can have numerous variations, according to the customer's choice.

Vien Dong
Map 3, C1. 359 Spadina Ave
℗ 593-6265. Inexpensive.
Streetcar **Spadina** (#510).
A Vietnamese place with lots of Cantonese influence and a few Gallic touches (frog legs, for example) and a variety of fresh, tropical fruit shakes.

24-HOUR FOOD

Shift workers, night owls and insomniacs all have reason to catch a bite or visit with friends in the depths of the night, and there is a pocket of mid-town all-night restaurants and cafés that offer a nourishing alternative to the ubiquitous, late-night doughnut shops. If you find yourself awake and hungry between 3am and 6am, the following restaurants will be open to serve you:

7 Charles Street West	p.160
Fran's	p.162
Golden Griddle	p.163
Mars Restaurant	p.164

UPTOWN

CAFÉS AND COFFEE HOUSES

----

7 Charles Street West
Map 4, H5. 7 Charles St W
℗ 928-9041. Moderate.
Subway **Bloor/Yonge**.
This old Victorian house has been renovated into a three-floor café that is open all day and night. The first floor is a

UPTOWN

traditional bistro-type dining area, the second an espresso bar and the third feels like a friend's attic, complete with a tiny pool table and wall murals. The food is simple, relatively inexpensive, and has an Italian twist. The desserts are lovely and there is a bargain-basement brunch on Sunday.

52 Inc.
Map 4, A8. 394 College St
960-0334. Moderate.
Streetcar **College** (#506).
Blink and you'll miss this tiny but worthwhile neighbourhood bar. The owners sell domestic art magazines and hang works by up-and-coming artists on the walls. The light menu includes a range of sandwiches named after Sixties art flicks (such as the *L'Avventura*, with roasted red peppers, asiago and watercress), and an extensive cocktail list also vies for patrons' attention.

Athens Pastries
Map 2, H6. 509 Danforth Ave
463-5144. Cheap.
Subway **Chester**.

True to its name, this narrow café-cum-bakery sells sweet and savoury Greek pastries with coffee, and that's about it. Huge trays of *baklava*, *spanakopita* and a delectable custard and filo confection empty out in rapid succession as sit-down or take-away customers file in for the filo fix.

Brownstone Café & Wine Bar
Map 4, H7. 603 Yonge St
920-6288. Moderate.
Subway **Wellesley**.
The *Brownstone* is proof positive that neighbourhood cafés are in every nook and corner of the city, even on busy Yonge Street. Light meals with plenty of vegetarian options are available throughout the day, and when the sun slips down coffee drinks give way to a thoughtful and reasonably priced wine list.

The Coffee Mill
Map 4, G5. 99 Yorkville Ave
967-3837. Moderate.
Subway **Bay** (Bellair exit).
This Hungarian establishment

UPTOWN

dates back to Yorkville's coffee house days, when the likes of Joni Mitchell and Neil Young were getting their start in that very neighbourhood. It serves a variety of coffees, its influences more Viennese than Italian, and the goulash is still one of the best bargains in town.

Dooney's Café
Map 4, B5. 511 Bloor St W
Ⓣ536-3292. Moderate.
Subway **Spadina**.
This is the David to *Starbuck's* Goliath. When the latter tried to usurp *Dooney's* lease, the café's regular patrons organised and stirred up the neighbourhood and kept the *Dooney's* dream alive. The interior is cosy with exposed-brick throughout, and the full menu boasts items like fat slices of French toast smothered in maple syrup and fresh fruit, pizzas, sandwiches and pastas.

Café Elise
Map 4, C6. 673 Spadina Ave
Ⓣ598-5522. Cheap.
Subway **Spadina**.
Generations of students from the nearby University of Toronto have gotten existential over the beverages and light meals served at the venerable *Café Elise*. Stews, curries, sandwiches and pastas are the rib-sticking mainstays.

Espressimo Caffebar
Map 4, H3. 1094 Yonge St
Ⓣ944-0101. Moderate.
Subway **Rosedale**.
It may not have the most imaginative name in the city but this charming little coffee house whooshes up fortifying espresso drinks for patrons worn out from shopping at the beautiful antique stores that line this strip near the tony Rosedale neighbourhood.

Fran's
Map 4, H9. 20 College St
Ⓣ923-9867;
Map 2, G6. 21 St Clair W
Ⓣ925-6337. Inexpensive.
Subways **College & St Clair** respectively.
This 24-hour restaurant chain is a Toronto institution – the St Clair outlet regularly served Fran's famed apple pie to the King of Denmark when the Royal Danish family was in

Toronto during World War II. For some reason, the simple grilled cheese sandwich with a side of fries is magical at 4.30am.

Future Bakery & Café
Map 4, B5. 483 Bloor St W
ⓣ 922-5875 (and three other locations). Inexpensive.
Subway **Spadina**.
Popular among Toronto's students and ageing intellectuals, this bakery, restaurant and café serves up Ukrainian and eastern European dishes (pierogies, cabbage rolls, kasha) and desserts until 2am.

Golden Griddle
Map 4, I8. 45 Carlton St
ⓣ 977 5044;
Map 3, K6. 11 Jarvis St
ⓣ 865-1263. Inexpensive.
Subway **College & Union** respectively.
A road-house type atmosphere where the late-night, early-morning types that roll in are an attraction all to themselves. This 24-hour joint serves mainly an array of pancakes, but a full menu is also available.

Iliada Café
Map 2, H6. 550 Danforth Ave
ⓣ 462-0334. Moderate.
Subway **Chester**.
The Greek coffee served here, which comes in a tiny cup three-quarters full of fine coffee grounds, makes espresso seem like baby formula. Regular coffee and espresso-type beverages are also available.

Jet Fuel Coffee Shop
Map 4, M8. 519 Parliament St
ⓣ 968-9982. Cheap.
Streetcar **College/Carlton**.
This is one of the oldest independent coffee establishments in town. It only serves beverages that can be made with an espresso machine (tea included), and imports a few baked goods for dunking. An excellent choice for relaxing with a huge, inexpensive latte and a newspaper.

Lettieri Espresso Bar Café
Map 4, G5. 94 Cumberland St
ⓣ 515-8764, and 3 other locations. Inexpensive.
Subway **Bay** (Bellair exit).

UPTOWN

163

Amidst the surge of espresso-bar chains that have blighted Toronto as of late, this one is actually deserving of praise. The paninis are delicious, and make for the cheapest meal in Yorkville. The atmosphere is nothing to write home about, but the coffee drinks are good and the selection of pastas and salads is fresh and authentically Italian.

Living Well

Map 4, I6. 692 Yonge St
ⓣ 922-6770. Moderate.
Subway **Yonge**.
The two terraces fill up fast in summer, and the casual clientele select from a full menu of inexpensive, well-prepared snacks and entrees, particularly custom-made sandwiches and pastas.

Maggie's

Map 4, A8. 400 College St
ⓣ 323-3248. Inexpensive.
Streetcar **College (#506)**.
Although you can get very nice lunches here, the real draw is *Maggie's* inexpensive, all-day breakfasts, featuring comfort food like eggs Benedict, omelettes and French toast served with mounds of fresh fruit and free refills on regular coffees and tea.

Mars Restaurant

Map 4, A8. 432 College St
ⓣ 921-6332;
Map 2, G5. 2363 Yonge St.
Cheap.
Streetcar **College (#506)**.
A full-service diner frequented for its cheap and filling all-day breakfast special: two eggs prepared any way you like, sausage and bacon, and thick slices of toast with jam. The outlet at Yonge and Eglinton trades heavily on the fifties diner theme with equally retro burgers, fries and breakfasts.

The Peartree Restaurant

Map 4, M8. 507 Parliament St
ⓣ 962-8190. Moderate.
Streetcar **Carlton/College (#506)**.
A neighbourhood café with a well-treed, open-air patio for summer lingering. The international menu features stir-fries, pastas and plenty of Tex Mex-influenced entrees. The Sunday brunch is hugely popular with locals, so come early.

Soda Market Café

Map 2, H6. 425 Danforth Ave
ⓣ466-5227. Moderate.
Subway **Chester**.
This attractive lunch spot
offers a menu of substantial
but inexpensive items such as
large omelettes with a variety
a fillings and a choice of
home-fried potatoes or salad,
pizzas, and a platter of Greek
dips and grilled pita in
addition to lattes, espressos,
cappuccinos and juices.

ASIAN FUSION

Silk Road

Map 2, H6. 341 Danforth Ave
ⓣ463-8660. Inexpensive.
Subway **Chester**.
Dishes from Central Asia to
Japan grace the menu here,
with an emphasis on the
regional dishes of China. Try
the dainty vegetarian appetiser
plate, "Granny Wong's hot
pot", a spicy stew of tofu,
vegetables and meat, or the
mu shu pancakes, which arrive
with your choice of fillings
and a generous dish of black
bean paste to smear on your
rice flour crepes. There is also

a wide variety of noodle
dishes, most of which can be
prepared for vegetarians.

Spring Rolls

Map 4, I6. 687 Yonge St
ⓣ972-7655. Moderate.
Subway **Yonge-Bloor**.
A cut about the Asian noodle
houses that jostle along this
strip of Yonge Street, *Spring
Rolls* offers a broad range of
Asian cuisines and influences
(Cantonese, Szechwan,
Vietnamese, Thai, Japanese)
prepared with above-average
skill and panache.

Tempo

Map 2, F7. 596 College St
ⓣ531-2822.
Moderate/Expensive.
Streetcar **College** (#506).
Some of the most desirable
restaurant seats in town are
the bar stools at *Tempo*
because that's the only place
you can order Chef Tom
Thai's tasting menu. Table
service in the minimalist
interior or shady street-side
patio gives way to equally
outstanding offerings, with
Japanese items like sushi and
sashimi plates, and delectable

UPTOWN

hybrids such as tea-smoked bass with a maple glaze or monkfish fired up with Cajun spices.

Zyng Noodle House
Map 4, I6. 730 Yonge St
Ⓣ 964-8410. Inexpensive.
Subway Yonge-Bloor.
Select from a myriad of broths, noodles and garnishes to custom design your own Asian noodle soup. The oversized bowls provide a fast and inexpensive lunch or light dinner.

CANADIAN AND AMERICAN
- -

Patriot
Map 4, F5. 131 Bloor St W, 2nd floor
Ⓣ 922-0025.
Moderate/Expensive.
Subway Bay/Museum.
Patriot features one of Toronto's hottest young chefs, David Chrystian, whose talent lies in innovative and unexpected pairings of tastes and textures. Here he reinterprets Canadian regional dishes such as salt cod from the Maritimes or *poutine* and *tortier* from Quebec, with audacious creativity. The cellar features an excellent selection of Ontario wines, the service is good and the wood and glass interior is calming and peaceful.

True Grits Soul Shack
Map 4, A5. 603 Markham St
Ⓣ 536-8383.
Moderate/Expensive.
Subway Bathurst.
Creole and Southern US specialities like grits, collard greens, and candied yams are dished up with laid-back elan in this comfy Victorian renovation. The walls are packed with funky *naif* paintings and the furniture is a flea market mish-mash. Lots of fun.

CARIBBEAN
- -

Irie
Map 2, H7. 808 College St
Ⓣ 531-4743. Moderate.
Streetcar College (#506).
Jamaican standards like jerk chicken, pork or shrimp, rice and rotis are expertly prepared

in this modest restaurant at the end of the thriving College Strip. There are plenty of vegetarian options and a rich dessert menu.

FRENCH

Arlequin
Map 4, F3. 134 Avenue Rd
℗928-9521. Expensive.
Subway **Bay (Cumberland exit).**
Traditional French food gets a kick in the pants from the occasional Middle Eastern embellishment. The *prix fixe* menu is supplemented by clever a la carte items and a take-out counter up front for those who just can't stay.

Bistro 990
Map 4, G7. 990 Bay St
℗921-9990. Expensive.
Subway **Wellesley.**
This cosy favourite of corporate types and the odd movie star offers robust examples of bistro fare, with a strong emphasis on meaty dishes (rabbit, lamb). The caramelised onion tart with a melt-in-the-mouth flake

pastry crust is a show stopper. *Prix fixe* menus take the sting out of what can be an expensive outing.

Ellipsis
Map 2, E7. 503 College St
℗929-2892.
Moderate/Expensive.
Streetcar **College (#506).**
Bistro classics (steamed mussels, lamb and navy-bean ragout) served up in serene, pared-down surroundings. Sunday brunch is hugely popular, so be prepared to wait.

Provence
Map 4, M8. 12 Amelia St
℗924-9901. Expensive.
Streetcar **Carlton (#506).**
This renovated Cabbagetown cottage produces a small but highly competent menu with pronounced *nouvelle* cuisine leanings: plenty of attention to vegetables, meats served *au jus* rather than in heavy sauces and lots of fresh-fruit desserts. Vegetarian options are a select but recent addition to the menu.

UPTOWN

GREEK

Avli

Map 2, H6. 401 Danforth Ave
℡ 461-9577.
Moderate/Expensive.
Subway **Chester**.
An authentic Greek restaurant with a strong emphasis on fancy starters, a combination of which could easily make a full meal. Classic seafood dishes, a variety of pot-pies and sublime baklava round out the meal, all served up with Hellenic elan. The wine list is good but ask about the owner's cellar for something really special.

Kalendar Koffee House

Map 2, E7. 596 College St
℡ 923-4138. Moderate.
Streetcar **College (#506)**.
Dark wood panelling and intimate booths provide an old-world atmosphere, which is in sharp contrast to the light, Mediterranean menu: pizza, pasta, Greek dips. Kalendar uses *naan* bread as a stand-in for pitta and employs a roti-like *dahl pori* instead of a wrap for hot sandwiches. Daily specials place a welcome emphasis on fresh seasonal ingredients. Spend some time looking over the beer and wine list and sample some of the exotic Quebec and Ontario micro beers or estate vintages.

Ouzeri

Map 2, H6. 500A Danforth Ave
℡ 466-8158.
Moderate/Expensive.
Subway **Chester**.
The later the hour the more festive the atmosphere at this raucous joint. A long list of starters and an extensive wine list are highlights.

Pan on the Danforth

Map 2, H6. 516 Danforth Ave
℡ 466-8158.
Moderate/Expensive.
Subway **Chester**.
This long, thin eatery is where Greek classics meet Athenian *nouvelle cuisine* with clever combinations and a light touch, such as chicken stuffed with feta cheese and spinach. Attentive service on even the busiest nights.

Pappas Grill

Map 2, H6. 440 Danforth Ave
Ⓣ 469-9595. Moderate.
Subway Chester.
All the standard items –
souvlaki, mezze appetisers,
grilled seafood – served with
baskets of pitta and lashings of
olive oil.

INDIAN/SRI LANKAN

Gujurat Durbar

Map 2, H7. 1386 Gerrard St E
Ⓣ 406-1085. Inexpensive.
Streetcar Carlton (#506).
This vegetarian restaurant in
the midst of the East End's
Little India serves up aromatic
dishes from India's northwest
Gujarati region. Your best bet
is the generously
proportioned *thali*, which
features a variety of daily
curries, dhal, pickles and rice.

Indian Rice Factory

Map 4, B2. 414 Dupont St
Ⓣ 961-3472. Moderate.
Subway Dupont.
This venerable Toronto
favourite is family-run and it
treats its regulars like extended
family members. The spicing

is on the mild side and the
offerings are the usual
samosas, curries, and
vindaloos but the atmosphere
is warm and friendly, and the
staff are eager to please.

Nataraj

Map 4, B5. 394 Bloor St W
Ⓣ 928-2925. Moderate.
Subway Spadina.
Delhi-specific dishes with a
tandoori twist. The air is
perfumed with delectable
naan baking on the sides of
the tandoori oven, which is
on view to diners through a
window to the kitchen. Try
the spicy stews, addictive
shrimp pakoras, and sugar-
rush desserts.

Rashnaa

Map 4, L7. 307 Wellesley St E
Ⓣ 929-2099. Moderate.
Streetcar Carlton (#506).
This tiny restaurant,
crammed into a small
Cabbagetown cottage, offers
intriguing southern Indian
and Sri Lankan dishes,
including stringhoppers – a
red lentil linguini served in
nests with coconut chutney –
and a variety of *dhosas, a*

UPTOWN

169

habit-forming Sri Lankan crepe that comes with a variety of fillings. One of the city's best dining bargains.

ITALIAN

Bar Italia
Map 2, E7. 584 College St
☎ 535-3621. Moderate.
Streetcar **College (#506).**
A recent renovation banished the pool tables in favour of more banquettes, and the chic little patio out front makes prime people-watching theatre. The food remains reliably delicious: Antipasti, risottos, pastas and panini are dished up amid the clatter of wine glasses by a solicitous staff.

Café Diplomatico
Map 2, E7. 594 College St
☎ 534-4637. Moderate.
Streetcar **College (#506).**
This vestige of an earlier time has managed to hold its own among new, chi-chi neighbours. Substantial, no-nonsense pizza with a selection of fresh toppings served inside or on the packed patio.

Café Nervosa
Map 4, G5. 75 Yorkville Ave
☎ 961-4642. Moderate.
Subway Bay (Bay/Bellair exit).
One of the few reasonably priced restaurants left in Yorkville, *Café Nervosa* is also a great spot for people-watching, inside or out. Salads and pasta dishes are featured but the pizzas are the menu's best bet.

Giovanna
Map 2, E7. 637 College St
☎ 538-2098.
Moderate/Expensive.
Streetcar **College (#506).**
Deceptively simple, northern Italian cooking is the proprietor's claim to fame. Velvet cream and mushroom sauces on homemade pasta coupled with light, tender vegetable dishes are elegant triumphs. A wood-burning oven produces light, crisp pizzas with a wide variety of available toppings. Patio tables are available but the clattering of the passing streetcar makes conversation difficult. Otherwise, the ambience is pleasant and the staff are friendly, prompt and knowledgeable.

Grano

Map 2, G6. 2035 Yonge St
☎ 440-1986.
Moderate/Expensive.
Subway Davisville.

The pastas, seafood and meat dishes are all delicious at this homey, uptown slice of Tuscany, but the reason people come back to *Grano's* time and time again is their brilliant antipasti: fried zucchini blossoms, golden rice balls with a mozzarella centre or the perfectly grilled eggplant are incomparable. The charming back patio is only closed during the depths of winter.

Il Fornello

Map 4, I1. 35 Elm St
☎ 486-2130 (and 3 other locations). Moderate.
Subway Yonge/Dundas.

Spoiled locals tend to forget how good *Il Fornello* pizzas are. Their thin, crisp crusts, browned to perfection in wood-fired ovens, are tops. The variety of toppings is diverse without being exotic, and on the off chance you don't want pizza, standard Italian fare (tortellini,

lasagnes, daily specials) is available.

Joya

Map 2, E7. 577 College St
☎ 588-6458.
Moderate/Expensive.
Streetcar College (#506).

A long, skinny addition to hipster heaven on the College Strip, *Joya* also has the advantage of a good grill with a recognisable Italian accent. Decor is very five minutes from now and the staff look like models, but the prices are very reasonable and the patio people-watching is prime.

Spiga

Map 2, G6. 1378 Yonge St
☎ 960-1500.
Inexpensive/Moderate.
Subway St Clair.

There is nothing fancy about this establishment. It dishes up basic, hearty Italian fare in maternal-sized portions for a very good price. Expect plump ravioli, pizzas mounded with toppings and a long list of pastas augmented by a basic wine list. For the lunchtime crowd *Spiga's* has a little

UPTOWN

lunch-counter/bakery next door where, for even less cost than the dining room, one can order take-out or eat in.

Teatro

Map 2, E7. 505 College St
☎971-1475. Expensive.
Streetcar **College (#506).**
A new addition to the poseur-friendly patios of College Street, this smallish establishment is currently more a place to be seen in than a fine restaurant. The mains are grazing-sized and feature such items as steak *tartare*, ornate salads dappled with slices of star fruit and a bouillabaisse gently perfumed with Pernod. Lots of very pretty surface with little substance served up at prime rates.

JAPANESE

Mariko

Map 2, H6. 348 Danforth Ave
☎463-8231. Moderate.
Subway **Chester.**
This Japanese bistro and sushi bar is a favourite neighbourhood haunt

amongst Riverdalers because of its health-conscious, vegetarian-friendly menu, its attractive East/West decor, and the unfailing courtesy of its staff. The bento boxes can be on the pricey side but the *udon* and *soba* noodle soups are a bargain.

Rikishi Japanese Restaurant

Map 2, F6. 833 Bloor St W
☎538-0760. Moderate.
Subway **Christie.**
Stuck out amid Portuguese, Cuban and Somalian sports bars, this little gem not only serves well-prepared traditional Japanese dishes, but it also offers far more than the standard two or three vegetarian options. Non-carnivores can choose from over 30 makki options and a variety of bento boxes. Wait staff are extremely helpful and attentive.

Sushi Delight

Map 2, H6. 461 Danforth Ave
☎406-0288.
Inexpensive/Moderate.
Subway **Chester.**
Sushi snobs may turn their

noses up at this little outlet, but the food is well prepared, the portions are substantial, and the price is right. A bento box order makes a very filling meal and there are plenty of vegetarian options on the a la carte menu. Daily special options are particularly affordable. Service is friendly and courteous if a little hurried at times.

LATIN AMERICAN AND SPANISH

Boulevard Café
Map 4, C7. 161 Harbord St
Ⓣ 961-7676.
Moderate/Expensive.
Streetcar **Spadina (#510)**.
Bus **Wellesley (#94)**.
This is your opportunity to sample Peruvian cuisine and familiarise yourself with a menu filled with seafood (shrimps, sea bass, oysters), charcoal-grilled chicken and staples like corn, beans and avocados prepared with a light touch, a little heat and plenty of citrus. Cosy surroundings in a converted annex house with dining rooms upstairs,

downstairs and along a sidewalk terrace.

La Carreta
Map 2, H6. 469 Danforth Ave
Ⓣ 461-7718. Moderate.
Subway **Chester**.
This jazzy Cuban joint offers a pleasing alternative to the souvlaki palaces that cram Danforth Avenue. The food is an intriguing mix of African, Spanish and Caribbean island influences. Huge grazing platters, including a vegetarian selection, make great introductions to the different dishes. Sangria, potent Cuban rum cocktails, and liquor-laced coffees take pride of place on the drinks menu.

Segovia
Map 4, H5. 5 St Nicholas St
Ⓣ 960-1010.
Moderate/Expensive.
Subway **Wellesley**.
Cavernous and darkly discrete; this old-time favourite has become a hot uptown venue for power lunches. The paella is somewhat staid but the cod brandine is a classic. There is also a tapas bar upstairs.

UPTOWN

MIDDLE EASTERN

Aida Falafel
Map 4, A5. 553 Bloor St W
☎ 925-6444. Cheap.
Subway **Bathurst**.
The interior is eye-poppingly bright, but the plump falafels served in warm, whole-wheat pittas drizzled with tahini sauce and spiked with cayenne pepper are Toronto's finest. Even better, there's a price break when you order more than one. There's also a full range of grilled vegetables, lentils, rice and stuffed vine leaves.

By the Way Café
Map 2, B5. 400 Bloor St W
☎ 967-4295. Moderate.
Subway **Spadina**.
An eclectic mixture of Middle East classics including Jewish delicacies, as well as substantial daily soups, salads and daily special, keep this spot packed on summer evenings, weekends and for Sunday brunch. It is a prime site for people-watching – and conversation kibbutzing – in the Annex neighbourhood. Plenty of vegetarian options.

Jerusalem
Map 2, E5. 955 Eglinton Ave W
☎ 783-6494. Moderate.
Subway **Eglinton West**.
This Israeli restaurant has been delighting diners for more than two decades. The combination platters for two are an excellent bargain and give the best example of this establishment's fusion of Middle Eastern and traditional Jewish dishes. The service is quick, friendly and helpful.

Kensington Kitchen
Map 4, C7. 124 Harbord St
☎ 961-3404. Moderate.
Streetcar **Spadina** (#510).
Bus **Wellesley** (#94).
Airy, converted house with upstairs and downstairs dining amid carefully selected knick-knacks and crimson-ochre carpets. The menu is pan-Mediterranean, with Lebanese, Greek and Moroccan classics, with plenty of choices for vegetarians.

UPTOWN

SEAFOOD

Joso's

Map 4, G3. 202 Davenport Ave
Ⓣ 925-1930. Expensive.
Subway Bay (Cumberland exit).
This much-loved seafood
restaurant, described at length
by Margaret Atwood in her
novel *Robber Bride*, is famed for
two things: its squid-ink pasta
and the plethora of breasts and
buttocks in *Joso's* paintings and
statues that decorate the place.

La Pecherie Mövenpick

Map 4, F5. 133 Yorkville Ave
Ⓣ 926-9545. Expensive.
Subway Bay (Cumberland exit).
La Pecherie offers first-rate
selections of ocean-fresh
seafood, expertly prepared.
Mounds of fresh fish are on
display as if they were the
models of a still-life painting,
but apart from that the decor
is somewhat demure and
restrained. Staff are attentive
and handy with a fish knife,
de-boning patron's fish fillets
at the table upon request.
Pastas, chicken dishes and
salads are also featured, as is an
excellent wine list.

STEAKHOUSES

George Bigliardi's

Map 4, I8. 463 Church St
Ⓣ 922-9594. Expensive.
Streetcar Carlton/College (#506).
Smack in the middle of the
rainbow coloured world of
Toronto's gay village is this
monument to granite-jawed
manhood. This establishment
is particularly well known for
its chateaubriand, but seafood
is also available.

THAI

Green Mango

Map 4, H6. 730 Yonge St
Ⓣ 928-0021. Cheap.
Subway Yonge/Bloor.
The popularity of this
cafeteria-like establishment
necessitated a recent move to
larger quarters. *Green Mango* is
perfect for inexpensive, quick
lunches. Spicy noodles are
dressed up with a selection of
tofu, chicken or vegetables
and they also serve fresh (ie
unfried) spring rolls and sticky
rice desserts.

UPTOWN

VIETNAMESE

Indochine
Map 4, I5. 4 Collier St
☎ 922-5840. Moderate.
Subway **Yonge/Bloor.**
The French accent in much
of classic Vietnamese cooking
is fairly pronounced here,
especially with regards to the
shellfish, but gentle touches of
fragrant lemon grass,
coriander and curry prevail in
the soups, noodle dishes and
the interesting pot pies offered
in this tasteful dining room
setting.

Bars

For a city that didn't serve mixed drinks until 1948 and is still subject to Canada's often puzzling liquor regulations, Toronto has managed to eke out a remarkably vital **bar scene**. You'll find everything from grizzled taverns, some of which still maintain a separate entrance for women, to sleek cocktail bars. During the cold winter months, people huddle inside, but in the summer many bars spread out open patios for all-day carousing.

Most bars and lounges featuring entertainment have a **weekend cover charge** after 9pm ranging between $5 and $10. Cover charges may apply during the week if there is a special act, performance, or top guest DJ. The **legal drinking age** throughout Ontario is nineteen, and last call at all establishments is 2am. This, however, does not necessarily herald an end to the night's festivities. After-hour bars and clubs riddle the city, and the people who will generally be able to guide you to them are the very bartenders serving your last orders. Be aware, though, that speakeasies (known locally as booze cans), roughly defined as unlicensed, after-hour clubs serving alcohol, are flat-out illegal and can be raided. All Toronto bars are required to sell **food**, presumably to soak up all that booze, but the quality and service of this can often be sorely lacking. Let observation be your guide; if you don't see anyone eating, the food probably isn't worth ordering.

Laws pertaining to **drinking and driving** are strict, so if you end up getting sloshed, leave your car in a parking lot or better yet, don't take it along in the first place. Cabs are far easier to find than parking spots, and public transportation roams the city's main arteries 24 hours a day.

DOWNTOWN

Acme Bar & Grill
Map 3, E4. 86 John St
Ⓣ 340-9700.
Streetcar King (#504).
A cross between a jazz club and a sports bar, with a selection of over eighty different single-malt scotches. A good spot to go after watching the ballgame at the nearby SkyDome.

Apothecary Music Bar
Map 3, D4. 340 Adelaide St W
Ⓣ 586-9858.
Streetcar Queen (#501).
One of the City's great neighbourhood bars, with a diverse, young clientele. The music gets loud after 9pm; sometimes there are live alternative jazz bands, but usually there's a DJ spinning anything from drum'n'bass to funk.

Betty's
Map 3, M4. 240 King St E
Ⓣ 368-1300.
Streetcar King (#504).
The threat of a lawsuit forced the owners to abbreviate the name from *The Betty Ford Clinic* to just plain *Betty's*, but regulars still remain devoted to this long, thin pub/bistro. It has a tree-canopied patio out back in the summer and in the winter its blond wood booths and tables are packed for most of the day. Excellent sandwiches, hot snacks and burgers can be washed down with a strong microbrew selection.

Black Bull Tavern
Map 3, D3. 298 Queen St W
Ⓣ 593-2766.
Streetcar Queen (#501).
The rows of gleaming

motorcycles parked outside should give you an idea of who patronises this place. But bikers aside, the *Black Bull* has a pleasant summer patio, good pool tables, and a full range of grilled food – burgers and fries, chicken, and the like.

Blue Agave Lounge
Map 2, F7. 783 Queen St W
Ⓣ 504-3359.
Streetcar **Queen** (#501).
Locals value the *Blue Agave's* balance of sophistication and relaxation out on the western stretch of Queen West. A full menu is available for those who bring an appetite.

The Bovine Sex Club
Map 3, A3. 542 Queen St W
Ⓣ 504-4239.
Streetcar **Queen** (#501).
Despite its comically evocative name, the *Bovine* doesn't proclaim its existence with a sign nor does it have anything to do with cows or sex. The exterior is encrusted with bicycle parts and scrap metal offering no glimpse of the playground within, which is filled with TV monitors

playing oddball videos, kinetic kitsch sculptures, tree branches twinkling with fairy lights, and a couple of long, well-stocked bars. There are pool tables, pinball machines and a wide range of music styles to keep you entertained.

Cameron House
Map 3, C3. 508 Queen St W
Ⓣ 703-0811.
Streetcar **Queen** (#501).
This place is half beer hall, half cocktail lounge and all entertainment. Artists have been rearranging the facade for twenty years now, the only constant being the huge metal ants marching up the side of the building. DJs play the front, and live music goes on in the back on weekends.

C'est What?
Map 3, K5. 67 Front St E
Ⓣ 867-9499.
Subway **Union Station**.
This handy little walkdown features 28 microbrews on tap and a variety of ales brewed on the premises. Some, like the hemp beer, are more experimental than others. Board games, deep couches

and live music every night make this a home away from home.

Dennison's Brewing Company

Map 3, I3. 75 Victoria St
Ⓣ 360-5877.
Subway Queen.

Four establishments grouped under one Romanesque roof: the brewery, which produces German-style lagers; *Conchy Joe's*, a casual oyster bar serving oysters, steamed mussels and fresh fish; *Louis' Brasserie*, which serves pasta, snacks and steaks; and downstairs is *Growler's Pub,* with its gleaming brass fittings, dark wood interior and standard pub grub.

Element Bar and Lounge

Map 3, B3. 533 Queen St W
Ⓣ 359-1919.
Streetcar Queen (#501).

Some patrons on the late end of the Gen X spectrum tried to dismiss *Element* as a tad too *Wallpaper*, but it works a sleek Retro-Mod interior to advantage and attracts a youngish but sophisticated crowd. Excellent DJs play trip-hop, trance and other forms of electronic beats on weekends.

Garage Paradise

Map 3, F3. 175 Richmond St W
Ⓣ 351-8101.
Streetcar Queen (#501).

Surviving against all odds, this former garage, existing in the midst of a group of expensive restaurants and nightclubs, is a slacker among prom queens. Zero attitude and eclectic music. Open Thurs–Sat only.

Imperial Pub

Map 3, I2. 54 Dundas E
Ⓣ 977-4667.
Subway Dundas.

A favourite of downtowners and students from the nearby polytechnic, this traditional tap house serves up beer and meaty pub food in two bars (there's also a large rooftop patio during the summer). The upstairs Library Lounge is a literary salon of sorts, attracting some of Canadian literature's heavy hitters who give wall-shaking poetry readings.

DOWNTOWN

McVeigh's New Windsor Tavern

Map 3, J3. 124 Church St
ⓣ 364-9698.
Streetcar **Dundas** (#505).
A three-decade old Irish pub, featuring Celtic music and food and dark, creamy Irish ales. Resolutely unfashionable and authentic to the core. Particularly festive on the afternoon of Christmas Eve, when all the businesses close for the holidays and all the Irish musicians in town come here.

NASA

Map 3, A1. 609 Queen St W
ⓣ 504-8356.
Streetcar **Queen** (#501).
A theme lounge whose decor is meant to evoke the Sixties space race. The DJs serve up solid house music to a youthful crowd.

The Octopus Lounge

Map 2, E7. 875 Queen St W
ⓣ 504-4798.
Streetcar **Queen** (#501).
Tucked behind a little Italian restaurant that shares the same street address, the *Octopus Lounge* is valued as a great getaway for patrons who don't want to dress up to go out and dance the night way. Latino funk steams up '*Pus*'s garage-like windows, the staff is down-to-earth, and the crowds are friendly.

The Paddock

Map 3, A3. 178 Bathurst St
ⓣ 504-9997.
Streetcar **Queen** (#501).
Rising phoenix-like from a grotty recent past to reclaim its original, authentic Deco glory, *The Paddock* boasts the world's longest Bakelite-topped bar, a solid micro-brewery and above-average pub grub and bar snacks. Often frequented by rising stars in the music and film biz.

Reservoir Lounge

Map 3, J5. 57 Wellington St E
ⓣ 955-0887.
Subway **Union Station**.
This subterranean, exposed-brick walk-down is a hot spot for swing, blues and boogie woogie music. The space for dancing is a bit cramped but the bar is long and has ample room to bend an elbow.

DOWNTOWN

The Rotterdam Bar & Bistro

Map 3, A4. 600 King Street W
☎ 504-6882.
Streetcar King (#504).
This wonderful old building is home to the Amsterdam Brewing Company, which features its own hearty brews as well as a beer store so you can get take out. Formerly famed as the only place in town you could buy beer on a Sunday, the *Rotterdam* is now a great spot for after-theatre drinks or Sunday brunch.

Stonecutter's Arms

Map 3, J3. 284 Richmond St E
☎ 860-0940.
Streetcar Queen (#501).
A Scottish pub with live music on weekends and a good selection of microbrews on tap.

Velvet Underground

Map 3, B3. 510 Queen St W
☎ 504-6688.
Streetcar Queen (#501).
The glitziest of several goth bars along the Queen West strip, complete with large metallic angels, voodoo gods, DJs and cages. Posing is encouraged.

Wheat Sheaf

Map 3, A4. 667 King St W
☎ 504-9912.
Streetcar King (#504).
Publicans have been pulling pints here since the 1840s, making it the oldest tavern in Toronto. Totally unpretentious surroundings and a full menu.

UPTOWN

Allen's

Map 2, H6. 143 Danforth Ave
☎ 463-2838.
Subway Broadview.
The bar is dark and woody in a New York City kind of way, with a selection of smoky Irish whiskies and a good draught ale line-up. The dinner menu offers sophisticated reinterpretations of homey Irish and North American classics with vegetarian options, and the occasional live Celtic music features impressive acts from Canada and Ireland. *The* place to raise a glass of stout on St Paddy's Day.

UPTOWN

Ciao Edie

Map 2, F7. 489 College St
Ⓣ 927-7774.
Streetcar **College** (#506).
Regulars affectionately
describe *Edie* as a *Trader Vic's*
on acid. The way-cool walk-
down is unselfconsciously
decorated in original seventies
garage sale finds (the lamps in
the window alone should be
enough to excite your
curiosity), the music is trip-
hop and trance, and the action
starts late.

College St Bar

Map 2, F7. 574 College St
Ⓣ 533-2417.
Streetcar **College** (#506).
There is nothing fashionable
about this comfortable
watering hole. It is popular
with university types but don't
let that put you off.

Dora Keogh Irish Pub

Map 2, H6. 141 Danforth Ave
Ⓣ 778-1804.
Subway **Broadview**.
Whereas *Allen's* is Irish by way
of New York, the *Dora* is
straight from Dublin,
complete with a snug. This
comfortable Hibernian pub
has a nice line of domestic
and imported premium beers
and single malts. Well-padded
banquettes, copper-topped
tables and a stone fireplace
invite lingering.

Graffiti Bar & Grill

Map 4, B9. 170 Baldwin St
Ⓣ 506-6699.
Streetcar **Spadina** (#510).
There is something
permanently edgy about
being a Kensington Market
bar, and people-watching
definitely takes over any
other scheduled enter-
tainment. Lots of draught on
tap and a grill menu
featuring plenty of burgers,
sandwiches, pizzas and pasta
until 2am.

Liquids + Oysters

Map 2, F7. 577 College St
Ⓣ 588-6458.
Streetcar **College** (#506).
A slender, hip walk-up lightly
furnished in retro Sixties chic
and serving a youngish
clientele. A good little
hideaway above an equally
trendy restaurant.

UPTOWN

183

Madison Avenue Pub

Map 4, C5. 14 Madison Ave
ⓣ 927-1722.
Subway St George.

The *Madison* was once three joined Annex houses and is now a massive multi-floor, five-patio pub. Patrons argue that it takes a full day to fully explore the possibilities of the place: there's pool tables and juke boxes, a piano bar on the main floor and a dance floor in the basement. Food-wise, it's a pub-grub menu with half-price dinner specials 5–8pm daily.

Myth

Map 2, H6. 417 Danforth Ave
ⓣ 461-8383.
Subway Chester.

A cavernous space with a huge suspended TV screen that silently plays Hollywood films with Greek mythological content. Young patrons line up to shoot pool or schmooze at the long bar, while more sedate couples ensconce themselves at tables to dally over the mezza-heavy menu (Greek salads and dips), which also features some pizza and pasta dishes. DJs spin on the weekends.

Only Café

Map 2, H6. 972 Danforth Ave
ⓣ 463-7843.
Subway Donlands.

A good variety of micro-brewed draughts, hearty daily specials like chilli, and a good selection of bar appetisers, such as chips and calamari. A friendly and rumpled East-end outpost.

Orbit Room

Map 2, F7. 580A College St
ⓣ 535-0613.
Streetcar College (#506).

Intimate bar/lounge serving up spicy entrees like jerk chicken, and light appetisers. Live R&B Mon, Wed and Sun.

Pauper's Pub

Map 4, B5. 539 Bloor St W
ⓣ 530-1331.
Subway Spadina.

This former bank is now home to two floors and a rooftop's worth of beer and hearty pub grub. Local legend has it that the downstairs bar is haunted by the ghost of a bank clerk who committed suicide on the premises.

Pimblett's

Map 4, M9. 263 Gerrard St E
ⓣ929-9525.
Streetcar **Carlton / College**
(#506).

A renovated Victorian house transformed into a British-style pub. The dark, cosy room has a good selection of microbrews, and a few pasta dishes and hearty daily specials augment the better-than-average food.

Remy's

Map 4, G4. 115 Yorkville Ave
ⓣ968-9429.
Subway **Bay (Cumberland exit).**
From around late October to early May, this is not a happening bar. But as soon as the weather warms and the rooftop patio opens up, it's another story. Tucked along a little lane, the terrace is like a treehouse, and attracts the youthful and the young in spirit. The kitchen serves Tex-Mex fare and there is a respectable selection of premium and imported beers, spirits and wines.

Rooftop Lounge (in the Park Hyatt Hotel)

Map 4, G4. 18th floor, 4 Avenue Rd
ⓣ324-1568.
Subway **Museum or Bay.**
Long a retreat for establishment literati, the *Rooftop* offers a spectacular view of the city and hands down the very best classic martinis in Toronto. The bartender has been perfecting his method for almost four decades. Sofas, a fireplace and silken smooth service make this spot a treasured oasis.

Souz Dal

Map 2, F7. 636 College St
ⓣ537-1883.
Streetcar **College (#506).**
The food here takes a back seat to the cocktail menu, which features favourites like the Dean Martin (vodka, cranberry and melon liqueur) and the Curious George (vodka, banana, and cranberry). Tiny tables are dotted with votive candles and dishes of pistachios; the background music is trance, trip-hop and the like.

UPTOWN

The Tranzac Club

Map 4, B5. 292 Brunswick Ave
Ⓣ 923-8137.
Subway **Spadina**.

This Aussie-Kiwi establishment has a plethora of beers, a snacks-only menu, and is home to innumerable local events, theatrical performances, and live music of various descriptions. The drinking establishment of choice during the summer's Fringe Theatre Festival (see p.267).

The Winchester

Map 4, M8. 537 Parliament St
Ⓣ 9291-1875.
Streetcar **College/Carlton** (#506).

This beautiful old hotel has seen several ups and downs and is currently on another ascendancy. The entire ground floor has been refurbished and smartened up, with a long bar and dining in the front, booths in the middle and pool tables and a stage in back for the almost nightly live acts, which range from stand-up comedy to folk jazz and blues. A good value and a good time with an absence of attitude.

UPTOWN

Nightlife

Toronto's nightlife, like its restaurants, has blossomed only in recent decades, and the city's reputation for rolling up its sidewalks after 10pm is a hangover from earlier days. There are **clubs**, **lounges** and **discos** for every taste and disposition, whether or not they are immediately apparent. During the winter nightlife is decidedly an indoor phenomenon, but the explosion of pent-up energies during those first warm spring nights fills the club-lined downtown streets until dawn. Most of the dance clubs are located on the **Richmond Street** strip, just south of **Queen West**, which is home to a number of the live-band venues. The **College Street strip**, west of Palmerston, is also a likely spot to look for an up-and-coming club amid all the cafés and bistros, although their emphasis is more lounge oriented. Also in the mix are venues that are staunchly jazz, blues or R&B, and they vigorously eschew trends, preferring the classic night owl ambience of smoke-filled bars. Most clubs and all lounges serve alcohol and, like the bars, their **last call** is at 2am. That means that all drinks have to be consumed and bottles taken away by 3am. Most clubs, however, will stay open until 4am on weekends, though live music spots tend to wind down earlier.

After last call a common Toronto pursuit is searching out a **booze can** (speakeasy; see "Bars", p.177). Bear in mind that booze cans are not legal drinking establishments and are subject to police raids, so you won't see advertisements for them in the daily papers. The younger sibling of the booze can is the **rave**. After a fairly uninhibited run, raves have finally garnered unwanted attention from parents, police and city hall, and dance parties taking place in unlicensed spaces are subject to raids for anything from drugs to fire violations.

For those venues which are legal and above board, consult the listings in **NOW**, **eye**, or **TRIBE**, three free weekly newspapers which are available in stores, restaurants and in news boxes on the street. The most comprehensive listings are in *NOW*, which likes to emphasise live music; *Tribe* specialises in dance clubs, and *eye* does a bit of both. Finally, distinctions between clubs and bars can be a bit tenuous, since almost all clubs have bars, and most of the bars also book DJs or bands or both, either for specific theme nights during the week or on weekends.

When dialling any of the phone numbers listed in the *Guide*, the prefix ⓣ 416 must be dialled first.
See p.276 for more details.

LIVE MUSIC

Toronto's **live music scene** has a long and venerable tradition. Guitar guru Neil Young is a local boy who got his start in Toronto bars, as did Robbie Robertson and Joan Anderson, who later morphed into Joni Mitchell. Today, artists like Holly Cole, Ron Sexsmith, Molly Johnston and Sarah Harmer keep the live performance torch burning, along with local bands like Kevin Breit and the Sisters Euclid, Flashing Lights, Do Make Say Think, Rheostatics and the Bare Naked Ladies.

Thanks to the healthy live music scene, almost every band doing a North American tour stops off here. The city has a well-established reputation for rock and indie bands, but its real forte is its eclectic range. In the late Seventies and early Eighties British New Wave bands established a large and solid fan base in Toronto, and consequently many Anglo groups tend to show up here as well. Blues and R&B are on the wane but jazz is making a comeback. There has also been a bit of a dance revival, and salsa, mambo, tango and merengue bands are tapping into the vibe in a big way, with a smidgen of swing thrown in for those with less hip control. Of course, the city's large Afro-Caribbean population ensures a fairly consistent offering of dance hall reggae and soca. It is a rare venue that doesn't **charge a cover**, which is $10 on average but may be more depending on the band or performer.

The 360

Map 3, D3. 326 Queen St W
Ⓣ 593-0840.
Streetcar Queen (#501).
This venue has not expended much extra effort to spruce up its grungy appearance, but the place is nevertheless an extremely hot venue to see rock musicians and innovative cabaret acts.

Bamboo

Map 3, D3. 312 Queen St W
Ⓣ 593-5771.
Streetcar Queen (#501).
Once a rattan furniture warehouse, this friendly and lively place now boasts a large, live-music dance club (mostly reggae and salsa bands), a dining room serving Caribbean-Asian fusion fare, and two delightful patios.

Big Bop

Map 3, A3. 651 Queen St W
Ⓣ 504-6699.
Streetcar Queen (#501).
This vast space is filled with urban rockers and contains several different stages, all of which cater to the live rock scene. The main stage was recently decorated with sumptuous mural-sized

LIVE MUSIC

reproductions of famous nineteenth-century paintings – making the walls the best-dressed thing in the joint.

Black Swan

Map 2, H6. 154 Danforth Ave
ⓣ 469-0537.
Subway Broadview.
One of the few remaining R&B outposts, this Riverdale neighbourhood institution also does lashings of folk on Sundays.

Chicago's Diner

Map 3, D3. 335 Queen St W
ⓣ 598-3301.
Streetcar Queen (#501).
A no-frills, testosterone-laden blues bar, serving patrons seven days a week until 1am.

El Macombo

Map 4, C9. 464 Spadina Ave
ⓣ 968-2001.
Streetcar College (#506).
The stuff of legends insofar as live acts are concerned, including luminaries like the Rolling Stones, B.B. King, Blondie, and hometown faves like Nash the Slash. The tables are sticky, the carpet is scary, but the bands are (usually) great.

El Rancho

Map 2, E7. 430 College St
ⓣ 921-2752.
Streetcar College (#506).
The nightclub here sizzles with live tangos and salsa, and the restaurant features luscious Spanish and Continental creations. Eager beginners throng here for lessons on weekends.

Guvernment

Map 3, K7. 132 Queens Quay E
ⓣ 869-0045.
Subway Union Station.
Down on the shores of Lake Ontario, this huge barn of a dance club books live bands for its downstairs cavern and has a multitude of DJs spinning in the two discos upstairs.

Horseshoe Tavern

Map 3, D3. 368 Queen St W
ⓣ 598-4753.
Streetcar Queen (#501).
Lots of Toronto bands got their start here, and it is still a favourite place for the now-famous to sit in for a set or stage a special one-off

LIVE MUSIC

concert. The interior is relentlessly unglamorous, but the phenomenal bar staff is a major compensation.

Lee's Palace

Map 4, B5. 529 Bloor St W
⊤ 532-7383.
Subway Bathurst.
Lee's continued popularity has nothing to do with the decor, the food or even the draught beer. Its reputation is entirely based on the outré bands it consistently books. Patrons can also check out the DJ dance action upstairs at the aptly named Dance cave.

Opera House

Map 2, H7. 735 Queen St E
⊤ 466-0313.
Streetcar Queen (#501).
This former vaudeville theatre is the chosen outpost for hardcore rock acts who like to thrash the night away. It is also a popular venue for the S&M/leather crowd and is home to the annual Leatherball.

Phoenix Concert Theatre

Map 4, L2. 410 Sherbourne St
⊤ 323-1251.
Streetcar Dundas (#505).

An imaginative renovation – and equally imaginative booking agents – makes this venue a popular place to catch a concert. Big-name acts looking for intimate venues, guitar legends and world music divas give it up in the main stage space, which looks like a cross between a Wild West saloon and an old vaudeville theatre.

Plaza Flamingo

Map 4, A8. 423 College St
⊤ 603-8884.
Streetcar College (#506).
Flamenco at the *Flamingo* is a possibility, either as entertainment or as lessons, and so are all the Latino dances you can muster the energy for – a buffet is available for those who need to refuel before starting another salsa.

The Rex Hotel Jazz Bar and Grill

Map 3, F3. 194 Queen St W
⊤ 598-2475.
Streecar Queen (#501).
In fierce arguments about which is the best jazz club in town, this one is consistently near the top of the list. A

LIVE MUSIC

191

well-primped crowd lounges in the spiffed-up interior, but any reservations about pretensions evaporate once the music – which is always top-notch – begins.

Savage Garden
Map 3, B3. 550 Queen St W
Ⓣ 504-2178.
Streetcar Queen (#501).
This industrial goth bar has lots of cages, metal sculptures and live thrash bands. Not for the timid.

Sneaky Dees
Map 4, A8. 431 College St
Ⓣ 603-3090.
Streetcar College (#506).

This no-attitude slacker palace has live rock bands, pinball, pool and Tex-Mex grub seven days a week until 4am.

Top O' The Senator
Map 3, I2. 249 Victoria St
Ⓣ 364-7517.
Subway Queen.
The upstairs bar to *The Senator* restaurant (see p.156), serving light entrees and snacks along with a good line in scotch and beer. But the main claim to fame is the superior jazz. When the big names play a Toronto club it is usually here.

CLUBS

New strains of clubs are springing up in Toronto like never before, ensuring a quality night out whatever your tastes. Weekends tend to be busy, and the more popular clubs can have long lines winter or summer. On weekends especially, be prepared to pay a cover charge for clubs, usually $5–10. Some clubs book live bands on occasion, but more stick to the DJ formula. Lounges rarely have live music – space being at more of a premium – but they generally don't have cover charges either. Check the listings in the free *NOW* or *eye* papers (see p.188) to see which DJs are playing where.

Bauhaus

Map 3, E5. 31 Mercer St
ⓣ 977-9813.
Streetcar King (#504).

The latest club in this industrial space, *Bauhaus* is a two-storey outfit with funk and soul downstairs and hip-hop and house upstairs in the smaller disco.

The Docks

Map 2, H7. 11 Polson St
ⓣ 461-DOCK. Cab only, south of the Gardiner expressway on the Toronto Harbour.

This massive complex – the lakefront patio is 41,000 square feet – is like a theme park for clubbers. The music wavers from old school disco and R&B to Top 40 and dance, just to make sure no one gets left out. If you get tired of the nightclub, disco or restaurant, you can go rock climbing, check out your swing on the driving range, or visit a haunted house.

Easy and the Fifth

Map 3, F3. 225 Richmond St W
ⓣ 979-3000.
Streetcar Queen (#501).

Movie stars and supermodels are fond of this expensive, well-appointed nightclub, which is also known for its restaurant. It has a wonderful rooftop patio, and some patrons enjoy the frisson of entering off an alley filled with tuxedoed bouncers and going up to the club in a freight elevator.

El Convento Rico

Map 2, E7. 750 College St
ⓣ 588-7800.
Streetcar College (#506).

Walking into this lively joint, replete with red velvet, flocked wallpaper and spot welding, makes you feel like you've stumbled on the best party in town – and you may well have. The crowd ranges from earnest suburbanites to dishy Latino drag queens, and the DJs spin Latin house and disco classics until 4am six nights a week (until 10pm Sun).

Fluid Lounge

Map 3, F3. 217 Richmond St W
ⓣ 593-6116.
Streetcar Queen (#501).

This is the sort of place that gets flooded every weekend

CLUBS

with suburban kids looking for a Big City experience. One is a mock-serious lounge and the other is awash in yards and yards of red sateen. Funk, Latin Beat and hip-hop are the nominal sounds.

Joker

Map 3, F3. 318 Richmond St W
⊤ 598-1313.
Streetcar Queen (#501).
A stylish behemoth of a club whose weekend patrons are willing to line up around the block. The music is generally heavy-handed techno with smatterings of hip-hop and R&B in the third floor disco.

Kajmere

Map 3, C4. 393 King St W
⊤ 586-0990.
Streetcar King (#504).
Another one of the recent crop of opulently decorated clubs, *Kajmere* does its own interpretation of the Gothic Revival, including a huge pipe organ in the DJ's booth. House and other forms of dance music reign here.

The Living Room

Map 3, F4. 330 Adelaide St W
⊤ 979-3168.
Streetcar King (#504).
A hipster heaven with an eclectic range of musical tastes brought to you by a retinue of DJs. Wednesday is ruled by acid jazz, Seventies disco and funk samples. There's European trip-hop on Thursday; Friday it's hip-hop and R&B; and Saturday and Sundays house is king.

SYN

Map 3, F4. 214 Adelaide St W
⊤ 595-5115.
Streetcar King (#504).
This two-storey establishment (dance floor downstairs, lounge complete with comfy chairs and fireplace upstairs) is a nightclub for a somewhat older crowd than the patrons of *Joker* and *Whisky Saigon*. Tame enough despite the flirty name.

This Is London

Map 3, C3. 364 Richmond St
⊤ 351-1100.
Streetcar Queen (#501).
Like *Easy and the Fifth*, you have to enter this club off a

small alleyway. When it opened people were appreciative of its stylish interior, DJ selections of disco, soul and Top 40, but the real buzz was about the women's washrooms: They take up the whole top floor, and hairdressers and make-up artists are on hand for touch-ups. Not a good choice of clubs if your date already spends too much time powdering her nose.

Whisky Saigon

Map 3, E3. 250 Richmond St W
Ⓣ 593-4646.
Streetcar Queen (#501).
This former factory offers four floors of music and dancing. The musical range covers everything from Eighties Retro to the latest electronica. The dance floors are a heaving mass of under-dressed, sweaty bodies but the rooftop patio is an amazing sanctuary.

CLUBS

Performing arts and film

Toronto is one of North America's most vibrant centres for the **performing arts**. The city's forte is its **theatre scene**, which is the third largest in the English-speaking world after London and New York. **Dance**, **opera**, **classical music** and **film** are also well represented, and the city is justifiably proud of the many **festivals** it sponsors throughout the year. The most renowned is the **Toronto International Film Festival**, which has become not only one of the world's best, but also one of the best attended. The high season for most of the performing arts begins in late September and runs through May, adding vibrancy to Toronto's often-dreary winter months. Summer is ruled by a plethora of outdoor festivals and events; see "Festivals and annual events", p.262, for more information.

THEATRE

With over six hundred opening nights a year, Toronto offers an exceptionally varied array of **theatre** productions, from opulent international hits to idiosyncratic fringe affairs. Classical drama rubs shoulders with edgy improvisational comedy, and big, Broadway-bound musicals co-exist with Baroque period pieces.

As if the wealth of choice during peak season were not enough, Toronto also boasts a number of **summer festivals**. The biannual Du Maurier Limited World Stage, held in April (☎973-3000), is a major international event, hosting alternative theatre companies from more than twenty countries; and the annual Fringe Theatre Festival of Toronto showcases approximately eighty workshops and alternative performances in ten days in early July. Finally, although they aren't within the confines of Toronto proper, the Stratford Festival and the Shaw Festival, both located two hours from Toronto in the towns of Stratford and Niagara-on-the-Lake respectively, are two of the largest and most respected theatre festivals in North America; see pp.202 & 204 for full details.

Prices for all theatrical endeavours – which range from $12 for smaller companies to $90 for prime seats at prime stages – can be cut in half for same-day performances at the **T.O. TIX booth** (Tues–Sat noon–7.30pm; ☎536-6468), inside the mammoth Eaton Centre shopping facility (see p.39). Go to the Centre's "Mews" level and look for the booth across from the *Mr Greenjeans* restaurant. Tickets go on sale at noon and it's a good idea to get in line a half-hour before. If this is still beyond your means, look for performances listed as PWYC ("Pay What You Can"). These have a suggested ticket price of about $8, but the boldest or poorest can get away with offering a few bucks or maybe even nothing at all.

There are four main **theatre districts** in Toronto: the downtown theatre district, encompassing the area around Yonge and Front streets, is the oldest and includes some of the most established companies; the adjacent East End district occupies the southeast corner of the city and features

THEATRE

primarily small, fringe companies; and the Annex neighbourhood, east of Bathurst between Dupont and Bloor, which is home to some of the best alternative companies. Finally, Harbourfront's Premier Dance Theatre is home to Toronto's newest classical repertory theatre company, Soulpepper.

DOWNTOWN

----

12 Alexander Street Theatre

Map 4, I8. 12 Alexander St
ⓣ 975-8555.
Subway Wellesley.
Tucked away in the heart of Toronto's gay and lesbian quarter, this is home to the gay-specialist "Buddies in Badtimes" company. When not spouting the best in original queer-culture performance, the theatre is landlord to visiting alternative theatre companies.

Elgin Theatre and Winter Garden

Map 3, I3. 189 Yonge St
ⓣ 314-2901. Tours Thurs 5pm, Sat & Sun 11am.
Subway Queen.
The Elgin and Winter Garden are one of the last functioning double-decker theatres in the world, with the latter built on top of the former in a highly economical use of one city lot. The theatres were given a full restoration by the Ontario Heritage Foundation, and while the downstairs Elgin is a treat with its red plush and gilt-plaster ornaments, it is the upstairs Winter Garden that really takes your breath away. This tiny gem was constructed to look like a garden, its ceiling replete with real leaves and its pillars clad to look like tree trunks. The Elgin specialises in visiting dramatic and musical productions, while the Winter Garden uses its more intimate setting to stage special events. Tours of the theatres are also available; see p.41 for details.

THEATRE

Hummingbird Centre
Map 3, I5. 1 Front St E
Ⓣ 872-2262.
Subway Union Station.
Formerly known as the
O'Keefe Centre, the
Hummingbird kick-started
the then moribund Toronto
theatre scene when it opened
its neo-Expressionist doors in
1960. At 3200 seats it is too
large for intimate drama,
making it the downtown
venue of choice for family-
oriented musicals like *The
Wizard of Oz*. It is also the
home of the Canadian Opera
Company and the National
Ballet (see p.207).

Pantages Theatre
Map 3, I2. 236 Yonge St
Ⓣ 362-3218 or 872-2222 for
reservations.
Subway Queen or Dundas.
Just up the street from the
Elgin and Winter Garden (see
opposite), the Pantages was
saved from demolition and
restored to its former
vaudeville glory by impresario
Garth Drabinsky for his
Toronto production of
Phantom of the Opera. These
days it is used for visiting

companies and special guest
acts, such as the talented
Dame Edna.

Princess of Wales Theatre
Map 3, E4. 300 King St W
Ⓣ 872-1212.
Subway St Andrew.
Built in 1993 to accommodate
the helicopter in *Miss Saigon*,
and currently home to the
blockbuster musical *The Lion
King*, this beautiful new
addition to Toronto's
playhouses has a deceptively
intimate feel despite its 2000
seats. The murals and loge
reliefs by artist Frank Stella are
an added treat.

Royal Alexandra Theatre
Map 3, F4. 260 Yonge St
Ⓣ 872-1212.
Subway St Andrew.
The dowager of Toronto
theatres, the "Royal Alex", as
she is known to locals, was
saved from demolition in 1963
by local businessman Ed
Mirvish. Designed in 1906,
this graceful Beaux Arts
building has been fully restored
to its Edwardian splendour,
and puts on everything from

THEATRE

classical repertory theatre to exuberant musicals like *Mamma Mia*. The dramatically cantilevered balcony ensures clear sightlines from every seat.

St Lawrence Centre for the Arts

Map 3, J5. 27 Front St E
☎ 386-3100.
Subway Union Station.
The St Lawrence Centre is home to the Canadian Stage Company and contains two stages: the Bluma Appel Theatre specialises in presenting new works by contemporary artists, and upstairs the studio-sized Jane Mallett Theatre presents experimental and workshop productions.

EAST END

- - - - - - - - - - - - - - - - - - - -

Alumnae Theatre

Map 3, N5. 70 Berkeley St
☎ 962-1948.
Streetcar King (#504).
Original theatre with low-budget charm has long been the Alumnae Theatre's mandate. Low on frills, high on fringe.

Canadian Stage

Map 3, N5. 26 Berkeley St
☎ 368-3110.
Streetcar King (#504).
In addition to being the second stage of the Canadian Stage Company, which presents its more experimental pieces here, this location often houses avant-garde or workshop performances, and is an excellent place to see young talent.

Young People's Theatre

Map 3, L5. 165 Front St E
☎ 862-2222.
Streetcar King (#504).
Originally a stable, this muscular, Romanesque-style building was saved from the wrecking ball in 1977. The innovative productions are geared towards a young audience, but are often as intriguing as (if not better than) many of the city's more mainstream offerings.

THEATRE

THE ANNEX

Factory Theatre

Map 3, A4. 125 Bathurst St
℡ 504-9971.

Streetcar King (#504).

Originally an auditorium for factory workers , this spot, with its pressed-tin decorative ornaments and seemingly fragile balcony, has a special charm. Since opening in 1970, the Factory has staged more then 400 Canadian plays, and its downstairs sister, the Factory Studio Café, has nurtured a reputation for innovative contemporary theatre.

Poor Alex

Map 4, B5. 296 Brunswick St
℡ 923-1644.

Subway Spadina.

The Poor Alex Theatre has been the launching pad for many a career and is especially in the thick of things during the annual Fringe Festival (see p.267). As likely to house productions by Albey and Pinter as original plays by talented unknowns, this Annex institution creates an inviting atmosphere for audiences tired of big-hair musicals and special-effect gimmicks.

Tarragon Theatre

Map 4, A2. 30 Bridgman St
℡ 531-1827.

Subway Dupont.

A renovated factory space, this has contributed to Toronto's thriving theatrical community by consistently presenting challenging, innovative theatre.

Theatre Centre

Map 2, F7. 1032 Queen St W
℡ 872-1111.

Streetcar Carlton (#506).

Once considered too far from the theatre-thriving Annex neighbourhood to be successful, Theatre Centre staged Michael Hollingsworth's *The Life and Times of Mackenzie King* in 1992 and sold out the entire run. Crowds have continued to come back for more, and the theatre has maintained its reputation for offering some of the best premieres in town.

THEATRE

THE STRATFORD FESTIVAL

Stratford's idyllic aspects – from its Elizabethan gardens to its preening swans – existed before the opening night of the first **Stratford Festival** in 1953. But it's the Festival that is responsible for putting the town (two hours southwest of Toronto on the banks of the Avon River) on the map. For more than three decades North America's largest classical repertory company has been thrilling audiences with remarkable productions that have revamped some old favourites. Two Shakespearean tragedies and two comedies are performed a season, augmented by other classical staples (Moliere, Sheridan, Johnson) as well as the best of modern and musical theatre. The Stratford Festival also hosts a lecture series, backstage and costume-warehouse tours, music concerts, an author reading series, and meet-and-greet sessions with the actors.

The Stratford Festival runs from mid-May to early November. **Tickets** are $53–67 for musicals and $48–62 for dramas, but prices can drop substantially for preview performances. The best money-saving option, however, is the Festival's two-for-one performance deal, where tickets for select performances are half-price. Contact the box office for more information at ☏ 1-800/567-1600.

By **car**, the most direct route to Stratford from Toronto is Hwy-401 West to Interchange 278 in Kitchener. From Kitchener take Hwy-8 West, and then switch to Hwy-7/8 West to Stratford; in total, it's a two-hour journey. Stratford also boasts a small municipal **airport** (☏ 519/271-2040), and there are two **trains** daily from Toronto (☏ 366-8411). Train ticket prices, normally $52 return, can be knocked down by forty percent if booked five days in advance.

Theatre Gargantua

Map 4, A8. 365 College St
ⓣ 260-4660.
Streetcar College (#506).
On Sundays, this charming little Gothic Revival church is home to the Saint Stephen-in-the-Field Anglican congregation, but from Monday to Saturday it houses the Theatre Gargantua troupe, whose richly textured play cycles have been performed here since the early Nineties.

Theatre Passe Muraille

Map 3, A3. 16 Ryerson Ave
ⓣ 504-7529.
Streetcar Queen (#501).
The unusual configuration of this former factory allows set designers a broad scope for dramatic possibilities. One of the best alternative theatres in the city.

ELSEWHERE IN TORONTO

New York Theatre

Map 4, I6. 651 Yonge St
ⓣ 531-9802.
Subway Wellesley.
A stage for long-running, middle-brow shows that are somewhere between musical dinner theatre and vaudeville: amusing, light entertainment with catchy tunes.

Summer theatre as an excuse for a city getaway is not restricted to Stratford or Niagara-on-the-Lake (see boxes opposite and overleaf). The Association of SummerTheatre 'Round Ontario (ASTRO) in association with Theatre Ontario stages professional productions in old opera houses, theatres indoors and out and even the redoubtable Old Red Barn in many Ontario towns and villages that are within easy driving distance of the city. Call ASTRO direct (416-408-4556, www.theatreontario.org) for more information.

THEATRE

THE SHAW FESTIVAL

The second largest repertory theatre company in North America after the Stratford Festival is the **Shaw Festival** in Niagara-on-the-Lake, a genteel Upper Canadian town nestled among the vineyards and fruit orchards of the Niagara Peninsula.

Begun in 1962, when a town lawyer named Brian Doherty staged George Bernard Shaw's *Don Juan in Hell* and *Candida*, this is the only festival in the world devoted solely to the works of Shaw and his contemporaries. Indeed, it is mandated to produce only plays written in Shaw's lifetime (1856–1950), which the company refers to as "plays about the beginning of the modern world".

Like the Stratford Festival, the Shaw has a generous selection of backstage activities, including tours, concerts, fairs, and a number of free programmes that introduce the company to its audience.

By **car** from Toronto (two hours), drive towards Niagara along the Queen Elizabeth Way (QEW). Once across the Garden City Skyway at St Catherines, take the Niagara-on-the-Lake exit (38B). A left onto York Road and a right onto Hwy-55 East (Niagara Stone Road) will take you to downtown Niagara-on-the-Lake. There's also a Greyhound **bus** service between Toronto and Niagara Falls; about $40 return. Once in Niagara Falls, it's necessary to transfer to a Charterways Bus (☏ 905/688-9600) for the short trip to Niagara-on-the-Lake. Keep in mind that the last bus back to Toronto leaves Niagara Falls daily at 10.10pm, making it more practical to stay the night.

Ticket prices are $22–65. Substantial discounts are available for previews, matinees, lunchtime and Sunday-night performances; contact the box office for information ☏ 1-800/511-SHAW.

CLASSICAL MUSIC, OPERA AND DANCE

Toronto's ongoing attempts to build a permanent opera house in the face of governmental indifference – sometimes benign, sometimes overtly hostile – suggests at the very least the tenacity of the city's music-lovers. Against all odds, Toronto maintains a wide-ranging programme of highbrow **opera**, **dance** and **classical music**. Ticket prices vary from $20 to well over $115, but, as with theatre tickets, T.O. Tix (☎536-6468) sells spare seats at half-price for that day's performances. As well, check the Music listings in *NOW* for smaller venues that nevertheless feature wonderful performers such as the Orpheus Choir (☎530-4428), the Music Umbrella concerts series (☎461-6681), and the free lunchtime recitals given in different churches throughout the city.

CLASSICAL MUSIC

George Weston Recital Hall

Map 2, G3. 5040 Yonge St
☎872-2222.
Subway North York Centre.
The classical wing of the Ford Centre for the Performing Arts, this performance hall competes with the Roy Thompson (see overleaf)for top-name classical, jazz and popular music acts.

Glenn Gould Studio

Map 3, E5. 250 Front St W
☎205-5555.
Streetcar King (#504).
Named for the great pianist, this small box-type hall in the Canadian Broadcasting Centre is so sprung for sound that enthusiastic performances leave audiences literally vibrating. The programming is first-rate and generally showcases Canadian talent, particularly since most performances are later broadcast on CBC Radio.

Massey Hall

Map 3, I3. 178 Victoria St
☎ 872-4255.
Subway **Dundas.**

A turn-of-the-century recital hall that boasts great acoustics and has hosted a wide variety of performers, everyone from Enrico Caruso and Maria Callas to Jarvis Cocker. The austere architecture is offset by Moorish details, like the fanciful moulding along the balconies.

Roy Thompson Hall

Map 3, F5. 60 Simcoe St
☎ 593-4828.
Subway **St Andrew.**

This is primarily home to the Toronto Symphony Orchestra (☎ 593-4828), but also to the Toronto Mendelssohn Choir (☎ 872-4255) and Toronto's riveting Tafelmusik Baroque Orchestra (☎ 964-6337). Finished in 1982 to a design by Arthur Erickson, it looks like an upturned soup bowl, but at night it is transformed as the glass-panelled walls glow transparent and cast light over the pavement. Inside, the circular hall has excellent sightlines, but its acoustics have not garnered rave reviews.

OPERA

- - - - - - - - - - - - - - - - - - - -

Autumn Leaf Performance

PO Box 1231 Station "F"
☎ 535-9998.

This company bills itself as practitioners of the "x-treme art of opera". Under the artistic direction of Thom Sokoloske, Autumn Leaf goes for the jugular with its sometimes Dadaist sensibilities and daring approach to performance. Call for a schedule and a list of venues.

Canadian Opera Company

Map 3, I5. 1 Front St E
☎ 363-6671.

Canada's national opera troupe, the COC has dazzled international audiences for years with its ambitious productions, devotion to young talent, and the musical erudition of its director, Richard Bradshaw. Seats are often scarce, particularly for the eagerly anticipated season premieres, so reserve as far in advance as possible – tickets generally run from $30 to $115. Rush tickets are only available to seniors and students, and are not released until two hours before a performance. Half-price tickets for same-day performances can be obtained through T.O. TIX (☎ 536-6468) but depend on availability.

Opera Anonymous

Map 2, F7. 44 Spencer Ave, Suite 2

☎ 256-5664.

This company specialises in accessible, theatrical renditions of contemporary English-language operas. A roaming troupe, they set up in Toronto's more intimate theatres; call for a performance schedule and a list of venues.

Opera Atelier

Map 4, F4. 87 Avenue Rd

☎ 925-3767.

A Baroque opera/ballet company known for sumptuous productions that are loved by opera buffs and first-timers alike. There are only a handful of productions a year, but their daring and artistic merits have attracted a devoted following. Ticket prices range from $45 to $90.

Tapestry Music Theatre

Map 2, E7. 60 Atlantic Ave, Studio 112

☎ 537-6066.

This company is dedicated to supporting and producing new Canadian works for the opera and music-theatre stages.

DANCE

Du Maurier Theatre

Map 3, F8. 231 Queens Quay W

☎ 973-4000.

Streetcar **Harbourfront**.

Part of the Harbourfront Centre (see p.73), this modern theatre centre stages primarily dance recitals but also the occasional theatrical or musical performance.

National Ballet Company

Map 3, I5. 1 Front St E

☎ 345-9595.

Subway **Union Station**.

CLASSICAL MUSIC, OPERA AND DANCE

The NBC's prima ballerinas, notably Karen Kain and Veronica Tennant, are revered as national treasures. The company has proven that it is one of the most accomplished corps anywhere, performing classical ballet and contemporary dance with equal artistry.

Premier Dance Theatre

Map 3, G8. 207 Queen's Quay W ⊤973-4921.
Streetcar **Harbourfront.**
A beautiful new facility built specifically for dance performances, this space also hosts a number of dramatic events, including Toronto's brava classical repertory troupe, Soul Pepper Theatre.

Toronto Dance Theatre

Map 4, M8. 80 Winchester St ⊤967-1365.
Streetcar **Carlton** (#506).
In a city once infamous for its repressive "Sunday Blue Laws", which, among other things, forbade theatrical performances on Sunday, it is fitting irony that this, like many of Toronto's contemporary theatres, is housed in a former church. Tucked deep in the heart of the historic Cabbagetown neighbourhood, the Toronto Dance Theatre and its affiliated school have a deserved reputation for producing daring and original productions.

FILM

Toronto vies with New York as North America's second most popular **film** set – only Los Angeles attracts more camera crews – passing for other cities in a number of films, including New York in *Moonstruck*, Boston in *Good Will Hunting* and even Tangiers in *Naked Lunch*.

Movie buffs will feel right at home here: Toronto has contributed stars (Jim Carrey, Mary Pickford) and directors (Atom Egoyan, David Cronenberg, Norman Jewison) to the film industry, and a number of **film festivals** (the

FILM

premier event being the Toronto International Film Festival; see p.214) keep Toronto on cinema's cutting edge.

First-run cinemas in Toronto range from multiplex shoe boxes (invented by Torontonian Garth Drabinsky) to old-fashioned picture palaces, although the latter are regrettably dwindling in number. To combat the impact of VCRs on the cinema trade, Toronto has instituted "Half Price Tuesdays", cutting the usual price of $10 for a first-run evening performance to $5 (consequently, Tuesday-night seats are hard to come by if you arrive late). Matinee performances are reduced to half-price on weekdays.

Many of the city's **second-run cinemas** are operated under the umbrella of the **Festival Group**, a coalition of independent theatres that screen film favourites and whatever else might strike its members' fancy. If you are spending more than a few weeks in Toronto and are devoted to the fifth art, it's worth buying a Festival Group membership for $6. Admission for members is $4; $6.50–7 for non-members. For more information call the Festival Group at ☎690-2600.

FIRST-RUN CINEMAS

Backstage
Map 4, H6. 31 Balmuto Ave
☎922-6361.
Subway Yonge-Bloor.
This compact four-screen theatre is the last stop for first-run films before they are retired to video or the repertory houses. Locals check it out for quirky

independent films that don't quite fit the arthouse market.

Beach Cinemas
Map 2, I7. 1651 Queen St E
☎699-5971.
Streetcar Queen (#501).
A plump suburban multiplex serving the cinema needs of the growing number of young families in this east-end neighbourhood.

FILM

Canada Square

Map 2, G5. 2200 Yonge St
Ⓣ 483-9428.

Subway **Eglinton.**

A sprawling thirteen-screen cineplex offering a blend of foreign, independent and mainstream films.

Capitol

Map 2, G5. 2492 Yonge St
Ⓣ 487-8852.

Subway **Eglinton.**

A wonderful Art Deco, single-screen cinema with a balcony, espresso bar and deep, comfortable seats. Programming is eclectic but commendable, with an emphasis on foreign and independent cinema.

Carlton

Map 4, I9. 20 Carlton St
Ⓣ 598-2309.

Subway **College.**

When Garth Drabinsky's Cineplex chain muscled in on the Toronto scene, a number of arthouse cinemas closed. To compensate for this, Drabinsky set aside the Carlton to show first-run art films, and its eleven screens are still doing just that. The café and espresso bar make a nice change from standard candy-bar fare, although that too is available. The smaller cinemas here can feel cramped.

Cumberland 4

Map 4, F5. 159 Cumberland St
Ⓣ 964-5971.

Subway **Bay.**

This multiplex (contrary to its name, it actually has five screens) in the heart of Yorkville is an uptown version of the Carlton and caters to arthouse film fans. Larger screens and more leg room make for more comfortable viewing than at the Carlton.

Eaton Centre

Map 3, I2. M1 Dundas St W
Ⓣ 593-4535.

Subway **Dundas.**

The largest of the Cineplex theatres, this eighteen-screen cinema is a favourite among the city's youth. Programming tends to reflect the customers, who do not seem put off by the small screens and cramped seating arrangements.

FILM

Eglinton

Map 2, G5. 400 Eglinton W
Ⓣ 487-4721.
Subway Eglinton West.
A single-screen, old-time cinema worth visiting for its nostalgia value alone. Specialises in quality Hollywood releases.

Hyland

Map 2, G6. 1501 Yonge St
Ⓣ 962-2891.
Subway St Clair.
A single-screen theatre specializing in PG fare. Very busy during weekend matinees. Parents should be warned: the lobby is filled with video games and candy dispensers.

Market Square

Map 3, K5. 80 Front St
Ⓣ 364-2300.
Subway Union Station.
This six-screen theatre gears itself towards mainstream films. Full screens and good-sized theatres make for comfortable viewing.

Paramount

Map 3, E3. 259 Richmond St W
Ⓣ 444-3456.
Streetcar Queen (#501).

Perfect venue for film-goers who want to feel like extras in *Blade Runner*. Half the spectacle is in the theatre itself, with a mammoth pixel board cube showing film clips to the club-hoppers outside, an almost vertical ride up the escalator to the cinemas, and a sound system that blasts you out of your seat. All this is expensive. Ticket prices at this cinema are $12.

Plaza

Map 4, H5. Hudson's Bay Centre, Yonge & Bloor sts
Ⓣ 964-2555.
Subway Yonge-Bloor.
Built in the Seventies, this three-screen theatre has large cinemas that feature first-run blockbusters. A great place to catch matinees, although some patrons find its underground location a bit eerie.

Regent

Map 2, G5. 551 Mount Pleasant St
Ⓣ 480-9884.
Subway Davisville.
Wonderful Art Deco single-screen cinema with a great

FILM

chrome box office and illuminated marquee. Features mainstream fare.

Silvercity Yonge
Map 2, G5. 2300 Yonge St
ⓣ 544-1236.
Subway Eglinton.
Another premium-priced movie venue that attempts to be an entertainment complex unto itself, this one aimed squarely at the youth market. For those adults in attendance, ticket prices are a hefty $12.

Uptown
Map 4, H6. 764 Yonge St
ⓣ 922-6361.
Subway St Clair.
One of the last cinema palace theatres left in the city. The main theatre upstairs has a huge curved screen left over from the panorama days, opulent gold curtains, red plush and plenty of plaster ornaments. Its 921 seats ensure that this is where the biggest blockbusters open; and during the Toronto International Film Festival it is packed to capacity.

Varsity
Map 4, H6. 55 Bloor St W
ⓣ 961-6303.
Subway Yonge-Bloor.
A recent expansion has turned this two-screener into an eleven-cinema behemoth, replete with displays of Hollywood costumes, premium prices and full-service (drinks and snacks delivered to your seat) screening rooms. The cinemas are well appointed with deep, comfortable seats.

York
Map 2, G5. 101 Eglinton Ave E
ⓣ 486-5600.
Subway Eglinton.
The two-storey screen makes the York a likely place to see films where size really does matter. The sound system is not for the timid.

SECOND-RUN CINEMAS

Bloor Cinema
Map 4, A5. 506 Bloor St W
ⓣ 532-6677.
Subway Bathurst.

FILM

This cinema won't win any beauty contests but it is an undeniably cool if somewhat worn place to view films. Frequently plays host to the numerous film festivals in Toronto (see Chapter 16).

The Fox
Map 2, I7. 2236 Queen St E
Ⓣ691-7330.
Streetcar **Carlton (#506).**
This former vaudeville theatre, located in the Beaches area, is an alternative to its multiplex cousin up the road (see p.209). There's no glitzy marquee and the popcorn is best avoided, but the seats are comfortable and the film selection is top-shelf.

Kingsway Theatre
Map 2, C6. 3030 Bloor St W
Ⓣ236-1411.
Subway **Royal York.**
Small and a bit worn at the heels, this film theatre makes up for its lacklustre interior by offering a top-notch selection of films.

The Music Hall
Map 2, H6. 147 Danforth Ave
Ⓣ778-8272.
Subway **Broadview.**
The space is still used for live performances and musical concerts, but has been recently converted for use as a cinema as well. Perhaps the last working-class music hall left in Toronto.

Revue Cinema
Map 2, E6. 400 Roncesvalles Ave
Ⓣ531-9959.
Subway **Dundas West.**
This cinema has long had a reputation for some of the finest programming outside the film-festival circuit. Well worth the trip.

The Royal
Map 2, F7. 606 College St
Ⓣ516-4845.
Streetcar **Carlton (#506).**
Situated on the hippest block in the city, the Royal has recently had new seats installed and its Forties interior touched up.

FILM

THE TORONTO INTERNATIONAL FILM FESTIVAL

At any given point in the year, someone is holding a film festival in Toronto. The most famous is the **Toronto International Film Festival** (℡ 968-3456), which in two decades has gone from being an obscure celluloid celebration for hard-core film fans to being one of the most respected festivals in the world – and the largest in North America.

A ten-day affair, the festival begins during the second week of September. **Same day** tickets are available from the applicable cinemas' box offices each day or as **rush tickets** immediately before screenings for $13, or $22 for **Gala screenings**. The lines for TIFF screenings can be fearsome, but when you do get in, the directors and stars introduce their pictures and then make themselves available for question-and-answer periods after a film's first showing (all films screen twice). Many regular TIFF attendees plan their holidays around the festival and tend to buy books of tickets in advance, a more economical way of doing the festival. There are a variety of plans to choose from, and if you purchase before July 21st there is a modest discount: the cheapest of these is a book of ten tickets for $90, but the most economical option is the Daytime Pass, which gets you into 25 screenings (8am–6pm shows only) for $125. The big Hollywood product screens at tony venues like Roy Thompson Hall or the Elgin Theatre, and attendance here demands a Gala Pass, which sells for about $200. For **other film festivals** throughout the year, see the "Festivals and annual events" chapter, p.262.

Gay Toronto

O ver the past 25 years, Toronto's relationship with **gays and lesbians** has evolved from blunt intolerance to enthusiastic celebration. The gay community now has significant economic, political and social clout, and Toronto boasts the largest "out" population of any city in Canada. Toronto's main gay-and-lesbian neighbourhood is focused on the intersection of Church and Wellesley streets, about one block east of Yonge Street, where the lion's share of gay community services, bars and restaurants are located.

At the northeast corner of Church and Wellesley is **Cawthra Park**; attractive by day, it admittedly turns a bit cruisey at night. At the northern edge of the park is a sobering AIDS memorial: slender aluminium posts set in a circular pattern amid flower beds list the names of locals who have succumbed to the disease. At the southwest corner of Church and Wellesley is the *Second Cup*, an outlet of the Canada-wide coffee-shop chain of the same name. Known locally as "The Steps", it has become a prime meeting spot in the neighbourhood.

Throughout the city, look for the **free gay weeklies**, *fab* and *Xtra!*, distributed in news boxes and in many downtown bars and restaurants. Three **Web sites** in particular cater to the gay community: Ⓦ *www.gaycanada.com* has extensive listings of what's going on in Toronto, Ⓦ *www.gaytoronto.com* is a basic introduction to the gay community, and the Canadian Lesbian and Gay Archives Web site, ⓦ *www.clga.ca/archives*, focuses primarily on doctrines of gay rights and advocacy.

Gay theatre in Toronto makes its home at the 12 Alexander Street Theatre (see p.198), where the "Buddies in Badtimes" company puts on a repertoire of queer-culture performances.

CONTACTS

The 519 Community Centre
Map 4, I7. 519 Church St
ⓣ 392-6874.
Subway **Wellesley**.
Once a private club, this solid building in the heart of the gay quarter is now the hub for the city's gay outreach and awareness programmes.

AIDS Committee of Toronto (ACT)
Map 4, I8. 399 Church St
ⓣ 340-2437.
Streetcar **Carlton (#508).**
This community resource centre is an authoritative source for AIDS–related information in Toronto. In an

effort to provide for those afflicted with the disease and their families, the centre offers legal and financial advice, access to advocacy groups, and a research library. French and Spanish are also spoken.

Pride Committee of Toronto
Map 4, I7. 65 Wellesley St E, Suite 304
ⓣ 927-7433;
ⓦ *www.torontopride.com*
Subway **Wellesley**.
Mission Control for the annual Gay Pride celebrations (see opposite), an organisational feat that requires eleven months of planning and fund-raising events. A great place to find out about upcoming events in the gay community.

GAY PRIDE

In 1971, Toronto's first **gay-pride celebration** was held at Hanlan's Point in the Toronto Islands – a paltry one hundred people showed up. Today the celebration stretches over an entire week at the end of June and attracts an annual attendance of over 700,000. Festivities promoting gay awareness fill the week and culminate with the Gay Pride Parade, which begins at the intersection of Church and Wellesley and trucks down Yonge Street before terminating at Church Street. To show solidarity with Toronto's gay population, the mayor rides at the front of the parade, and the premier of Ontario writes warm letters of support in the prefaces of publications like *Canada's Gay Guide*, which is available in bookstores throughout the city.

ACCOMMODATION

619 Parliament St
Map 4, M9. 619 Parliament St
☎ 964-0426.
Streetcar **Carlton (#506).**
An inexpensive, Victorian guest house in Cabbagetown, complete with amenities like cable, videos, microwaves and massage boys on call. About a ten-minute walk from the Gay Village. ❸.

Banting House
Map 4, K8. 73 Homewood Ave
☎ 924-1458; ⓕ 924-3304.
Subway **Wellesley.**
A pretty Victorian house with cosy furnishings located two blocks from the Church and Wellesley intersection. The price includes breakfast, and rooms with en-suite bathrooms are available. ❹.

ACCOMMODATION

Cawthra Square Bed & Breakfast
Map 4, J7. 10 Cawthra Sq
ⓣ966-3074 or 1-800/259-5474;
ⓕ966-4494.
Subway Wellesley.
An attractive row house with well-kept, attractive furnishings. Located at the heart of the Gay and Lesbian Village. ❺.

Victoria's Mansion
Map 4, I6. 68 Gloucester
ⓣ 921-4625.
Subway Wellesley.
The rainbow flag flies proudly over this downtown Victorian mansion. The rooms are all equipped with fridges, microwaves and coffee-makers, and Victoria herself is on hand to make her guests feel at home. ❺.

GAY BARS AND CLUBS

Bar 501
Map 4, I7. 501 Church St
ⓣ944-3272.
Subway Wellesley.
On Sundays in the summer, the drag-queen show here spills out onto the sidewalk. A great place to catch up on neighbourhood gossip in a pared-down, clubhouse-like atmosphere.

Bar Babylon
Map 4, I7. 553 Church St
ⓣ923-2626.
Subway Wellesley.
Three floors of funky fun keep this youth-oriented bar/lounge happening. The martini menu has over 250 concoctions to choose from and the kitchen features delicious innovations like a fabled lentil and cous-cous soup.

The Barn / Stables
Map 4, J8. 418 Church St
ⓣ977-4684.
Subway Wellesley.
Another three-floor party house, this one drawing an all-ages leather and denim crowd. Both live music and DJs are featured.

Black Eagle

Map 4, J8. 457 Church St
ⓣ 413-1219.
Subway **Wellesley**.
A popular leather and denim cruise bar with multiple bars and a roof-top patio to cool off on when things get too hot.

Byzantium

Map 4, I7. 499 Church St
ⓣ 922-3859.
Subway **Wellesley**.
A stylish address divided into equal parts martini bar and restaurant. This extremely long, narrow space promotes mixing and mingling.

Hair of the Dog

Map 4, J8. 425 Church St
ⓣ 964-2708.
Subway **Wellesley**.
The neighbourhood's newest watering hole is a two-storey bar and restaurant that strays over to the upscale side. A nice place to go on a date.

Pope Joan

Map 4, M8. 547 Parliament St
ⓣ 925-6662.
Streetcar **Carlton (#506)**.
A cavernous space, this is one of the few lesbian bars in town. On the weekends DJs play disco and dance tracks for an appreciative crowd.

Remington's Men of Steel

Map 3, I1. 379 Yonge St
ⓣ 977-2160.
Subway **Dundas**.
A cheesy gay strip bar that took over its location from a former cheesy straight strip bar. Predictably garish.

Slack Alice Bar & Grill

Map 4, I7. 562 Church St
ⓣ 969-8742.
Subway **Wellesley**.
As laid-back and poseur-free as its name would suggest. Does a nice line of martinis and an international menu that ambles between Continental and Middle Eastern; delicious daily specials.

Tango

Map 4, I7. 508 Church St
ⓣ 972-1662.
Subway **Wellesley**.
A hot new lesbian bar on the strip, *Tango* pitches to a younger crowd but welcomes women of all ages.

GAY BARS AND CLUBS

The Toolbox

Map 2, H7. 508 Eastern Ave
ⓣ 466-8616.
Streetcar Queen (#501).
There are lots of leathery
dominants here looking for
their latex counterparts. If
you go, bring a sense of
adventure.

Wilde Oscar's

Map 4, I7. 518 Church St
ⓣ 921-8142.
Subway Wellesley.
The fabulous patio here
grudgingly shuts down in
winter, but the two floors'
worth of bistro and bar inside
are perfectly comfortable
during the chilly months. The
menu emphasises burgers
(including a very tasty veggie
burger).

Woody's

Map 4, I6. 467 Church St
ⓣ 972-0887.
Subway Wellesley.
This place has an excellent
selection of microbrews and
draft ales, daily specials and a
popular weekend brunch.
Not that anyone comes here
for the food: a popular gay
hangout, there's a men's bare-
chest competition at midnight
on weekends, and a Sunday
tea dance with drag
performers, singers and
outlandish themes.

Zelda's Bar and Restaurant

Map 4, I7. 542 Church St
ⓣ 922-2526.
Subway Wellesley.
Owned and operated by the
same crew that brought you
Zelda's on Wellesley (now
Zelda's Satellite Lounge, 76
Wellesley St E), the new and
expanded space offers more
room for more patrons having
more fun. A very popular
neighbourhood hangout
offering reasonably priced
drinks and food.

GAY BATHS

Bijou
Map 4, I9. 64 Gerrard St E (at Church)
℡971-9985.
Subway **Wellesley**.
Recently the object of police attention, the *Bijou* nevertheless continues to offer its own brand of steamy entertainment.

The Cellar
Map 4, I7. 78 Wellesley St E
℡975-1799.
Subway **Wellesley**.
The hours are convenient – it's open twenty-four hours a day, seven days a week – as long as you can find the place. Its entrance is underneath the *Pizza Pizza* at Wellesley and Church. There's no sign, just a back door.

Shops and galleries

Whether you're after computers or couture fashions, antiques or the avant-garde, Toronto is a terrific place for the shopaholic. The city is Canada's biggest and most cosmopolitan, and the wealth of **shopping** possibilities spans the whole of the metropolitan area. The hours of business are fairly consistent: Most shops are open seven days a week 10am–7pm Mon–Wed, 10am–9pm Thurs–Fri, 10am–6pm Sat and noon–6pm Sunday.

Of the shopping districts, the intersection at **Yonge and Dundas** is a magnet for youth and teems with under-twenties who flock here from the suburbs and beyond. With the Eaton Centre stretching a full city block to the southwest, The Gap's flagship store to the north, and most of the city's major music stores to the east, anything a teen could want is within easy reach.

Trekking north from here on Yonge to Bloor Street West takes you to the cusp of **Yorkville**, a nest of streets, including Cumberland Avenue, Yorkville Avenue, and Scollard Street, that runs between Yonge and Avenue Road. Although Yorkville was the Flower Power epicentre in Toronto during the Sixties, the area is now filled with costly boutiques, piano bars and a large percentage of Toronto's Beautiful People. Even if you can't afford to buy anything here, it makes for a pleasant stroll.

SHOPPING CATEGORIES

Back down on the lower-west side of the city, the expanse of **Queen Street West** between University Avenue and Bathurst Street is an eclectic jumble of shops, cafés, bars, galleries and street-side stands. Particularly laid-back, this is the place for trend-setting designer gear, the latest in fusion cuisine, and the hippest clubs. An incursion of chain stores is slowly gentrifying the area, however, so the best of the independent shopping scene has been pushed west of Spadina Avenue.

If you're visiting from outside of Canada, be sure to save all your receipts when shopping as in many instances you can claim a tax refund; see pp.275–76 for more details.

ANTIQUES

507 Antiques
Map 2, H7. 50 Carroll St
Ⓣ 462-9989.
Streetcar Queen (#501).
A mammoth cache of
architectural salvage, large
wrought-iron pieces and
garden statuary. Most of the
stock isn't particularly
portable, but there are rooms
of smaller furniture at the
back, and little decorative
accessories are scattered
throughout.

Absolutely
Map 4, H2. 1132 Yonge St
Ⓣ 324-8351.
Subway Rosedale.
The narrowness of the store is
accentuated by the stacks of
wonderful finds piled high
along the walls and in every
possible nook and cranny.
Huge sea sponges perch atop
delicate Victorian pedestals,
antique hat forms adorn
Georgian desks, and huge
Belle Epoch gilt mirrors
reflect everything back,
doubling the sense of
wondrous clutter.

L'Atelier
Map 4, H1. 1224 Yonge St
Ⓣ 966-0200.
Subway Summerhill.
Small and elegant, L'Atelier
specialises in late eighteenth-
and early nineteenth-century
furniture and decorative
objects, largely from England
and France.

Clutters Art Deco
Gallery
Map 2, H7. 692 Queen St E
Ⓣ 461-3776.
Streetcar Queen (#501).
This hip store is crammed
with top-notch (and
surprisingly affordable) Art
Deco furniture, chandeliers,
lights and bronze statuary.

The Door Store
Map 3, L3. 43 Britain St
Ⓣ 863-1590.
Streetcar Dundas (#505).
Two floors of woodwork,
stained glass, wrought iron
(perfectly rusted to a warm
ochre), fireplaces and details.
Pieces range from the tiny
(Victorian bronze keyhole

ANTIQUES

covers) to the huge (Art Nouveau garden gazebos).

Harbourfront Antique Market

Map 3, D7. 390 Queens Quay W
Ⓣ 260-2626.
Streetcar Harbourfront (#509 from Union Station) or Spadina (#510) from Spadina subway station.
There are more than one hundred permanent antique dealers on the ground floor of this covered market, which is perhaps the best place to get a sense of the going prices for high-quality antiques.

The Paisley Shoppe

Map 4, G5. 77 Yorkville Ave
Ⓣ 923-5830.
Subway Bay (Bellair exit).
Housed in the last of Yorkville's Regency cottages, this Toronto institution specialises in furniture, decorative accessories, and tableware items from the eighteenth and nineteenth centuries.

Prince of Serendip

Map 4, H3. 1073 Yonge St
Ⓣ 925-3760.
Subway Rosedale.
Patrons are treated with warmth and attentiveness at this aptly named store. Wares in the huge bay window at the front include substantial Victorian furniture and gigantic chandeliers, and the intriguing, dim interior extends back into a garden, where you can find a selection of outdoor statuary.

Red Indian Art Deco

Map 3, A3. 536 Queen St W
Ⓣ 504-7706.
Streetcar Queen (#501).
You never know what you'll find crammed into this narrow, deep store, but it's always worth a look. Finds have included matching Eames chairs, rare Fornasetti pieces, and a series of ceramics by Jean Cocteau.

ANTIQUES

BOOKS

NEW BOOKS

The Beguiling
Map 4, A5. 601 Markham St
Ⓣ533-9168.
Subway **Bathurst**.
A comprehensive selection of 'zines, illustrated novels and underground comics with some quirky postcards and ephemera thrown in.

Bookcity
Map 2, H6. 348 Danforth Ave
Ⓣ469-9997.
Subway **Chester**.
A solid neighbourhood bookstore with a good range of new-release literature, magazines and children's selections.

Chapters
Map 4, G5. 110 Bloor St W
Ⓣ920-9299.
Subway **Bay**.
Part-owned by the behemoth American chain Barnes and Noble, this is the big-box book emporium in Toronto. Browsers are encouraged to linger in a cosy atmosphere that includes deep couches, skylights, a fireplace and a café on the ground level.

David Mirvish Books on Art
Map 4, A5. 596 Markham
Ⓣ531-9975.
Subway **Bathurst**.
A browser-friendly art book store with exceptional sections on contemporary and Canadian art as well as some terrific bargains. A must-stop shop for serious collectors.

Indigo Books, Music & Café
Map 2, G5. 2300 Yonge St
Ⓣ544-0049.
Subway **Eglinton**.
Also at **Map 3, H4.** 468 King St W
Ⓣ364-4499.
Map 4, G5. 50 Bloor St W
Ⓣ925-3536.
This forward-thinking chain of large bookstores decks locations out in bleached wood and buffed aluminium with the *de rigueur* cafés. It gets high

marks for its children's books and championship of Canadian authors. Gift sections include beautiful selections of stationery and pens.

Nicholas Hoare

Map 3, K5. 45 Front St E
Ⓣ 777-2665.
Subway **Union Station**.
A beautifully appointed store replete with Gothic folly flourishes, this bibliophile refuge provides comfy chairs and sofas in front of a working fireplace for browsers. Their large selection runs the gamut, and the staff is particularly helpful.

Pages

Map 3, E3. 265 Queen St W
Ⓣ 598-1447.
Streetcar **Queen (#501)**.
The bookstore of choice for the sophisticated reader, this place has the edgiest and most comprehensive collection of contemporary literature and art and social criticism in town. There are also good travel, film, music, art and architecture sections, as well as an extensive range of magazines. The erudite owner

and his staff answer even the most arcane questions with grace and ease.

This Ain't the Rosedale Library

Map 4, I7. 483 Church St
Ⓣ 929-9912.
Subway **Wellesley**.
A funky neighbourhood bookstore offering lots of magazines, contemporary literature, and an excellent resource/research section with an emphasis on gay culture. The easy-going owners are usually available to discuss their twin passions: Canadian literature and baseball.

World's Biggest Bookstore

Map 3, I1. 20 Edward St
Ⓣ 977-7009.
Subway **Dundas**.
When giant bookstore chains collide (Smith's, Coles and Chapters in this case) they spawn entities like this – with over 150,000 titles, it's easy to spend the better part of a day combing through this barn-like structure. If you can't find what you want elsewhere, you're sure to find it here.

BOOKS

USED BOOKS

Acadia Art and Rare Books

Map 3, N3. 232 Queen St E
☎ 364-7638.
Streetcar **Queen** (#501).
The neighbourhood is a tad scary, but it's worth stepping over a few winos to find this place. Really low prices for really high-quality antiquarian books and prints. This is where other dealers shop for stock, and the owner appreciates a knowledgeable customer.

D & E Lake

Map 4, L5. 237 King St E
☎ 863-9930.
Streetcar **King** (#504).
This is what an antiquarian bookstore and print gallery should look like: a Dickensian brick building with paned windows and creaky floors. The owner can spellbind you with the length of cigarette ash he'll allow to dangle over a precious first edition. This is a collector's first stop: the wide selection includes military, art and architecture,

and medical books, all in excellent condition.

Eliot's Bookstore

Map 4, H7. 584 Yonge St
☎ 925-0268.
Subway **Wellesley**.
Bookstore with a good general and scholastic collection alongside a used magazine selection that is particularly strong on arts and music.

TRAVEL BOOKS

Ulysses Travel Bookshop

Map 4, G5. 101 Yorkville Ave
☎ 323-3609.
Subway **Bay** (Bellair exit).
An excellent selection of maps, guides, and travel literature, as well as all those clever little travel accessories you never know you need until you go on a trip.

Pearly's Maps

Map 2, F5. 1050 Eglinton Ave W
☎ 785-6277.
Subway **Eliglinton West**.
Purveyors of the excellent Pearly's map books, which give detailed depictions of city

BOOKS

streets, as well as CD-ROM travel guides and travel products for the well-packed globetrotter.

GAY AND LESBIAN BOOKS

Glad Day Bookshop
Map 4, H6. 598A Yonge St
☎ 961-1624.
Subway **Wellesley.**
Dedicated exclusively to gay and lesbian literature, erotica and magazines, this establishment has been a cornerstone of the gay community for almost two decades. A good place to find out about upcoming events.

FEMINIST BOOKS

Toronto Women's Bookstore
Map 4, C7. 73 Harbord St
☎ 922-8744.
Streetcar **Spadina (#510).**
Housed comfortably in a Victorian row house, this hub of Toronto feminist literature also boasts an extensive bulletin board with listings for women's health services, community issues, and upcoming rallies and events.

CLOTHES

INDEPENDENT DESIGNERS

Comrags
Map 2, F7. 654 Queen St W
☎ 360-7249.
Streetcar **Queen (#501).**
Toronto fashion pioneers Judy Cornish and Joyce Gunhouse are famed for their ongoing reinterpretations of the "little dress". Their Queen West West retail space shows off a full range of their creations, from casual to formal wear.

Fashion Crimes
Map 3, D3. 395 Queen St W
☎ 592-9001.
Streetcar **Queen (#501).**
Designer Pam Chorley has held her own on the trendy Queen Street West strip with a

CLOTHES

Independent Toronto designers are surprisingly affordable.
Most boutiques' regular prices are on average only 10–15
percent higher on comparable goods at ho-hum mass-
merchandisers like The Gap, Talbots, or Banana Republic.
If you are lucky enough to catch a sale, the affordability,
quality craftsmanship, fabrics and forward-looking
designs make the merchandise irresistible.

"More Is More" fashion philosophy that runs counter to any and all Minimalist trends. Her romantic clothing line ranges from form-flattering, bias-cut gowns and dresses to the Baroque theatricality of her bridal frocks. There's also a full range of idiosyncratic accessories to choose from.

Hoax Couture

Map 4, G5. 114 Cumberland St
ⓣ 929-4629.
Subway Bay (Bellair exit).
Chris Tyrell and Jim Searle's designs have focused on sleek, innovative eveningwear for both men and women in recent years with an emphasis on superb craftsmanship. Their latest line of full-length leather jackets is superb.

Nina Mdviani

Map 4, F4. 162 Cumberland St,
Renaissance Court
ⓣ 960-4900.
Subway Bay (Cumberland exit).
This designer began her career doing costumes for theatre and opera in Warsaw, so "dramatic" is perhaps the first adjective used to describe her work. Her innovative "nipple fabric" – a puckered, stretch sheer that Nina tie-dyes and fashions into scarves, tops and tube sheaths – is a must-have. Great stuff if you want to make a statement.

Wenches & Rogues

Map 4, F5. 110 Yorkville Ave
ⓣ 920-8959.
Subway Bay (Cumberland exit).
Many of Canada's top independent designers for men and women's clothing

CLOTHES

can be found in this two-storey Yorkville boutique, including David Dixon, Misura, and Crystal Siemens.

DESIGNER/HAUTE COUTURE

Chanel Boutique
Map 4, G5. 131 Bloor St W
☎ 925-2577.
Subway Bay.
Purveyors of the ultimate power suit for Ladies Who Lunch, Chanel offers dependable excellence at astronomical prices.

Chez Catherine
Map 4, F4. 55 Avenue Rd
☎ 967-5666.
Subway Bay, (Cumberland exit).
This high-calibre store carries one of the finest collections of couture labels in the city, with special emphasis on Gianfranco Ferre and Krizia.

Prada
Map 4, G5. 131 Bloor St W
☎ 513-0400.
Subway Bay.
Prada is the latest fashion darling, and this lovely store

stocks a full line of pricey, trend-setting clothes and accessories. In particular, take time to ogle the shoe and handbag collections.

CHAIN STORES

Club Monaco
Map 4, F5. 157 Bloor St W and Avenue Rd
☎ 591-8837.
Subway Museum.
The creation of Canadian designer Alfred Sung, this place is where many talented young designers are cutting their fashion teeth. Geared towards young adults, these upscale casual threads form the basic building blocks of many a wardrobe.

Le Chateau
Map 3, D3. 336 Queen St W
☎ 971-9314, and three other downtown locations.
Streetcar Queen (#501).
Savvy young shoppers who want 'The Look' for less head straight to Le Chateau, a Canadian chain for men and women that specialises in four-season club gear and the

CLOTHES

kind of clothes that make parents crazy. A children's line is now available as well.

Roots

Map 3, I3. In the Eaton Centre, 220 Yonge St
Ⓣ 977-0041.
Subway Dundas.

Roots' signature wear has long been its supple leather bomber jackets, shoes and bags. Over the past few years it has expanded into quality cotton and wool lines with a *sportiff* flair. There are several locations throughout the city, so if you don't see what you want here, ask them to call other stores.

Zara

Map 4, H5. 50 Bloor St W, Holt Renfrew Centre
Ⓣ 916-2401.
Subway Bloor-Yonge.

Europeans may be familiar with this Spanish store for men's and women's fashion, but it is still relatively new for North Americans. Zara offers exceptional, up-to-the-minute designs for bargain-basement prices.

VINTAGE
- - - - - - - - - - - - - - - - - - - -

Courage My Love

Map 3, B1. 14 Kensington Ave
Ⓣ 979-1992.
Streetcar Dundas (#505).

Vintage clothing for men and women augmented with an eclectic selection of beads, amulets and buttons. The clientele here ranges from high school girls looking for funky prom dresses to fashion-magazine editors looking for cheap chic. The most venerable of the Kensington Market *schmatta* shops.

Divine Decadence

Map 4, H5. 55 Bloor St W
Ⓣ 324-9759.
Subway Bay.

With a stunning collection of vintage haute couture, this Toronto favourite is patronised by socialites, movie stars and anyone who loves beautiful clothes. There's Chanel from the Thirties, Dior from the Sixties, and Edwardian and Victorian pieces with all the appropriate period accessories.

CLOTHES

So Hip It Hurts

Map 3, E3. 323 Queen St W
☎ 971-6901.
Subway Osgoode.
A good source for party
gladrags and costume jewellery.
The name alone pulls the
curious in off the street.

THRIFT

Honest Ed's

Map 4, A5. 581 Bloor St W
☎ 537-1574.
Subway Bathurst.
Toronto's ultimate discount
store. Three carnival-like
floors graced with goofy jokes
and pictures of owner Ed
Mirvish with show biz
personalities ranging from
Claire Bloom to Peter Tosh.
The signs exhort shoppers to
lighten up and buy something
cheap, and there are some
amazing buys if you have the
time to rummage through the
troves of clothes and
accessories.

Tom's Place

Map 3, B1. 190 Baldwin Ave,
☎ 596-0297.
Streetcar Spadina (#510).
A Kensington Market
institution, Tom's Place
offers a huge selection of
men's and women's designer
clothes at discount prices.
The actual price tags are
more or less suggestions for
bartering with the deeply
courteous Tom. The more
he likes you the better the
deal. The staff is top-notch
and alterations are speedily
performed on site.

CRAFTS

Arts on King

Map 3, K5. 169 King St E
☎ 777-9617.
Streetcar King (#504).
Local, regional and national
craftspeople display their wares
in this cavernous old warehouse
space. Downstairs there's
jewellery, glass, ceramics and
assorted knick-knacks; upstairs
features art exhibitions. A good
spot to search for a unique gift.

CRAFTS

Bounty

Map 3, F8. 235 York Quay
Centre
ⓣ 973-4993.
Streetcar Harbourfront (#509
from Union Station).
This consignment shop
features stained and blown
glass, jewellery, baskets, fired
clay, ironware, furniture and
much more. The stock is
mostly by local artisans.

First Hand

Map 3, G8. 207 Queens Quay
W, Queens Quay Terminal
Building
ⓣ 203-7773.
Streetcar Harbourfront (#509
from Union Station).
Contemporary Canadian crafts
and visual arts in all kinds of
media are on display here,
representing over 200 artists of
varying degrees of renown.

DEPARTMENT STORES AND MALLS

DEPARTMENT STORES

The Bay

Map 3, I3. 176 Queen St
ⓣ 861-9111.
Subway Yonge-Bloor
Map 4, I5. Bloor and Yonge
ⓣ 972-3333.
Subway Bloor-Yonge.
With two locations (each
takes up a full city block), The
Bay has become a formidable
downtown presence. The
name was shortened from
Hudson Bay Company, the
world's oldest corporate entity
and former owner of most of
the Canadian North. You can
still purchase the Hudson's
Bay Blanket here (a must-have
item during the fur trade), but
the rest of the basic
department-store stock is
decidedly contemporary.

Eaton's

Map 3, I2. 290 Yonge St
ⓣ 343-2111.
Subway Dundas.
Eaton's, Canada's oldest
department store chain,
recently bit the dust, and this

flagship store is actually owned by Sears, Eaton's former rival. Happily, the store has kept both the old name and its emphasis on upscale quality, but the new emphasis is on mainstream fashion, perfumes, cosmetics and accessories instead of the traditional homeware items.

Holt Renfrew

Map 4, H5. 50 Bloor St W
ⓣ 922-2333.
Subway Bay.
Toronto's premier one-stop shopping destination for both men and women. Specialises in signature collections from the likes of Jean-Paul Gaultier, Gucci, Sonia Rykiel and Armani, as well as upper-echelon Canadian designers like Brian Bailey, Catherine Regehr and Lida Baday.

MALLS

- - - - - - - - - - - - - - - - - - -

BCE Place

Map 3, I5. 181 Bay Street.
Subway Union Station.
One of the most dramatic

complexes in the city, the BCE was designed by Spanish architect Santiago Calatrava, who found a way to incorporate – rather than bulldoze – the walls of the Commerce Bank of the Midland District (Toronto's oldest stone building) and a block of Victorian shops into the development. A galleria of shops and office space, the BCE has a vaulted ceiling that allows sunlight to pour in – a welcome antidote to the subterranean fluorescent lighting of the Underground City (see overleaf).

Eaton Centre

Map 3, I2 & I3. 290 Yonge St
ⓣ 343-2111.
Subway Queen or Dundas.
Anchored by Eaton's department store (see opposite) at its northern boundary, this enormous mall covers the distance between two subway stops, contains hundreds of stores on three main levels, and takes the better part of an afternoon just to walk from one end to the other. This is perhaps the best place to shop

THE UNDERGROUND CITY

The largest mall in Toronto is invisible from the surface, buried beneath the streets in eleven kilometres of tunnels known as the **Underground City**, which stretches south–north from Front to Dundas, and east–west between Yonge and Richmond. The entrances to the Underground City are brightly marked with the coloured **PATH** logo.

This subterranean network of plazas co-evolved with the banking towers that dominate the street level. Developers had the idea of creating shopping environments for the hundreds of thousands of workers who pour into the city's core daily from the subways, commuter trains and expressways. No matter how bad the weather, you can always go shopping, see a film, visit a gallery, or find something to eat in the well-planned labyrinths beneath Toronto.

if you have limited time, simply because every chain store of any significance is here. The layout follows one general rule: high-end shops are on the third level, mid-price shops on the second, and the cheap stuff is on the bottom.

Hazelton Lanes

Map 4, F4. 55 Avenue Rd
℡968-8600.
Subway Bay (Cumberland exit).
When Elizabeth Taylor is in Toronto, Hazelton Lanes fills her one-stop shopping needs. It's *that* kind of a place: high-end stores mixed in with a few restaurants and cafés. In the winter its inner courtyard transforms from outdoor café to skating rink.

FOOD AND DRINK

GOURMET FOOD AND WINE STORES

Alex Farm Products

Map 2, H6. 377 Danforth Ave
🕾 465-9500.
Subway Chester.
A cheese fanatic's dream, this place's specialities include thirteen different types of sheep-milk cheeses, a remarkable array of goat cheeses flown in from France weekly, and a Trappist raw-milk cheese made by Canadian monks that is delicious. There's a second location at the St Lawrence Market (🕾 368-2415); see "Markets", p.241.

Caviar Direct

Map 3, K5. St Lawrence Market 🕾 361-3422.
Subway Union Station.
An emporium for Beluga and Persian caviars, this place also touts the Canadian variety, a golden caviar from the sturgeon of Lake Huron. Be sure to try a piece of "Indian candy" (smoked salmon cured in maple syrup).

Dinah's Cupboard

Map 4, H5. 50 Cumberland St
🕾 921-8112.
Subway Bay.
A high-class Toronto food shop perfect for putting together an urban picnic. Choose from a wide selection of teas and coffees, fancy baked goods, and deli items like sandwiches and salads.

Holt Renfrew Gourmet

Map 4, H5. 50 Bloor St W
🕾 922-2333.
Subway Bay.
One side of this shop is a lunch counter and take-away deli, and the other is filled with a wide range of condiments and prettily packaged herbs. Especially good for its range of sweets.

Pusateri's

Map 2, G5. 1539 Avenue Rd
🕾 785-9100.
Subway Lawrence.
Serious food critics have

FOOD AND DRINK

proclaimed this family-run operation as what New York's Balducci's used to be: foodie heaven. Every item is absolutely top quality. Special features include an olive oil tasting bar, cooking demonstrations by the city's leading chefs, and, unique outside of Italy, an entire wall of Italian *parmigian reggiano* cheese wheels.

SEN5ES

Map 4, H5. 15 Bloor St W
Ⓣ 935-0400.
Subway Bloor-Yonge.
The hope is that your five senses will be so stimulated here that you won't blanche at the astronomical prices. The pastries, all baked on site, are artful, as are creations like caviar-speckled sour cream atop perfect blinis. Dean & DeLuca products are available for the label-conscious, and there's full-service dining upstairs.

Vintages

Map 4, F4. Hazelton Lanes, 87 Avenue Rd
Ⓣ 924-9463.
Subway Bay.

A well-stocked wine store that showcases top-flight vintages and rare years. Special features include the exotic Ontario ice wine – an intensely sweet dessert wine made from grapes frozen on the vine – as well as an excellent selection of cognacs, brandies and fine spirits.

BAKERIES AND PATISSERIES

Carousel Bakery

Map 3, K5. St Lawrence Market
Ⓣ 363-4247.
Subway Union Station.
Absolutely the best place for brioche, Carousel also gets high marks for its speciality breads and focaccia.

Daniel et Daniel

Map 4, M9. 248 Carlton St
Ⓣ 968-9275.
Streetcar Carlton (#506).
Classically French, this place creates superb cakes, jewel-like fruit tarts and dainty pastries. Be on the lookout for traditional French confections timed to

coincide with feast days like Epiphany, when cakes are baked with little tokens and gifts inside.

Dufflet Pastries

Map 2, F7. 787 Queen St W
☎ 504-2870.
Streetcar **Queen (#501).**
This tiny outlet, named for Toronto's best-loved dessert baker, is a must for serious sweet tooths. Those in the know can spot a Dufflet cake, pastry or *bombe* from twenty paces.

Yung Sing Pastry

Map 3, E1. 22 Baldwin St
☎ 979-2832.
Subway **Queens Park.**
Lunchtime crowds throng to this tiny take-out-only bakery, which features spicy beef-stuffed buns, pork or veggie spring rolls, lotus-nut shortcake, and the richest egg custard tarts you've ever tasted. A complete lunch here won't cost more than $3.

HEALTH FOOD STORES

- - - - - - - - - - - - - - - - - - - -

The Big Carrot

Map 2, H6. 348 Danforth Ave
☎ 466-2129.
Subway **Chester.**
Toronto's only health food supermarket, this place has a full selection of organic produce, fish and meat, bulk foods and a vegetarian deli counter. An attached space sells beauty and personal hygiene products as well as herbal medicines.

The House of Spice

Map 3, B1. 190 August Ave
☎ 593-9724.
Streetcar **College (#506).**
Cherished in Toronto for its breathtaking range of products – spices, coffees, teas, oils, condiments and exotic tinned foods – as well as for its exceptional prices. The owner keeps a stack of photocopied recipes from her own collection at the register for curious customers. Worth a visit just to savour the sights and smells.

FOOD AND DRINK

INUIT/FIRST NATIONS GALLERIES

Fehley Fine Arts

Map 4, G4. 14 Hazelton Ave
☎ 323-1373.
Subway Bay.
Fehley's is an international leader in the complex area of Inuit art, representing artists and sculptors from across the enormous expanse of the Canadian Arctic. Although the sculptures here tend to be the star attractions, don't miss the graphic-art pieces.

The Guild Shop

Map 4, G5. 118 Cumberland St
☎ 921-1721.
Subway Bay.
Long distinguished as an outlet for Canadian artists and craftspeople, the Guild is also the city's oldest dealer of Inuit and Native art. The Inuit statuary is exceptional, often very affordable, and the curator is more than happy to expound on the pieces' significance. An excellent place for the beginning collector.

Isaacs Inuit Gallery

Map 4, E5. 9 Prince Arthur Ave
☎ 921-9985.
Subway Bay.
Serious collectors have long patronised Isaacs, which carries Inuit sculpture, prints, drawings and wall hangings.

Maslak-McLeod Gallery

Map 4, E5. 25 Prince Arthur Ave
☎ 944-2577.
Subway Bay.
This gallery carries some of the most important names in First Nations and Inuit paintings, including masters like Norval Morrisseau and Abraham Aghik.

Native Stone Art

Map 3, E3. 4 McCaul St
☎ 593-0924.
Streetcar College (#506).
This gallery/shop sells a wide selection of First Nations crafts, leathers, jewellery and carvings.

INUIT/FIRST NATIONS GALLERIES

MARKETS

Unlike many large North American cities, Toronto has preserved its historic **markets**. Not just places to pick up a few groceries, the markets are meeting places and excellent stages for people-watching.

The Farmers Market (also called North Market)

Map 3, K5. 92 Front St E
Ⓣ 392-7219.
Subway Union Station.
The vendors here produce what they sell, offering up fresh honey, pots of herbs, home-baked goods, fresh cheeses, and fruits and vegetables straight off the farm. Open on Sat only, 5am–5pm.

Kensington Market

Map 4, A9 & B9. Dundas St W and Kensington Ave
Streetcar Dundas (#505).
This is a United Nations of food: one street is stuffed with Ethiopian, Vietnamese, Trinidadian, Bahamian, Chinese, Portuguese and Jewish food shops, while around the corner merchants from throughout Latin America congregate with vendors from the Middle East, Mediterranean and Central Europe. If you can't find it here, the odds are you won't find it anywhere. Closed Sun.

St Lawrence Market

Map 3, K5. Front and Church streets
Ⓣ 392-7219.
Subway Union Station.
Once the spot of Toronto's first city hall, this market boasts two levels of stalls, shops and bins filled with tantalising goods. The busiest and most festive day to visit is Saturday, when buskers of every description play to the crowds. Ubiquitous Peruvian flute ensembles vie with traditional Canadian fiddlers; students from the music conservatory practise for cash; and an assortment of regulars sing for their supper. Apart from the array of international goods, you can sample treats

MARKETS

241

specific to Ontario, like peameal-and-bacon sandwiches (bacon coated in a cornmeal crust) and fiddlehead ferns. The lower level also has a crafts market where vendors sell hats, scarves, jewellery and wooden toys. Closed Sun.

MUSEUM SHOPS

The Art Gallery of Ontario Gallery Shop
Map 3, E2. 317 Dundas St W
ⓣ 979-6610.
Subway St Patrick.
In addition to items themed around current exhibits, the museum's shop stocks work by local potters, glass blowers and silversmiths. There's also an excellent selection of children's toys, posters, books, cards and multimedia teaching aids.

Gardiner Museum Shop
Map 4, F6. 111 Queen's Park
ⓣ 586-5699.
Subway Museum.
Perhaps the best place in town to find innovative, one-off ceramics at fair prices. The Gardiner's gift shop carries consignment items from some of the best

ceramicists working in Canada today.

The ROM Shop
Map 4, F6. 100 Queen's Park
ⓣ 586-5775.
Subway Museum.
The gift shop at the Royal Ontario Museum sells works by local artists on consignment, including raku, porcelain, textiles and native crafts. The book selection has an excellent range of titles dealing with Canadian and First Nation history and culture, and the children's section, located downstairs, is chock-full of educational books and toys themed on the museum's collections, particularly the dinosaur wing.

MUSIC

NEW

L'Atelier Grigorian
Map 4, G5. 70 Yorkville Ave
Ⓣ 922-6477.
Subway Bay.
The comprehensive selection
of classical and ancient music
here includes many imported
labels and hard-to-find titles.
Nothing comes cheap, but if
you really need that four-disc
set of Byzantine liturgical
music, this is the place to be.

HMV
Map 3, I1. 333 Yonge St
Ⓣ 586-9668.
Subway Dundas.
The four comprehensively
stocked floors here are packed
with nearly all musical genres.
Listening posts play selections
from top-40 tracks, and if the
staff isn't familiar with a title
they will consult their
computers to find it for you.

Metropolis Records
Map 3, C3. 162A Spadina Ave
Ⓣ 364-0230.

Streetcar Spadina (#510).
This modest walk-up carries
only trip-hop, drum'n'bass
and other electronic club
sounds on both vinyl and CD.
Also a handy spot to pick up
fliers on clubs, lounges and
the odd after-hours joint.

Sam the Record Man
Map 3, I1. 347 Yonge St
Ⓣ 977-4650.
Subway Dundas.
Rock star signatures dapple
the walls here, which may
account for the owner's
reluctance to wash them
down. The store is grotty and
the staff can be surly, but
these shortcomings don't
deter the loyal customers,
who burrow excitedly
through the extensive
collections of rock, jazz,
classical and world music.

Tower Records
Map 3, I3. 2 Queen St W
Ⓣ 593-2500.
Subway Queen.
This aggressive superstore
offers competitive prices on

MUSIC

243

top-40 titles, but is not particularly well organised. The book section is good, though, if somewhat inconsistent, as is the selection of laser discs, videos and DVDs.

Traxx

Map 4, H9. 427 Yonge St
☎ 977-4888.
Subway Wellesley.

A favourite among Toronto's DJs and clubbers, Traxx specialises in house, techno, hip-hop, rap, and drum'n'bass. They carry both CDs and vinyl, and the counters are littered with club flyers.

Because many entertainment corporations use Toronto's diverse, cosmopolitan population as a test market for North America, Toronto has some of the best prices for new-release compact discs in the world – frequently half of what they are in Europe and a few dollars cheaper than in the States.

USED

Driftwood Music

Map 3, F3. 247 Queen St W
☎ 598-0368.
Subway Osgoode.

This remarkably well organised and reasonably priced store carries used CDs, tapes and some vinyl. The selection is good in all categories, but the emphasis is on rock.

Kop's

Map 3, F3. 229 Queen St W
☎ 593-8523.
Subway Osgoode.

A highly popular fixture on the Queen West strip, this boxy store is crammed with new and used CDs, some cassettes, and a collection of vinyl upstairs. The stock is rock-heavy, but there are some interesting finds in the jazz and blues sections.

MUSIC

Rotate This

Map 3, B3. 620 Queen St W
Ⓣ 504-8447.
Streetcar Queen (#501).
A bit further down the Queen West strip than Kop's and therefore less likely to be filled with young things from the suburbs on a Saturday afternoon. Diverse selection of many genres.

Second Vinyl

Map 3, E3. 2 McCaul St
Ⓣ 977-3737.
Subway Osgoode.
Despite the name, this store carries only a limited selection of vinyl records. One side of the store is devoted to used jazz and classical CDs, and the other is filled with rock and alternative titles.

She Said Boom

Map 4, B8. 372 College St
Ⓣ 944-3224.
Streetcar Carlton (#506).
An emporium devoted to popular culture and sounds, filled with new and used CDs and books.

Vortex

Map 2, G5. 2309 Yonge St
Ⓣ 483-7437.
Subway Eglinton.
One of the oldest used CD stores in the city, this second-story walk-up has a sprawling collection that will delight browsers.

Wild East

Map 2, H6. 360 Danforth Ave
Ⓣ 469-8371.
Subway Chester.
This Riverdale walk-up specialises in unusual titles and musical curiosities ranging from electronica to vintage recordings. New and used CDs are available, and customers are encouraged to listen to titles before buying. The selection is large and varied, and the owner is famous for his encyclopaedic knowledge of music.

MUSIC

SPECIALITY SHOPS

He & She Clothing Gallery

Map 3, M3. 263 Queen St E
ⓣ 594-0171.
Streetcar Queen (#501).
For work or play, these exuberantly sleazy outfits are deliberately provocative and loads of fun. There's a full range of stiletto pumps in sizes big enough to accommodate both sexes.

Kidding Around

Map 4, G5. 91 Cumberland Ave
ⓣ 926-8996.
Subway Bay (Bay exit).
A delightfully goofy store where you can buy quality rubber chickens, talking door knockers, and metal lunch boxes decorated with Sumo wrestler prints and vintage TV shows.

Le Casa del Habano Toronto

Map 4, F5. 170 Bloor St W
ⓣ 926-9066.
Subway Museum.
The Toronto location of this international chain carries a select range of Cuban cigars for the connoisseur. A favourite stop for American visitors craving a puff off a Cuban cigar.

Northbound Leather

Map 4, H7. 7 St Nicholas St
ⓣ 972-1037.
Subway Wellesley.
Spiffy duds in latex, leather and PVC, with a full complement of masks, whips and other props for erotic home theatre. Beautiful workmanship, high-quality materials, and a broad-minded, attentive staff. There's a second location at 586 Yonge St (ⓣ 924-5018).

Spytech Spy Store

Map 2, G5. 2028 Yonge St
ⓣ 482-8588.
Subway Eglinton.
Spytech is dedicated to electronic surveillance gadgets like bugging or anti-bugging devices, teensy cameras and night-vision goggles. A handy place if you're into espionage or just plain paranoid.

SPORTS

Hogtown Extreme Sports
Map 3, D4. 401 King W
Ⓣ 598-4192.
Streetcar King (#504).
This place specialises in skateboarding equipment, baggy clothes and snowboards. Tired boarders can slouch in the Skater's Lounge, which is basically a bunch of couches to hang out on while swapping skatepark stories.

Mountain Equipment Co-op
Map 3, D4. 400 King St W
Ⓣ 340-2667.
Streetcar King (#504).
A $5 annual membership buys you access to the city's most extensive range of top-flight sports equipment. If you're planning to dog-sled in the Arctic, bike across China, climb mountains or go deep-sea diving, you can buy everything you need here at better-than-average prices. Note the building itself, which is made from recycled materials.

Nike Toronto
Map 4, G5. 110 Bloor W
Ⓣ 921-6453.
Subway Bay.
A superstore devoted to all things Nike. Fans of the "swoosh" will find all the latest lines and models, all under one roof.

Spinning Wheels
Map 4, L8. 240 Carlton St
Ⓣ 923-4626.
Streetcar Carlton (#506).
The total outfitter for committed cyclists, stocking a solid range of bikes and all the necessary accoutrements.

SPORTS

Sports and outdoor activities

There is no shortage of **spectator sports** in Toronto. Ice hockey, basketball, baseball and Canadian football provide a calendar year's worth of excitement in both the professional and amateur ranks. Historic rivalries between regional and city teams are no longer the political allegories they once were, but partisan sentiment for the home team can make being in the stands almost as exciting as the action on the field.

There are currently two main **venues** for spectator sports in Toronto: the **Air Canada Centre**, at 40 Bay St, is home of the Toronto Maple Leafs hockey team and the Toronto Raptors basketball squad; and the **SkyDome**, 277 Front St W, hosts the Toronto Blue Jays baseball team and the Toronto Argonauts football team.

In the early stages of its urban development Toronto was on the vanguard of the parks movement, and the city has continued to build on its creative approach to providing excellent **recreational** facilities, courses and activities for all its citizens. For example, Torontonians enjoy nearly eight thousand hectares of park space, ninety indoor pools, more than two hundred outdoor swimming pools and nearly four hundred tennis courts. There are also all-night baseball diamonds, soccer pitches, hiking and cross-country skiing trails, ice-skating rinks, greenhouses and gardens and wildlife sanctuaries. To find a facility or to check on opening hours and fees, call the **Toronto Parks Hotline** (☎338-0338); **Metropolitan Toronto Parks and Recreation** (☎392-8000); or check the **Municipal Blue Pages** in the phone book.

HOCKEY

Hockey is Canada's national pastime, and with players hurtling around at nearly 50kph and the puck clocking speeds of over 160kph, this would be a high-adrenaline sport even without its relaxed attitude to combat on the ice. As an old Canadian adage has it, "I went to see a fight and an ice-hockey game broke out."

Once upon a time, the Toronto **Maple Leafs** were the only professional sports team in Toronto; they were also the best team in the National Hockey League (NHL) and were deified by Toronto's citizens. The Maple Leafs' old home, the fabled Maple Leaf Gardens, was, like the team, beginning to get a little worn around the edges, and in February of 1999 the squad moved to the Air Canada Centre (☎815-5500). This brand-new complex also hosts Toronto's professional basketball team (the Raptors) and is connected to Union Station by an underground walkway.

The regular season, which lasts from October to April, is composed of approximately ninety games. **Ticket** prices range from $20 and can exceed $300 if there is the merest chance of the Maple Leafs making it to the playoffs and contention for the Stanley Cup, the Holy Grail of professional hockey. In those years when the Leafs make the playoffs, tickets are virtually impossible to obtain.

CANADIAN FOOTBALL

Professional **Canadian football**, played under the aegis of the Canadian Football League (CFL), is overshadowed by the United States' National Football League (NFL). The best Canadian homegrown talents move south in search of more money, and the NFL's cast-offs tend to come north to fill the ranks. The two countries' football games vary only slightly. In Canada the playing field is longer, wider and has a deeper end zone, and there are twelve rather than eleven players on each team. There is also one fewer "down" in a game, meaning that after kick-off the offensive team has three, rather than four, chances to advance the ball ten yards and regain a first down. The limited time allowed between plays results in a more fast-paced and high-scoring sport, in which ties are often decided in overtime or in a dramatic final-minute surge.

Toronto's team, the **Argonauts** (or "Argos"), share the 63,000-seat SkyDome (☎595-0077) with the Toronto Blue Jays baseball team. The season takes place between August and November, and culminates in playoffs for the Grey Cup, Canadian football's championship trophy. **Tickets** for games range from $6 to $35 for a regular series and as much as $100 for a Grey Cup match.

BASEBALL

When the Toronto **Blue Jays** won their first World Series in 1992, over a million people crammed downtown to celebrate the victory. And when the Jays repeated the feat the following year, Toronto's new-found love for **baseball** was sealed. Some people consider baseball to be on a par with chess as an intellectually challenging game of strategy. Others consider its entertainment value to be marginally shy of watching paint dry. Somewhere in between are people who simply enjoy the relaxed pace of the game while sipping beer and snacking on hotdogs on a warm summer day.

The Blue Jays (affiliated with Major League Baseball's American League) play 81 home games a season, which lasts from April to October. Games are generally played in the afternoon or at night and can last anywhere from two to four hours. **Tickets** for a match at the Blue Jays' splendid home, the SkyDome (see opposite), start at around $20 and are usually easy to obtain.

BASKETBALL

Canadians are fond of annoying Americans with the fact that **basketball** was invented by a Canadian, James Naismith. It is with less enthusiasm, though, that they acknowledge that it was not until Naismith took his game south of the border in 1891 that it actually took off.

Toronto had a professional basketball team in the Thirties and Forties, but when the American divisions reorganised themselves into the National Basketball Association (NBA) in the Fifties, the Toronto franchise was dropped. Toronto didn't rejoin the professional ranks until 1995, when the Toronto **Raptors**, named for the dinosaurs made famous by Michael Crichton's *Jurassic Park*, joined the NBA.

The Raptors were recently acquired by the owner of the Toronto Maple Leafs, and the team plays its home games during the November through May season at the ultra-modern Air Canada Centre (see p.249). Ticket prices range from $11 to $500, and it's worth attending a game to marvel at the sheer athleticism of Raptor star Vince Carter, whom locals consider the heir apparent to Michael Jordan's basketball throne.

BASKETBALL

LACROSSE

Although Canada's national sport is now ice hockey, the first and perhaps most truly Canadian sport is **lacrosse**, which is currently enjoying a vigorous resurgence in popularity. This fast, rugged game was invented by the Iroquois peoples of the Six Nation Confederacy, whose games would include hundreds of players on both sides and were mistaken by the first European sports spectators for battles. The rules of play, simplified and codified in the mid-nineteenth century, state that the game's objective is simply to send the ball through the opponent's goal as many times as possible while preventing the opposing team from scoring. There are ten players to a team and the long-handled, racket-like implement, called the crosse, used to toss and catch the ball, is the most distinctive feature of the game. As in hockey, players face off in midfield, their crosses touching the ground, and the referee drops the ball between them. Other similarities lacrosse shares with hockey are body checks and penalties for slashing, tripping and fistfights. The local National Lacrosse League team, the Toronto Rock, are back-to-back series champions and their season runs from January through April; they play at the Air Canada Centre (see p.249). Tickets are around the $10 mark.

BICYCLING

In recent years **bicycles** have proliferated in Toronto, both as a means of transportation and for recreation. Indeed, the municipal government even has a **Cycling Committee**, which devotes itself to protecting the interests of cyclists in the city. The committee also sponsors a variety of group rides and bike-friendly activities; for more information call ⓣ392-7592. Bike lanes have made an appearance on the main traffic arteries throughout the city, and there are over

85 kilometres of cycling paths in Toronto's parklands. Maps of the various cycling routes are available free of charge at bike shops, Toronto Information kiosks and through **Metro Parks and Culture** (☎392-8186).

Because bicycles are considered vehicles, cyclists are subject to the same rules of the road as car drivers with one addition: cyclists under the age of eighteen must wear a protective helmet. Bicycles are allowed on streetcars, subways and buses except during weekday rush hours: 6.30–9.30am and 3.30–6.30pm. Bicycles can be **rented** on the Toronto Islands (see p.80) at Hanlan's Point and on Centre Island; onshore, your best bet is McBride Cycle, 180 Queen's Quay W (☎203-5651), which charges $12 for the first hour and $2 for every hour thereafter. Another competitively priced rental location is In-Line Skate and Bicycle Rental, 5 Rees St (☎260-9000).

SKATEBOARDING, SNOWBOARDING AND SKIING

Although the modernist plazas surrounding the downtown skyscrapers are a serious temptation for **skateboard** enthusiasts, boarding downtown is not always looked kindly upon by authorities – not to mention the locals. There are, however, plenty of skateboarding parks ringing the city. One of the largest is Rampage Skatepark, 3677 Keele St (☎613-1334; *www.rampageskatepark.com*), which has rentals, an equipment shop and ramps galore. A couple of others worth a shot include the Scarborough Skatepark, located at 5450 Lawrence Ave E (☎396-4031), and Shred Central, 19 St Nicholas St, a recent downtown addition that is half a block from Yonge and Wellesley.

Skateboarding's winter twin, **snowboarding**, as well as **cross-country skiing**, can be experienced without leaving the city limits. In the hilly northern bounds of Toronto, try the Raven Ski Snowboard Club, 206 Lord Seaton Rd,

Willowdale (☎225-1551); lessons are available for beginners. Two municipal centres that rent equipment and provide lessons are the North York Ski Centre (☎395-7931), located in Earl Bales Park at Sheppard and Bathurst streets, and the Centennial Park Ski Hill at Renforth and Rathburn streets (☎394-8754). Some city parks also have steep banks and cliffs suitable for beginner snowboarding. In particular, try the Broadview side of Riverdale Park (take the #504 or #505 streetcar to the Broadview station), although on a snowy Sunday you may have to make way for young tobogganers.

ICE SKATING

There are more than 25 **ice rinks** operating day and night in the city's parks for pleasure, figure skating and "shinny" (informal ice hockey). One of the most popular rinks is right out front of the New City Hall in Nathan Phillips Square (see p.34), which also has a skate rental facility. There is no charge to use any of the various park skating facilities, but if you don't have your own skates, a rental pair will set you back $5–7. For information on the various locations, hours of operation and ice conditions call the parks service number at ☎392-1111 (Mon–Fri 8.30am–4.30pm).

HIKING AND WALKING

There are six walking trails – referred to by the city as **Discovery Walks** – winding through the city's parklands, ravines and neighbourhoods (for more information call ☎392-1111). The meandering routes are perfect for families and are peppered with signs that explain the flora, fauna and historical significance of the trails. The **Central Ravines, Belt Line and Gardens Discovery Walk** winds through the Don River's wooded ravines and follows an old rail line north to the pastoral setting of Mount Pleasant Cemetery. Another favourite is the **Don Valley Hills and Dales Discovery Walk**, which is particularly popular with young families and weaves through a bird sanctuary before crossing the Don River and heading up into Riverdale Park, whose hills are a tobogganer's dream in the winter. The best coastal path is the **Western Ravines and Beaches Discovery Walk**, which leads to a shoreline boardwalk through natural ponds, marshes and lakeshore parks. From here – or any of the city's walking paths – it's hard to believe you're still within Toronto's city limits.

There are also special **walking tours** organised by the city, which include bird watching, spring garden tours, fall foliage and heritage walks. For information on city-run walks call ☎392-8186. Two private organisations that offer well-organised hiking and walking tours are the **Toronto Bruce Trail Club** (☎690-HIKE) and **Toronto Field Naturalists** (☎968-6255).

GOLF

Five public **golf courses** offer beginners and experienced duffers alike the opportunity to whack a few balls around. They are: Scarlett Woods Golf Course (☎392-2484), a par-62 course suitable for beginners at Scarlett Road and Jane Street, south of Eglinton Avenue East; the Humber Valley Golf Course (☎392-2488), a challenging par-70 course on Beattie Avenue east of Albion Road; Dentonia Park Golf Course (☎392-2558), an excellent eighteen-hole course on Victoria Park Avenue, just off Danforth Avenue; the Don Valley Golf Course (☎392-2465), another challenging eighteen-hole, par-71 course at the intersection of Yonge Street and William Carson Crescent, a five-minute walk from the

York Mills subway stop; and finally, the Tam O'Shanter Golf Course, the city's premier golfing facility, with eighteen holes ranked at par-70. It is located on Birchmount Road north of Sheppard Avenue East; via public transportation take either the Birchmount #17, Sheppard East #85 or Sheppard East #85A buses. All of Toronto's golf courses have public washrooms, clubhouses and pro shops with rental equipment. Adult passes range from $9 to $17 for nine holes, and from $15 to $25 for eighteen holes.

WATERSPORTS

Toronto is a port city with an active waterfront. **Sailing**, **windsurfing**, **water skiing**, and **cruise boating** are popular summer pursuits along the shores of Lake Ontario. Swimming in Lake Ontario is not recommended due to pollution, but the public beaches are still popular attractions for sunning and general carousing. Heading out on the lake on a sailboat, canoe or kayak is an easy proposition through the **Harbourfront Canoe and Kayak School**, 283A Queen's Quay West (☏ 203-2277), which runs classes, rentals and organised tours year-round.

If you happen to be visiting Toronto with your own boat in tow, the city operates four **public marinas**: Ashbridge's Bay Park (☏ 392-6095) is accessible by car from Lakeshore Boulevard East, just east of Coxwell Avenue; Bluffer's Park (☏ 392-2556), with its 500-slip public marina, is reached by driving south on Brimley Road to its end; and at the city's west end, there's Humber Bay West Park (☏ 392-9715), a waterfront park with fly casting and model-boat ponds, a fishing pier, and a public boat launch and moorings. It can be reached by car via Lakeshore Boulevard near Park Lawn Road. Finally, there is also a public marina on the Toronto Islands (☏ 203-1055), which charges a nominal fee for overnight stays.

Kids' Toronto

oronto does an excellent job of keeping visitors with **kids** in good spirits. The city's family-positive image is a result of Toronto's reputation for being both safe and clean. Also, the populous baby boom generation started rearing families at a particularly active point in Toronto's urban renewal and development. Consequently, the interests of families were taken into account when attractions were conceived and built. And, unlike in most large North American cities, a significant portion of Toronto's population lives downtown, meaning a park or playground is always close at hand.

MUSEUMS AND ATTRACTIONS

Allen Gardens Conservatory
Map 4, J9. Jarvis Street at Carlton Street
Ⓣ 392-1111.
Streetcar **Carlton** (#506).
Mon–Fri 9am–4pm, Sat & Sun 10am–5pm.
The six greenhouses here are in bloom year round, but the place is especially alive with children during its Victorian Christmas Flower Show, which runs from early December to early January; opening ceremonies include sleigh rides, carolling and games for children.

Children's Own Museum

Map 4, F6. 90 Queen's Park
ⓣ 966-9073.
Subway **Museum**.
Wed–Sat 10am–5pm, Tues
10am–8pm, Sun noon–5pm;
$3.75, children under 2 free.
The "museum" part of this
place's name is something of a
misnomer, and the space is
officially described as an
"interactive gallery dedicated
to kids". The complex is
enormous, and its open-
concept play space is filled
with various toy-filled
stations and cubicles. One
station, for example, is a
make-believe veterinary
office, filled with plush
animal toys needing medical
attention and children in tiny
lab coats playing vet. Other
exhibits include Main Street,
where there's a huge fake tree
children can climb around,
and the Neighbourhood
Theatre, which puts on
spontaneous puppet shows
and theatrical productions. If
it all gets to be too much –
for you or your kids – there is
a designated Quiet Space
with books, cushions and soft
furnishings.

Laser Quest

Map 2, J5. 1980 Eglinton Ave E
ⓣ 285-1333.
Subway **Warden to bus #68**.
Tues–Thurs 6pm–10pm, Fri
4pm–midnight, Sat
noon–midnight, Sun
noon–10pm, closed Mon.
A sci-fi fantasy game whereby
participants armed with laser
weapons pursue one another
through labyrinths, along cat
walks and up ramps. Heavy
mood mist, special audio-
visual effects and atmospheric
lighting accentuate the
experience. Admission is $7
per game. Each game lasts
about twenty minutes.

Lillian H. Smith Library

Map 4, C9. 293 College Street
ⓣ 393-5630.
Streetcar **Carlton (#506)**.
Everything here, from the vast
collections to the statues of
mythical beasts outside the
main door, is dedicated solely
to children's literature. Don't
miss the Osborne Collection
of Early Children's Books,
which has rare and first-
edition books dating from as
far back as the fourteenth
century.

Playdium Entertainment

Map 3, E3. 126 John St,
ⓣ 260-1400.
Streetcar Queen (#501).
Mon–Wed 9am–midnight, Thurs
9am–2am, Fri–Sat 9am–4am,
Sun 11am–11pm.
A converted warehouse
provides 52,000 square feet of
the latest video games,
interactive attractions and
simulators, and virtual reality
experiences. As if that wasn't
enough, kids can literally
climb the wall on the forty-
foot-high Cliffhanger wall,
designed for climbing, tightrope walking and – of course
– free falling.

SHOPS

Jacadi

Map 4, F4. 87 Avenue Rd
ⓣ 923-1717.
Subway Bay (Cumberland exit),
in Hazelton Lanes.
A branch of the *haute couture*
Parisian chain that introduces
kids to fashion's foibles at a
very young age. The clothes
are very well made, very nice
and very expensive.

The Lion, the Witch and the Wardrobe

Map 2, F5. 888 Eglinton Ave W
ⓣ 785-9177.
Subway Eglinton West.
A children's bookstore with a
big Narnia theme, The Lion
carries educational children's
books, games and tapes as well
as an adults' section of best-
selling books about children.

Mastermind

Map 2, G4. 3350 Yonge St
ⓣ 487-7177.
Subway Lawrence.
An excellent toy store
specialising in games and
other intellectual amusements
for kids.

Misdemeanors

Map 3, D3. 322 Queen St W
ⓣ 351-8758.
Streetcar Queen (#506).
Crushed velvet baby jumpers
(machine washable of course),
the ultimate in girlie-girl
dresses and pairs of angel
wings are some of the big
sellers in this wonderful store.
The children's hats section is
unbelievably large. For infants
through to "tweens".

Science City

Map 4, H5. 50 Bloor St W
ⓣ 968-2627.
Subway Bay.
Creative games and puzzles for all skill and age levels crowd this underground store, which is part of the Holt Renfrew Centre (see "Shops and galleries", p.235).

The Toy Shop

Map 4, H5. 62 Cumberland Ave
ⓣ 961-4870.
Subway Bay.
The creative, well-crafted toys sold here come from around the world and are geared toward children of all ages.

EATING

Môvenpick Marché

Map 3, I5. 42 Yonge St
ⓣ 366-8986.
Subway Union Station.
To get food, diners visit a variety of food stations, where orders are prepared before their eyes. Select from choices like pasta, Belgian waffles, stir-fries, pizza, omelettes, and mounds of fresh fruit and fruit smoothies – all of which get high marks for variety, freshness and quality. Young patrons can eat their meals seated at diminutive tables on tiny chairs, and there is a play area for toddlers who can't sit still while their elders finish up. Sunday from 10am to 3pm is family day, where a clown does face painting, makes balloon animals and performs magic tricks.

Old Spaghetti Factory

Map 3, J6. 54 The Esplanade
ⓣ 864-9761.
Subway Union Station.
Several generations of birthday parties have been held in this cavernous restaurant, which includes a section made from an old streetcar. The food is what the name suggests: spaghetti and other pasta dishes, with lots of portions and treats for kids.

EATING

Shopsy's TV City

Map 3, E4. 284 King St W
ⓣ 599-5464.
Streetcar King (#504).

Not the place for parents who hope to converse with their offspring over dinner. The booths are equipped with Sony PlayStations hooked up to dazzling monitors, and if that isn't enough, over thirty TV monitors scattered throughout the place play endless rounds of cartoons. The menu is kid-oriented, with deli and grill favourites.

EATING

Festivals and annual events

Toronto boasts a large number of **festivals and annual events**, particularly in the summer months, when hardly a weekend goes by without some kind of extravaganza. There's less going on in winter, but this is made up for by the height of the city's performing arts calendar (see "Performing arts and film", p.196). Although you're bound to stumble across some kind of festivity by just wandering the city, it's best to know what to look for; for a seasonal events guide call **Tourism Toronto** (☎203-2600) or **Ontario Tourism** (☎1-800/ONTARIO).

The Stratford and Shaw festivals, North America's two largest theatre festivals, are both held within a two-hour's drive of Toronto. For full details, see pp.202 & 204.

JANUARY

Robbie Burns Day

A traditional Scottish *ceilidh* (house party), held on January 25 – the Caledonian bard's birthday – at Mackenzie House, 82 Bond St, which was once the home of Toronto's first mayor, William Lyon Mackenzie. Festivities include poetry readings, music and dancing, and eating haggis to the screeching blows of bagpipes (☎ 392-6915).

International Boat Show

A remembrance of summer in the depths of winter, this boat show has become hugely popular among mariners and landlubbers alike. It is usually held during the third week of January at Exhibition Place (☎ 591-6772).

FEBRUARY

Chinese New Year

Traditional and contemporary performances by some of Toronto's best Chinese artists, as well as demonstrations of Chinese opera, cooking, folk dancing, music and crafts. The festival, which takes place at the Harbourfront, could also be in the last week of January, depending on the Chinese lunar calendar (☎ 973-3000).

Listen Up!

A week-long festival of storytelling events for all ages. Most of the readings, workshops and concerts are free. For a list of venues and a complete schedule, call ☎ 656-2445.

Kuumba – A Celebration of African Heritage Month

Toronto's various African cultures celebrate their roots throughout the entire month. All activities take place at the Harbourfront Centre (see p.73), and include music, dance, film, storytelling, a comedy cabaret and culinary events (☎ 973-3000).

Toronto Winterfest

A free community event designed to chase away winter blues with live music performances, ice-sculpting demonstrations, ice skating and children's games. Activities start mid-month at North York City Hall and Mel Lastman Square, both at 5100 Yonge St (☎ 395-7350).

MARCH

St Patrick's Day Parade

Held on the Sunday nearest March 17, this is the day when all Torontonians claim to be Irish as an excuse to indulge in step dancing, music, food and, of course, Guinness. The highlight of the festivities is the parade itself, a conglomerate of some 2000 costumed marchers and dozens of floats and entertainers. The route travels south on Yonge from Bloor, snakes down to Queen St, where it then veers west and terminates at Bay St (☎ 487-1566).

APRIL

World Stage

A biannual gathering of some of the world's best contemporary theatre groups. Performances, many of them world premieres, are interspersed with lectures, workshops and special events. The plays themselves are scattered among the city's many theatres; call ☎ 973-3000 for festival information.

Festival of Original Theatre and Film (FOOT)

FOOT, staged over the course of a week in early April, is promoted by the graduate students of the University of Toronto's Drama School. The festival includes screenings, readings, performances and seminars, all at the University's Robert Gill Theatre, 214 College St (☎ 978-7986).

Sprockets

An international film festival for children aged 8–14 organised by the same group that puts on the Toronto International Film Festival (see p.269). In addition to screening short and feature-length films, Sprockets features behind-the-scenes events that demystify the secrets of the movie-making process (☎ 967-7371).

Images Festival of Independent Film and Video

Held over the course of ten days from late April to early May, this festival explores the creative outer reaches of cinema; tickets are $5 (☎ 971-8405).

MAY

Jewish Film Festival

Staggered through the first week of May, this series of shorts, features and documentaries chronicles Jewish communities from around the world; tickets cost $8 (☎ 324-8600).

Inside Out: Gay and Lesbian Film and Video Festival

Held during the third week in May, this festival showcases films that deal with gay, lesbian or bisexual subject matter (☎ 977-6847).

Milk International Children's Festival

One of the largest family events in North America, this annual festival of the performing arts is usually held in late May and features theatre, dance, music and a guest lecture series all geared towards children. It takes place at the Harbourfront Centre (see p.73), and many of the events are free (℡ 973-3000).

JUNE

Metro International Caravan

Usually occurring in mid-June, this festival brings together the customs of Toronto's vast ethnic populations, with over thirty pavilions filled with exotic foods, music and arts and crafts (℡ 977-0466).

Du Maurier Downtown Jazz Festival

International jazz headliners fill the city's jazz venues for ten days in mid-June. Lunchtime concerts are often free, and the low-cost midnight concerts have evolved into some of the festival's most exciting events (℡ 363-8717).

Toronto International Dragon Boat Races

Two days of cultural performances from Toronto's Asian communities. The highlight is the dragon boat races held off Toronto's Centre Island (see p.79), when more than 160 elaborately decorated racing boats compete for prizes. Each 39-foot vessel is filled with 22 rowers, who take their cues from a team drummer, who pounds out what he thinks will be the winning cadence. Held the third week of June (℡ 598-8945).

Gay Pride Week

Amazingly, this is the biggest gay-pride celebration in North America – bigger than New York's or even San Francisco's. For seven days at the end of June the city hosts a slew of gay-and-lesbian events, which all culminate with a massive parade down Yonge Street and over to Church Street (☎92-PRIDE).

Benson and Hedges Symphony of Fire

A spectacular two-week-long fireworks competition at Ontario Place (see p.75). Nations from around the world show up to prove their pyrotechnic skills and to wow the considerable crowds. The explosives go off in a barge moored offshore, and each display is choreographed to music. There are six performances spanning the months of June and July. Showtime is 10.30pm, with pre-show activities beginning at 10pm. Reserved seats cost $21; general grounds admission is $9.95.

JULY

Canada Day

July 1 is Canada's birthday. A full roster of concerts and celebrations in Queen's Park commemorate the occasion outside the Ontario Legislature buildings (☎314-7524).

Toronto Harbour Parade of Lights

Also part of the city's Canada Day celebrations, this day-long festival at the Harbourfront Centre (see p.73) includes illusionists, music and children's performers. The day concludes with fireworks and a light parade put on by the boats in the harbour (☎973-3000).

The Fringe Theatre Festival

Early July is given over to the Fringe Festival, which features theatre performances by ninety companies from every corner of the globe. Shows are performed in selected Annex-area theatres; see p.201 (☎966-1062).

JULY

Celebrate Toronto Street Festival

This carnival-like street festival takes up the downtown blocks of Yonge Street for a weekend in early July, with bands, midway rides, giant inflatable things and clowns. Free admission (☎ 395-7350).

Outdoor Art Exhibition

On the second weekend in July, Nathan Phillips Square, outside of Toronto's City Hall, is filled with the works of over 500 artists, all vying for more than $20,000 in prizes. An excellent opportunity to discover new talent and maybe even buy a work of art (☎ 408-2754).

Molson Indy

Formula One fans line Lakeshore Boulevard at the end of July to watch the world's top drivers compete in this major event on the race circuit. A three-day admission pass will set you back $45 (☎ 922-7477).

Caribana Festival

Toronto is home to one of the biggest Caribbean festivals in the world. This ten-day affair at the end of July and early August features music, dance, fabulous food and crazy fashions. It all culminates in a huge street parade along Lakeshore Boulevard (☎ 465-4884).

Beaches International Jazz Festival

During the last weekend of the month, jazz artists from Canada and around the world perform free in the parks, patios and street corners of Toronto's The Beaches neighbourhood. See "The suburbs" (p.82) for a description of the area. For festival information call ☎ 698-2152.

JULY

AUGUST

Du Maurier Open Tennis Championship

See international tennis champs like Michael Chang and
Andre Agassi compete for millions of dollars in prizes at the
York University courts, at Steels Avenue and Keele Street.
The tournament takes place during the first ten days of
August, and tickets range from $5 all the way to $75 (☎665-
9777).

Taste of the Danforth

Upwards to a million people clog the stretch of Danforth
Avenue between Broadview and Jones the second weekend in
August to listen to live music, watch their children cavort in
various bauble-filled bubbles and, most importantly, to eat.
Over 100 participating restaurants set up sidewalk food stations
with little, inexpensive items that add up to a huge meal.

Canadian National Exhibition

An annual carnival signalling the beginning of the end of
summer. While it can be a bit much for adults, kids go wild for
the noisy arcades, rides and the plethora of junk food. Special
events include an air show and a concert series. The festivities
take place at the Canadian National Exhibition grounds on
Lakeshore Boulevard (☎393-6000).

SEPTEMBER

Toronto International Film Festival

This is the last major film festival still open to the public, making
it one of the world's most massively attended. Stars, directors,
producers and thousands of film nuts take over the city's
downtown cinemas for ten days, and while the festival has gained
a high-profile reputation as the launch pad for future

Oscar-winners, the overall ambience can still be described as "grassroots". See "Performing arts and film" (p.214) for more information (☎ 967-7371).

Cabbagetown Festival

The oldest and largest of Toronto's many neighbourhood festivals, this event includes a small film festival, a pub crawl, arts and crafts and lots of live music. The epicentre for activities is Riverdale Park during the second weekend of September (☎ 921-0857).

OCTOBER

International Festival of Authors

The world's largest and most prestigious literary event is held at the Harbourfront Centre (see p.73) during the third week of October. Over eighty of the finest authors (fiction, poetry, drama and biography) in the world congregate to give interviews, lectures and a full roster of readings (☎ 973-3000).

NOVEMBER

Royal Agricultural Winter Fair

A venerable Toronto institution held within the first two weeks of November, the Royal has been bringing the country to the city for more than three generations. It is now the world's largest indoor agricultural fair, complete with weird, exotic poultry, life-sized butter sculptures and major equestrian events (☎ 263-3400).

Santa Claus Parade

The unofficial beginning of the Christmas shopping season, this parade trucks down Yonge Street with clowns, brass bands, floats and, of course, Santa in tow. Usually held on the second weekend in November (☎ 599-9090, ext 500).

DECEMBER

The Christmas Story
This nativity pageant has been a tradition since 1938. Held in
the charming Church of the Holy Trinity (see p.39) behind the
Eaton Centre, The Christmas Story is told through mime,
narration, organ music and carols sung by an unseen choir
(℡598-8979).

Kensington Festival of Light
This lantern-lit neighbourhood pageant begins at dusk on the
Winter Solstice (December 21) and encompasses images and
performances from Hanukkah, Christmas, and winter solstice
celebrations from around the world (℡598-2829).

First Night Toronto
A no-alcohol, family-oriented New Year's Eve celebration held
in Nathan Phillips Square at Toronto's City Hall. Festivities
include concerts, singing, and children's activities (℡362-
3692).

Hogmanay! Happy New Year!
Hogmanay, which means "happy new year" in Gaelic, is an
annual New Year's Eve bash at the historic Scottish Mackenzie
House, 82 Bond St. Revellers enjoy traditional Scottish music,
holiday food, and tours of the house (℡392-6915).

City directory

AIRLINES Air Canada, 130 Bloor St W (925-2311); Air France, 151 Bloor St W (922-3344); American Airlines, 55 Bloor St W (1-800/443-7300); British Airways, 4120 Yonge St (250-0880); Cathay Pacific, 70 York St (864-0448); Delta Air Lines, 2 Bloor St W (923-5968); KLM Royal Dutch Airlines, 2 Bloor St W (323-1515); Lufthansa German Airlines, 26 Wellington Ave E (368-4777); Northwest Airlines, *Royal York Hotel*, 100 Front St (1-800/225-2525); United Airlines, *Royal York Hotel*, 100 Front St (1-800/241-6522).

ATMS Automated Teller Machines are everywhere. US and overseas visitors can use their ATM cards at most of them if their cards are linked to the Cirrus or Plus systems, which are clearly displayed on the machines.

BANKS Bank of Montreal, 2 King St W (867-5323); Banque Nationale du Paris, 121 King St W (360-8040); Bank of Nova Scotia, Scotia Plaza, 44 King St W (866-6430); Bank of Tokyo-Mitsubishi, Royal Bank Plaza, 200 Bay St (865-0220); Canadian Imperial Bank of Commerce (CIBC), Commerce Court, King St W at Bay (980-7777); Citibank, 1 Toronto St (947-2900); Chase Manhattan Bank of Canada, 100 King St W (216-4100); Deutsche Bank, 222 Bay St (682-8400); Hong Kong Bank of Canada, 70 York St (868-8000); Royal Bank, Royal Bank Plaza, 200 Bay St (974-3940); Toronto Dominion

Bank, Toronto Dominion Centre, 66 Wellington St W (☏ 869-1144). Bank hours may vary, but, at the very least, they are all open Mon–Fri 10am–3pm.

CONSULATES Australia, 360 Bay St (☏ 863-0649); Britain, 777 Bay St (☏ 593-1267); France, 130 Bloor St W (☏ 925-8041); Germany, 77 Admiral Rd (☏ 925-2813); Italy, 136 Beverly St (☏ 977-1566); Japan, Toronto Dominion Bank Tower, 66 Wellington St W (☏ 363-7038); Netherlands, 1 Dundas St W (☏ 598-2520); People's Republic of China, 240 St George St (☏ 964-7260); United States of America, 360 University Ave (☏ 595-1700).

CURRENCY EXCHANGE Most large downtown banks will change currency and traveller's cheques. American Express checks should be cashed at their downtown office, 50 Bloor St W (Mon–Wed & Sat 10am–6pm, Thurs & Fri 10am–7pm, closed Sun; ☏ 967-3411). Other currency exchange offices include Thomas Cook, 10 King St E (Mon–Fri 9am–5pm; ☏ 863-1611), and Currencies International, whose main branch is at 80 Bloor St W (daily 8.30am–7pm; ☏ 921-4872).

DENTIST For emergencies, call the Academy of Dentistry hotline (daily 9am–11pm; ☏ 967-5649).

DISABILITY While most public sights (museums, monuments, etc) are handicap-accessible, accessibility in restaurants, theatres and some hotels can be sporadic. For restaurants, check listings in *NOW*, the free weekly city guide, for the wheelchair-accessible symbol, or call ahead. The subway system is currently making its stations wheelchair-accessible. All the main stations have elevators and newer trains are wider to accommodate wheelchairs. Many downtown bus routes have kneeling vehicles; for local-transit handicap information, call ☏ 393-4636. For general information and assistance, call Beyond Ability International ☏ 410-3748 (24-hour hotline); ⓦ *www.beyond-ability.com*.

CONSULATES–DISABILITY

EMERGENCIES ☎ 911 for fire, police and ambulance. Other emergency numbers include: Assaulted Women's Helpline (☎ 863-0511); Child Abuse (☎ 395-1500); Rape Crisis (☎ 597-8808).

HOSPITALS Toronto General Hospital, 200 Elizabeth St (☎ 340-3111); Women's College Hospital, 76 Grenville Ave (☎ 966-7111); Hospital for Sick Children, 555 University Ave (☎ 813-1500). For minor medical injuries and illness visit First Canadian Medical Centre, 1 First Canadian Place (☎ 368-6787) or the Walk-In Medical Clinic, 1910 Yonge St (☎ 483-2000).

LAUNDROMATS The Laundry Lounge, 531 Yonge St (☎ 975-4747), has food, video games, colour TV, a wash-and-fold service and does dry cleaning and alterations; 24 hour Coin Laundry, 566 Mount Pleasant Ave (☎ 487-0233), is always open; and Splish Splash Cleaning Centre, 590 College St (☎ 532-6499), has plenty of good cafés in the vicinity to visit while you wait.

LEFT LUGGAGE The best places to dump your stuff for a few hours (24 hours maximum) are the lockers at Union Station, 65 Front St, or those at the Toronto Coach Terminal, 610 Bay St at Dundas. Alternatively, try the lockers on the Bloor-Yonge Street subway station or, even better, the lockers at the Metro Reference Library, 789 Yonge St. Most lockers cost a mere 25 cents.

LEGAL ADVICE The Law Society of Upper Canada maintains a lawyer referral service (Mon–Fri 9am–1pm and 2–5pm; ☎ 947-3330).

LIBRARY The main downtown branch of the Toronto Public Library is the Toronto Reference Library, 789 Yonge St (Mon–Thurs 10am–8pm, Fri & Sat 10am–5pm, Sun 1.30–5pm, closed Sun during summer; ☎ 393-7131).

PHARMACIES Shopper's Drug Mart, at 700 Bay St (☎ 979-2424) and 722 Yonge St (☎ 920-0098); for a holistic pharmacy, including herbal and traditional treatments, try Hooper's, 24 Wellesley St W (☎ 928-3366).

POLICE STATIONS Main Precinct, 40 College St at Yonge (☎ 808-2222; for emergencies call ☎ 911); also contains a Police Museum (☎ 808-7020), gift shop and information kiosk.

POST OFFICES Generally open Mon–Fri 9am–6pm, Sat 9am–noon. The proper term for "Post Office" is "Canada Post Outlet for Products and Services". The main Toronto branches are located at 31 Adelaide St E (☎ 214-2352); 595 Bay St (☎ 506-0911); and Commerce Court at 25 King St W (☎ 925-7452). Many pharmacies and stationery stores also have full-service postal counters.

PUBLIC HOLIDAYS New Year's Day (January 1), Good Friday (Friday before Easter Sunday), Victoria Day (May 24), Canada Day (July 1), Simcoe Day (first Monday in August), Labour Day (first Monday in September), Thanksgiving (second Monday in October), Christmas Day (December 25), and Boxing Day (December 26).

PUBLIC RESTROOMS Try the lobbies of downtown hotels, any shopping centre, subway stations (particularly Union Station), and the Toronto Reference Library.

RADIO CBC Radio One (99.1 FM) is Toronto's frequency for the Canadian Broadcasting Corporation, an excellent source for public affairs, news and arts programming. For just news try CFTR (680 AM) or CFRB (1010 AM). For easy rock, tune in to CHUM (104.5 FM) or MIX (99.9 FM). Harder rock is found on Q 107 (107.1 FM), and alternative sounds are on CFNY (102.1 FM). CISS (92.5 FM) does country, and for classical, try CFMX (96 FM) or CBC Two (94.5 FM). There are also excellent student stations that feature alternative and world artists, as well as news and events: CJRT (91.1 FM) from Ryerson Polytechnic, and CIUT (89 FM) from the University of Toronto.

RAPE CRISIS (see "Emergencies" above).

TAX Two taxes are levied on almost every purchase: the 8 percent Provincial Sales Tax (PST), and the 7 percent Goods and Service Tax (GST). Note

POLICE STATIONS—TAX

that the PST on hotel and motel accommodation drops to 5 percent. Foreign visitors can claim a refund for GST taxes levied on accommodation and accumulated purchases of a minimum of $200, but not on meals. To claim your rebate ask for a GST refund form at your hotel, travel information booths, or at the airport before departure (many retailers with a large tourist clientele also carry the forms). Keep all receipts, and submit them with your form within 60 days of purchase. You can also apply for a refund on the 8 percent Ontario Sales Tax if you are not an Ontario resident, but the accumulated purchases must add up to a minimum of $625 and the form is harder to get. For the Provincial Sales Tax refund form call 1-800/263-7965 or write to: Ontario Ministry of Finance, Retail Sales Tax Branch Box 623, 33 King St W, Oshawa, Ontario L1H 8H7.

TELEPHONES As of March 25, 2001 all local telephone calls will require the 416 area code as well as the number itself. New telephone numbers

assigned after this time will have a new Toronto area code, 647. From that date Toronto numbers must be preceeded by the area code when dialling, even locally. Basically, all calls in Toronto are now ten digits long. If looking to make a call, there's no shortage of public phones in Toronto. All are equipped for the hearing-impaired, and most accept pre-paid calling cards as well as credit cards. All phone books contain maps of the downtown core and the Toronto Transit Commission (TTC) routes. Local calls are 25 cents.

TELEVISION CBC TV (channel 5); CTV (channel 9); TV Ontario (channel 19); Global (channel 41); CITY TV (channel 57); CFMT (channel 47).

TICKETS The following Toronto ticket agencies cover local shows, concerts and sporting events; a service charge is added to all ticket prices. Ticketmaster (870-8000) is Canada's largest computerised ticket distribution system and the official agent for venues like the Elgin and Winter Garden Theatres, Maple Leaf Gardens and the SkyDome. Ticket King (☎872-1212 or ☎1/800-461-3333) takes care of the Royal Alexandra Theatre, the Princess of Wales Theatre, and special exhibits at the Art Gallery of Ontario. T.O. TIX (Tues–Sat noon–7.30pm; ☎596-8211; see "Performing arts and film," p.196), located inside the Eatons Centre, is a same-day, half-price ticket agent affiliated with the Toronto Theatre Alliance.

TIME Toronto is on Eastern Standard Time (EST), the same time zone as New York City. Daylight Savings Time runs from the first Sunday in April to the last Sunday in October.

TRAVEL AGENTS The Flight Centre is a good place to look for last-minute bargain fares. They have four downtown locations: 382 Bay St (☎934-0670), 335 Bay St (☎363-9004), 130 King St W (☎865-1616), and 1560 Yonge St (☎932-1899). For full-service assistance for cruises, air, rail and tours, try Carlson Wagonlit at 1220 Yonge St (☎224-0867).

TRAVELLER'S AID Downtown, go to Union Station, Room B23 (☎366-7788) or the bus terminal at Bay and Dundas (☎596-8647); both open daily 9.30am–9.30pm. At Pearson International Airport there are kiosks at each terminal: Terminal 1 (☎905-676-2868), Terminal 2 (☎905-676-2869), Terminal 3 (☎905-612-5890); all three are open daily 9am–10pm.

WOMEN'S RESOURCES The University of Toronto Women's Centre is located at 568 Spadina Ave (☎978-8201, call ahead as hours can be erratic); the Regional Women's Health Centre, an outreach clinic affiliated with Women's College Hospital, is at 790 Bay St (☎586-0211); and the Toronto Women's Bookstore, 73 Harbord St (☎922-8744; see "Shopping", p.229), keeps tabs on the scores of community organisations throughout Toronto and southern Ontario specifically concerned with women.

TIME—WOMEN'S RESOURCES

CONTEXTS

A brief history of Toronto

Beginnings

In prehistoric times, the densely forested northern shores of Lake Ontario were occupied by nomadic **hunter-gatherers**, who roamed in search of elk, bears, caribou and perhaps mammoths, supplementing their meaty diet with berries and roots. Around 1000 BC, these nomads were displaced by **Iroquois-speaking peoples**, who gained a controlling foothold in areas that are now modern-day southern Ontario, upper New York and Quebec. The settlers of this period (usually called the **Initial Woodland** period – 1000 BC to 900 AD) only differed from their predecessors in the advent of pottery and the construction of burial mounds. In the **Terminal Woodland** period (900–1600 AD), however, the Iroquois-speakers developed a comparatively sophisticated culture, which was based on the cultivation of corn (maize), beans and squash. This agricultural system enabled them to lead a fairly settled life, and the first Europeans to sail up the St Lawrence River stumbled across large communities

– often several hundred strong – inhabiting palisaded settlements comparable with Sainte-Marie (see p.117). Archaeologists have discovered the remains of over 190 Iroquois villages in the Toronto area alone.

Iroquois society was divided into matriarchal clans, which were governed by a female elder. The clan shared a long house, and when a man married (always outside his own clan), he moved to the long house of his wife. Tribal chiefs (*sachems*) were male, but they were selected by the female elders of the tribe and they also had to belong to a lineage through which the rank of *sachem* descended. Once selected, a *sachem* had to have his rank confirmed by the federal council of the inter-tribal league – or confederacy – to which his clan belonged. These **tribal confederacies**, of which there were just a handful, also served as military alliances, and warfare between them was endemic. In particular, the Five Nations confederacy, which lived to the south of Lake Ontario, was almost always at war with the Hurons to the north.

The coming of the Europeans

In the sixteenth century, British and French **fur traders** began to inch their way inland from the Atlantic seaboard. The French focused on the St Lawrence River, establishing Quebec City in 1608. From their new headquarters, it was a fairly easy canoe trip southwest to **Toronto** (whose name is taken from Huron for "place of meeting"), which was on an early portage route between Lake Ontario and Georgian Bay. The French allied themselves with the Hurons, and in 1615 **Samuel de Champlain** led a full-scale expedition to southern Ontario to cement the Huron alliance and boost French control of the fur trade. When he arrived, Champlain handed out muskets to his Huron allies, encouraging them to attack their ancient enemies, the Five

Nations. He also sent Étienne Brûlé, one of his interpreters, down to Toronto with a Huron war party, the first recorded visit of a European to Toronto.

In the short term, Champlain's actions bolstered the French position, but the Five Nations never forgave France's alliance with the Hurons, and thirty years later they took their revenge. In 1648, Dutch traders began selling muskets to the Five Nations, and the following year they launched a full-scale invasion of Huronia, massacring their Huron enemies and razing the settlement of Sainte-Marie among the Hurons to the ground.

The rise of the British

The destruction of Sainte-Marie was a grisly setback for the French, but it didn't affect their desire to control southern Ontario. In the second half of the seventeenth century, they rushed to encircle Lake Ontario with a ring of forts-cum-trading posts. The British did the same. Initially, the French out-colonised the British, and they furthered their ambitions by crushing the Five Nations confederacy in the 1690s, forcing them deep into New York state. In 1720, the French established a tiny fur-trading post at Toronto, the first European settlement on the site, and although it was soon abandoned, the French returned thirty years later to build a settlement and a stockade, **Fort Rouillé**. This was to be the high-water mark of French success. During the Seven Years' War (1756–63), the British conquered New France (present-day Quebec) and overran the French outposts dotted around the Great Lakes. The Fort Rouillé garrison didn't actually wait for the British, but prudently burnt their own fort down and high-tailed into the woods before the Redcoats arrived. The site lay abandoned for almost forty years until hundreds of Loyalist settlers arrived following the American Revolution.

THE RISE OF THE BRITISH

Early Toronto (1793–1812)

In the aftermath of the American Revolution (1775–83), thousands of Americans fled north to Canada determined to remain under British jurisdiction. These migrants were the **United Empire Loyalists**, and several hundred of them settled along the northern shore of Lake Ontario. The British parliament responded to this sudden influx by passing the **Canada Act** of 1791, which divided the remaining British-American territories in two: Upper and Lower Canada, each with its own legislative councils. Lower Canada was broadly equivalent to today's Quebec, and Upper Canada to modern-day Ontario. The first capital of Upper Canada was Niagara-on-the-Lake (see p.103), but this was much too near the American border for comfort, and the province's new lieutenant-governor, the energetic **John Graves Simcoe**, moved his administration to the relative safety of Toronto in 1793. He called the new settlement **York** in honour of Frederick, the Duke of York and a son of George III. Eton- and Oxford-educated, Simcoe was a man of style, and his first Toronto home contained the large canvas tent that had originally been made for Captain Cook's Pacific trips. Actually, the term "tent" hardly does it justice – the structure had wooden walls, insulating boards and proper doors and windows; Simcoe's soldiers were much impressed. Simcoe's wife, Elizabeth, also made a marked impression on the area: her witty diaries remain a valuable source of information on colonial life, and her watercolours are among the first visual records of Native American life along the Lake Ontario shoreline.

John Simcoe's aspirations for York soon withered. He thought the settlement's harbour was first-rate, but he was exasperated by the rude conditions of frontier life, writing, "the city's site was better calculated for a frog pond...than for the residence of human beings". The Simcoes and a fair number of their contemporaries abandoned York in 1796. Nicknamed "**Muddy York**", the capital failed to attract many settlers, and twenty years later it had just seven hundred inhabitants. The main deterrent to settlement, however, was the festering relationship between Britain and the US, which culminated in the **War of 1812**, whereby the Americans hoped to eject the British from Canada. The Americans thought this would be a fairly straightforward proposition and expected to be greeted as liberators. In both respects, they were quite wrong, but they did capture York without too much difficulty in 1813. Most of the American casualties came when the garrison of Fort York (see p.32) blew up their own munitions and accidentally pulverised the approaching US army. The Americans stayed for just twelve days, and returned for an even shorter period three months later. Neither occupation was especially rigorous, with the Americans content to do a bit of minor burning and looting. Even this, however, was too much for the redoubtable **Reverend John Strachan**, who bombarded the Americans with demands about the treatment of prisoners and the need for the occupiers to respect private property. The Treaty of Ghent ended the war in 1814, and under its terms the US recognised the legitimacy of British North America.

The Family Compact

The Canada Act had established an Upper Canada government based on a Legislative Assembly, whose power was shared with an appointed assembly, an executive council and an appointed governor. This convoluted arrangement ultimately condemned the government to impotence. At the same time, a colonial elite built up chains of influence around several high-level officials, and by the 1830s economic and political power had fallen into the hands of an

THE FAMILY COMPACT

anglophile oligarchy christened the **Family Compact**. This group's most vociferous opponent was a radical Scot, **William Lyon Mackenzie** (see p.42), who promulgated his views both in his newspaper, the *Colonial Advocate*, and as a member of the Legislative Assembly. Mackenzie became the first mayor of Toronto, as the town was renamed in 1834, but the radicals were defeated in the elections two years later, and a frustrated Mackenzie drifted towards the idea of armed revolt. In 1837, he staged the **Upper Canadian Rebellion**, a badly organised uprising of a few hundred farmers, who marched down Yonge Street, fought a couple of half-hearted skirmishes and then melted away. Mackenzie fled across the border and two of the other ringleaders were executed. But the British parliament, mindful of their earlier experiences in New England, moved to liberalise Upper Canada's administration instead of taking reprisals. In 1841, they granted Canada responsible government, reuniting the two provinces in a loose confederation and pre-figuring the final union of 1867 when Upper Canada was re-designated Ontario as part of the British **Dominion of Canada**. Even Mackenzie was pardoned and allowed to return. His pardon seemed to fly in the face of his portrayal of the oligarchs as hard-faced reactionaries; indeed, this same privileged group had even pushed progressive antislavery bills through the legislature as early as the 1830s.

Victorian Toronto

By the end of the nineteenth century, Toronto had become a major manufacturing centre and railway terminus. The city was dominated by a conservative mercantile elite who were exceedingly loyal to the British interest and maintained a strong Protestant tradition. This elite was sustained by the working-class **Orange Lodges**, whose reactionary influence was a key feature of municipal politics – spurring Charles Dickens, for one, to write disparagingly of the city's "rabid Toryism" when he visited in the 1840s. That said, the Protestants were enthusiastic about public education, just like the Methodist-leaning middle classes, who also spearheaded social reform movements, specifically Suffrage and Temperance. Like every industrial city of the period, Toronto had its slums, but there were fine mansions too, and the city centre was dotted with solid Victorian churches, offices and colleges.

The Victorian period came to an appropriate close with a grand visit by the future **King George V**, who toured Toronto with his extravagantly dressed entourage – all bustles and parasols, bearskin and pith helmets – in 1901.

The twentieth century

Edwardian Toronto boomed and the population soared from 30,000 in 1850, to 81,000 in 1882, and 230,000 in 1910. Most of the city's immigrants came from Britain, and when **World War I** broke out in 1914 the citizens of loyalist Toronto poured into the streets to sing "Rule Britannia". Thousands of volunteers subsequently thronged the recruiting stations – an enthusiasm which cost many their lives: no fewer than seventy thousand Torontonians fought in the war, and casualties amounted to around fifteen percent.

The carnage did not, however, dint the city's economy – rather the opposite in fact – and the boom times continued until the stock market crash of 1929 cut a swathe through the Canadian economy. During the **Great Depression** unemployment reached astronomical levels – between thirty and thirty-five percent – and economic problems were compounded by the lack of a decent welfare system. The hastily established Department of Welfare was only able to

THE TWENTIETH CENTURY

issue food and clothing vouchers, meaning that thousands slept in the streets. Fate was cruel too: Toronto experienced some of the severest weather it had ever had, with perishing winters followed by boiling hot summers.

At the start of **World War II**, thousands of Torontonians once again rushed to join the armed forces. The British were extremely grateful and Churchill visited Canada on several occasions, making a series of famous speeches here (see p.35). The war also resuscitated the Canadian economy – as well as that of the United States – and Toronto's factories were speedily converted to war production. Boatloads of British kids were also shipped to Toronto to escape the attentions of Hitler's Luftwaffe. After the war, Toronto set about the process of reconstruction in earnest. There was a lot to do. The city's infrastructure had not kept pace with the increase in population, and the water, transportation and sewage systems were desperately in need of improvement. Political change was also needed. The city was now surrounded by a jumble of politically independent municipalities, and the need for an overall system of authority was self-evident. After much vigorous horse-trading, the result was the creation of **Metropolitan Toronto** in 1953, its governing body an elected council comprising 24 representatives, 12 apiece from the city and suburbs. The dominant figure of Metro politics for the first ten years was the dynamic **Frederick G. Gardiner**, aka "Big Daddy", who authorised the construction of the Gardiner Expressway.

Nevertheless, for all its status as the capital of Ontario, Toronto remained strikingly provincial in comparison to Montreal until well into the 1950s. It was then that things began to change, the most conspicuous sign being the 1955 defeat of the incumbent mayor, Leslie Saunders, by **Nathan Phillips**, who became the city's first Jewish mayor. Other pointers were the opening of the city's first cocktail bars in 1947, and, three years later, a closely fought referendum whose result meant that public sporting events could be held on Sundays. Up until then, Sundays had been preserved as a "day of rest" and even Eaton's department store drew its curtains to prevent Sabbath-day window-shopping. The opening of the St Lawrence Seaway in 1959 also stimulated the city's economy, though not quite as much as had been anticipated on account of the development of road transport.

In the 1960s the economy exploded, and the city's appearance was transformed by the construction of a series of mighty, modernistic **skyscrapers**. This helter-skelter development was further boosted by the troubles in Quebec, where the clamour for fair treatment by the Francophones prompted many of Montreal's Anglophone-dominated financial institutions and big businesses to up-sticks and transfer to Toronto. Much to the glee of Torontonians, the census of 1976 showed that Toronto had become **Canada's biggest city**, edging Montreal by just one thousand inhabitants, and the gap has grown wider by the year. Meanwhile, Toronto's **ethnic complexion** was changing too, and by the early 1970s Canadians of British extraction were in the minority for the first time.

In the last twenty years, Toronto's economy has followed the cycles of boom and retrenchment common to the rest of the country, though real estate speculation was especially frenzied until the bottom fell out of the property market in 1988. In the mid-Nineties, the Progressive Conservatives took control of Ontario, and their hard-nosed leader, Mike Harris, pushed through another governmental reorganisation, combining the city of Toronto with its surrounding suburbs. This **"Mega City"**, as it has come to be known, has a population of 4.4 million and covers no less than 10,000 square kilometres. The change was deeply unpopular in the city itself, but Harris still managed to get himself re-elected in 2000 with the large-scale support of small-town and suburban Ontario. A hated figure amongst the province's liberals and socialists, Harris's conservative social policies are often blamed for the dramatic increase in the number of homeless people on the city's streets.

With or without Harris, Toronto has become one of the world's favourite capitals, sporting a flamboyance, self-confidence and vibrancy that would have amazed earlier generations. It is also a thoroughly cosmopolitan metropolis, with a strong environmental lobby that trains a beady eye on the developers. The environmentalists have steadfastly opposed a string of hare-brained schemes that would have pulverised their surroundings and, often because of them, Toronto is one of the continent's most likeable, liveable cities.

Literary Toronto

Although there has been a **literary scene** in Toronto since the mid-nineteenth century, Toronto as a theme in Canadian literature has emerged only in modern decades. From the diaries of **Elizabeth Simcoe** in the late eighteenth century to the fiery editorials of **William Lyon Mackenzie** and the fond sketches of **Henry Scadding** at the turn of the twentieth century, early writings about Toronto were almost entirely non-fiction. When writers did delve into fiction, their subjects were often lofty discussions on matters of church and state, not the pastoral aspects of Toronto life. As early Canadian novelist **Sara Jeanette Duncan** (1861–1922) wrote of the fictional Ontario town of Elgin in *The Imperialist*, "Nothing compared with religion but politics, and nothing compared with politics but religion." These were the only topics worthy of serious discussion.

Social realism became a popular literary theme in the aftermath of World War I, but this gritty real-world writing style was slow to take off in Canada, where people preferred historical romances and small-town settings. Two important exceptions were **Morley Callaghan** (1903–90) and **Hugh Garner** (1913–79), who wrote about their native Toronto from a class perspective, focusing on aspects of life that had none of the high moral tones or Gothic romance associated with nineteenth-century novelists. Garner and Callaghan also tended to hover on the left of the political spectrum, far from the peculiarly Canadian "Red Tory" brand of social satire best captured by humorist **Stephen Leacock** (1869–1944). The overwhelming emphasis was on small-town Ontario, which obscured the fact that the urban population of Toronto was awash in a sea of change. In Callaghan's *Such Is My Beloved* (1934), a description of the demographic shift in a Toronto parish between world wars has a contemporary ring, even though it describes a social construct that no longer exists:

> *The Cathedral was an old, soot-covered, imitation Gothic church that never aroused the enthusiasm of a visitor to the city. It had been in that neighbourhood for so long it now seemed just a part of an old city block. The parish was no longer a rich one. Wealthy old families moved away to new and more pretentious sections of the city, and poor foreigners kept coming in and turning the homes into rooming houses. These Europeans were usually Catholics, so the congregation at the Cathedral kept getting larger and poorer. Father Anglin really belonged to the finer, more prosperous days, and it made him sad to see how many of his own people had gone away, how small the collections were on Sunday and how few social organisations there were for the women. He was often bitter about the matter, although he should have seen that it was really a Protestant city, that all around his own Cathedral were handsome Protestant Churches, which were crowded on Sunday with well-dressed people, and that the majority of the citizens could hardly have told a stranger where the Catholic Cathedral was.*

The Hugh Garner co-operative housing development on Ontario Street is named in testament to Garner's novel *Cabbagetown*. The book is set in the Depression and takes its name from the Toronto neighbourhood that Garner famously described as "the largest Anglo-Saxon Slum in North America". An unexpurgated version of the novel did not appear until 1968, by which time the streets he described had either been turned into tracts of sanitised public housing or refurbished as upscale Victorian residences for moneyed professionals. The improbable transformation of the Cabbagetown neighbourhood (see p.67) is documented in Garner's 1976 novel *The Intruders*.

In the late Fifties and early Sixties, Toronto was the home base for a remarkable flowering of prose, poetry, painting and theatre. Many of Canada's leading poets, essayists and novelists – most notably **Margaret Atwood** – emerged from the milieu that crowded into the all-night poetry readings at the Bohemian Embassy on St Nicholas Street. Other major talents from that era were **Milton Acorn**, known across Canada as "The People's Poet", **Gwendolyn MacEwen**, and **b.p. nichol** and **Paul Dutton**, both of whom belonged to the **Four Horsemen**, a poetry performance group. These artists and their contemporaries made Toronto a hospitable place for creativity. They set up awards to encourage new writers and sustain established ones; they mentored one another and took many newcomers under their wings; and they encouraged a school of writing that considered place – in this case Toronto – to be fundamental to storytelling. For them, Toronto was not, as Robert Fulford said, "a place to graduate from". It was a place to stay. In this passage from **Michael Ondaatje's** *In the Skin of a Lion*, Commissioner Harris, who built Toronto engineering feats like the Bloor Street Viaduct and the Water Filtration Plant (see p.84), describes a vision:

> One night, I had a dream. I got off the bus at College – it was when we were moving College Street so it would hook up to Carlton – and I came to this area I had never been to. I

saw fountains where there used to be an intersection. What was strange was that I knew my way around. I knew that soon I should turn and see a garden and more fountains. When I awoke from the dream the sense of familiarity kept tugging me all day. In my dream the next night I was walking in a mysterious park off Spadina Avenue. The following day I was lunching with the architect John Lyle. I told him of these landscapes and he began to laugh. "These are real," he said. "Where?" I asked. "In Toronto?" It turned out I was dreaming about projects for the city that had been rejected over the years. Wonderful things that were said to be too vulgar or too expensive, too this, too that. And I was walking through these places, beside the traffic circle at Yonge and Bloor, down the proposed Federal Avenue to Union Station. Lyle was right. These were real places. They could have existed. I mean, the Bloor Street viaduct and this building here are just a hint of what could have been done here.

In 1965 **Stan Bevington** and **Wayne Clifford** took over a back-lane carriage house space from Marshall Mcluhan and founded **Coach House Press**, which became the incubator for all that was new and adventurous in Canadian literature. In addition to publishing the early works of Atwood and Ondaatje – whose *In the Skin of a Lion* is perhaps the definitive Toronto novel – Coach House began a tradition of giving talented new writers their first break: **Paul Quarrington**, **Susan Swan** and anthologist **Alberto Manguel** are just three examples. The company continued to expand its interests, putting out textbooks and a Quebec translation series featuring emerging Quebecois authors like **Jacques Ferron**, **Nichole Brossard** and **Victor-Levy Beaulieu**. A turbulent period of conflict on the editorial board and financial difficulties caused the press to be dissolved in 1996, but in 1997 Bevington announced the birth of **Coach House Press Books**, an establishment devoted to beautiful, handmade limited editions and, way at the other end of the publishing spectrum, online novels for the Internet.

Other Toronto-based novelists to achieve prominence during the Sixties and Seventies were **Timothy Findley** and **Robertson Davies**. Findley's third novel, *The Wars* (1977), established him as a major literary talent, and recent novels such as *Headhunter* (1993) and *The Piano Man's Daughter* (1995), both set in Toronto, make great use of local history, lore and settings.

Robertson Davies, one of the most significant novelists of the post-war era, uses quirky, thinly veiled descriptions of Toronto institutions like the University of Toronto in novels like *The Rebel Angels* (1981), which is imbued with a strong sense of place. Both Davies and Findley have a knack for recognising the rich stories that have yet to be told about the people and the city of Toronto. Rather than portraying Toronto as a stuffy, provincial town, the characters of a Findley or Davies novel are flamboyant, mystical, and are often based on obscure mementos of Canadian history.

In the Seventies and Eighties, new voices found their way into Canadian literature. The immigrant experience in Toronto has been covered since the early nineteenth century, but early writers usually saw themselves as importing values and mores, and they shared similar cultural backgrounds and religions. Writers like **Neil Bissoondath**, who was born in Trinidad, **Michael Ondaatje**, who was born in Ceylon, and **M.G. Vassanji**, who is originally from Kenya, contributed a different perspective of immigrant life in Toronto. In Vassanji's *No New Land*, customary activities become strange, and the landmarks native Torontonians see as everyday dull become exotic:

What would immigrants in Toronto do without Honest Ed's, the block-wide carnival that's also a store, the brilliant kaaba to which people flock even from the suburbs? A centre of attraction whose energy never ebbs, simply transmutes, at night its thousands of dazzling lights splash the sidewalk in flashes of yellow and green and red, and the air sizzles with catchy fluorescent messages circled by running lights. The dazzle and sparkle that's seen as far away as Asia and Africa in the bosoms of bourgeois homes where they dream of foreign goods and emigration. The Lalanis and other Dar immigrants would go there on Sundays, entire families getting off at the Bathurst station to join the droves crossing Bloor Street West on their way to that shopping paradise.

Toronto has an ambiguity about it that has long made capturing the city's essence difficult. Poet-turned-novelist **Anne Michaels**, however, beautifully explored the city's many faces in *Fugitive Pieces* (1996):

Like Athens, Toronto is an active port. It's a city of derelict warehouses and docks, of waterfront silos and freight yards, coal yards and a sugar refinery; of distilleries, the cloying smell of malt rising from the lake on humid summer nights.

It's a city where almost everyone has come from elsewhere – a market, a caravansary – bringing with them their different ways of dying and marrying, their kitchens and songs. A city of forsaken worlds; a language a kind of farewell.

It's a city of ravines. Remnants of wilderness have been left behind. Through these great sunken gardens you can traverse the city beneath the streets, look up to the floating neighbourhoods, houses built in the treetops.

It's a city of valleys spanned by bridges. A railway runs through back yards. A city of hidden lanes, of clapboard garages with corrugated tin roofs, of wooden fences sagging where children have made shortcuts. In April, the thickly treed streets are flooded with samara, a green tide. Forgotten rivers, abandoned quarries, the remains of an Iroquois fortress.

Public parks hazy with subtropical memory, a city built in the bowl of a prehistoric lake.

The above description would have confounded earlier generations of the city's writers, who lived in Toronto but uniformly placed their poems and novels elsewhere. Likewise, the perspective of outsiders who came to Toronto in the nineteenth and early twentieth centuries almost always stressed the city's perceived rigidities. From Charles Dickens to Ernest Hemingway and Wyndham Lewis, literary visitors often took Toronto's social and political milieu to be narrow and provincial. With the city's social and cultural maturation in the latter half of the twentieth century, however, the city has come to recognise a new literary pride; one that has allowed Toronto's artists to describe the city with passion, compassion and lyricism.

Books

Most of the following books should be readily available in the UK, US or Canada. We have given publishers for each title in the form UK/US publisher, unless the book is published in one country only; out-of-print titles are indicated by o/p. Note that virtually all the listed books published in the US will be stocked by major Canadian bookshops; we have indicated those books published only in Canada.

Impressions and memoirs

John Bently-Mays, *Emerald City: Toronto Visited* (o/p). Thoughtful critical essays about the city, its architecture and its inhabitants.

C.S. Clark, *On Toronto the Good: A Social Study* (Coles Canadiana Collection, o/p). Originally published in 1898, this is one of the city's earliest urban studies, exploring the evolution of the many aspects of city life that have made Toronto what it is today.

John Robert Colombo, *Haunted Toronto* (Houslow Press, Canada). Colombo is a poet, novelist and indefatigable anthologist of Canadiana. This collection of Toronto hauntings highlights the city's interest in the weird and fantastic.

Wayne Grady, *Toronto in the Wild: Field Notes of an Urban Naturalist* (Macfarlane/Walter & Ross). Toronto has a wide assortment of flora and fauna living in its ravines, parks, empty lots and rooftops. Grady chronicles them all in this picture-filled book.

William Kilbourn (ed), *The Toronto Book: An Anthology of Writings Past and Present* (Macmillan, Canada, o/p). A collection of over a century of informed, uninformed and imaginative descriptions of Toronto.

David McFadden, *Trip Around Lake Ontario* (Coach House Press, 1988; reprinted by Great Lakes Suite/Talon Books). Part of a trilogy detailing the author's circumnavigation of lakes Ontario, Erie and Huron written in a deceptively simple style.

George Rust D'Eye, *Cabbagetown Remembered* (Stoddart and Company, Canada). An intimate portrait and historical account of this popular Toronto neighbourhood (see p.67), its people and its landmarks. Wonderful photographs.

William White (ed), *The Complete Toronto Dispatches*, 1920–1924 (Charles Scribners Sons). Ernest Hemingway's first professional writing job was with *The Toronto Star* as both a local reporter and as a European correspondent. This is a collection of his dispatches for the paper.

History

Carl Benn, *The Iroquois in the War of 1812* (University of Toronto Press). In 1812 the United States, at war with Canada, invaded and briefly occupied York (Toronto). The role played by the Five Nations and Iroquois peoples in the war was pivotal in Canada's survival, and the ramifications of the War of 1812 affected the aboriginal people of Ontario for years to come.

William Dendy, *Lost Toronto* (Oxford University Press). This book documents the unfortunate loss of countless historically important Toronto buildings to the wrecking ball, fire and neglect. An eye-opener for those who can only think of Toronto's urban landscape as "modern".

HISTORY

Harold Innis, *The Fur Trade in Canada: An Introduction to Canadian Economic History* (University of Toronto Press). The words "dramatic, sweeping and engaging" are not usually associated with books on economic history, but in this case they fit the bill. Innis' study is invaluable for the insight it gives to pre-European Canada, and its trading customs with Ontario's native peoples.

Anna Jameson, *Winter Studies and Summer Rambles in Canada* (Coles Publishing Company, Canada). Originally published in 1839, these tart observations of early Toronto's colonial society are marked by a sense of wonderment at the vastness of Canada's untamed land.

Kenneth McNaught, *The Penguin History of Canada* (Penguin). A concise, annotated analysis of Canada's economic, social and political history.

Henry Scadding, *Toronto of Old* (Oxford University Press, o/p). Originally published in 1873, and written by a member of one of Toronto's founding families,

these sketches and pen-and-ink illustrations have an immediacy and charm that give insight to Toronto's early years.

Elizabeth Simcoe, *Mrs. Simcoe's Diary*, Mary Innis, editor (Macmillan, Canada). The wife of Upper Canada's first lieutenant-governor and an early resident of York (Toronto), Simcoe not only gave detailed observations of the landscape and the city's way of life, but she was also an astute political observer, offering portraits of major historical figures like Chief Joseph Brant.

Randall White, *Toronto the Good: Toronto in the 1920s* (Dundurn Press, Canada). A detailed portrait of the evolution of a modern city and its people. Stuffed with intriguing facts, observations and photographs.

George Woodcock, *A Social History of Canada* (Penguin). An erudite and very readable book about the peoples of Canada and the country's development. Woodcock is the most perceptive of Canada's historians.

Architecture and arts

Eric Arthur, *Toronto: No Mean City* (University of Toronto Press). One of the earliest and best-known studies of Toronto's architectural heritage, written by the father of the city's architectural conservancy movement.

Robert Fulford, *Accidental City* (Macfarlane, Walter & Ross, o/p). This entertaining book on the vagaries of the city's development pokes around in some unlikely nooks and crannies. The central thesis is somewhat bogus (almost all cities develop haphazardly), but it's a good read all the same.

Greg Gatenby, *Toronto, A Literary Guide* (McArthur, Canada). This walking-tour guide to Toronto is a wonderful way to get to know the city. Gatenby is the director and moving spirit behind the marvellous International Festival of Authors (see p.270).

Glenn Gould, *The Glenn Gould Reader*, Tim Page, editor (Lester & Orpen Dennys, o/p).

Sometimes chatty, sometimes pompous, Gould's voice and erudition shine through this collection of essays, articles and letters written from early adulthood to the end of his short life.

Liz Lundell, *The Estates of Old Toronto* (Boston Mills Press). A pictorial study of nineteenth-century domestic architecture in Toronto, as well as a social history. Most of the buildings, unfortunately, have been lost to time.

Patricia McHugh, *Toronto Architecture: A City Guide* (McClelland and Stewart). A comprehensive guide to Toronto architecture and neighbourhoods. Each photo-rich chapter functions as a walking tour through different sections of the city.

Dennis Reid, *A Concise History of Canadian Painting* (Oxford University Press). Not especially concise, this book is nonetheless a thorough trawl through Canada's leading artists, with bags of biographical detail and lots of black-and-white (and a few colour) illustrations of major works.

ARCHITECTURE AND ARTS

Harold Towne and David P. Silcox, *Tom Thomson: The Silence in the Storm* (McClelland and Stewart). A study of the career and inspirations of Tom Thomson, one of Toronto's best-known artists. Towne, the co-writer, was also a major Canadian artist.

Travel and specific guides

Katherine Ashenburg, *Going to Town: Six Southern Ontario Towns* (Macfarlane/Walter & Ross). A terrific day-trip guide to a variety of towns within driving distance of Toronto.

Elliott Katz, *The Great Toronto Bicycling Guide* (Great North Books). A useful guide to Toronto area bike paths as well as background information about the region itself.

Scott Mitchell, *Secret Toronto: The Unique Guidebook to Toronto's Hidden Sights, Sounds and Tastes* (ECW Press). Torontonians rolled their eyes at the title description: most of the entries weren't terribly secret. However, first-time visitors will find it a useful off-the-beaten-path guide.

Fiction

Margaret Atwood, *The Robber Bride* (McClelland and Stewart). Toronto readers had a field day with the thinly veiled descriptions of famous and infamous Torontonians. A snapshot of time and place, this book lives up to Atwood's high storytelling standards.

Austin Clarke, *The Origin of Waves* (McClelland and Stewart). Two Barbadians meet in a Toronto blizzard after a separation of almost fifty years. A warm novel of two lives and the journeys each has made.

Robertson Davies, *The Cunning Man* (McClelland and Stewart). Jonathan Hullah is a Toronto doctor befuddled by the death of one Father Hobbes, some twenty years earlier. As he recalls the circumstances surrounding the priest's death, Hullah also finds time to ruminate on theatre, art, God and the strange secrets of a doctor's consulting room.

Timothy Findley, *Headhunter* (Harper Collins). A sombre, futuristic novel that brings aspects of Conrad's *Heart of Darkness* to contemporary Rosedale, an haute bourgeois Toronto neighbourhood.

Gwendolyn MacEwen, *Norman's Land* (Coach House Press, o/p). MacEwen once called Canada the most exotic place in the world, and she defends this thesis admirably in this enormously creative novel about a character she first introduced in her short-story collection *Norman*.

Alie Munro, *Who Do You Think You Are?* (Penguin, US). Beautifully crafted novel from one of Canada's finest writers. There is no better evocation of small-town Ontario life.

Michael Ondaatje, *In the Skin of a Lion* (Vintage Books). This is the novel that introduces readers to the characters in the more famous *The English Patient*. It spans a period between the end of World War I and the Great Depression in East End Toronto.

Nino Ricci, *Where Has She Gone?* (McClelland and Stewart). The third in a trilogy that began with *Lives of the Saints*, this book is about an Italian-Canadian family's sometimes tragic attempts to find its identity.

Susan Swan, *The Wives of Bath* (Alfred J. Knopf). At a Toronto girls' school in the Sixties, the protagonist, Mouse, struggles with notions of feminine beauty as her best friend struggles with gender identity. A wry novel written in a genre the author describes as "sexual gothic".

FICTION

Index

Stay in touch with us!

ROUGHNEWS is Rough Guides'
free newsletter. In three issues a year
we give you news, travel issues,
music reviews, readers' letters and
the latest dispatches from authors on
the road.

I would like to receive ROUGHNEWS: please put me on your free mailing list.

NAME . . . .

ADDRESS . . . .

Please clip or photocopy and send to: Rough Guides, 62-70 Shorts Gardens,
London WC2H 9AH, England

or Rough Guides, 375 Hudson Street, New York, NY 10014, USA.

ROUGH GUIDES: Travel

Amsterdam
Andalucia
Australia
Austria
Bali & Lombok
Barcelona
Belgium & Luxembourg
Belize
Berlin
Brazil
Britain
Brittany & Normandy
Bulgaria
California
Canada
Central America
Chile
China
Corfu & the Ionian Islands
Corsica
Costa Rica
Crete
Cyprus
Czech & Slovak Republics
Dodecanese
Dominican Republic
Egypt
England
Europe
Florida
France
French Hotels & Restaurants 1999
Germany
Goa
Greece

Greek Islands
Guatemala
Hawaii
Holland
Hong Kong & Macau
Hungary
India
Indonesia
Ireland
Israel & the Palestinian Territories
Italy
Jamaica
Japan
Jordan
Kenya
Laos
London
London Restaurants
Los Angeles
Malaysia, Singapore & Brunei
Mallorca & Menorca
Maya World
Mexico
Morocco
Moscow
Nepal
New England
New York
New Zealand
Norway
Pacific Northwest
Paris
Peru
Poland
Portugal
Prague

Provence & the Côte d'Azur
The Pyrenees
Romania
St Petersburg
San Francisco
Scandinavia
Scotland
Sicily
Singapore
South Africa
Southern India
Southwest USA
Spain
Sweden
Syria
Thailand
Trinidad & Tobago
Tunisia
Turkey
Tuscany & Umbria
USA
Venice
Vienna
Vietnam
Wales
Washington DC
West Africa
Zimbabwe & Botswana

THE ROUGH GUIDE TO
Canada

ROUGH GUIDES: Mini Guides, Travel Specials and Phrasebooks

Miami
& the Florida Keys

MINI GUIDES

Antigua
Bangkok
Barbados
Big Island of Hawaii
Boston
Brussels
Budapest
Dublin
Edinburgh
Florence
Honolulu
Lisbon
London Restaurants
Madrid
Maui
Melbourne
New Orleans
St Lucia

First-Time
Asia

EVERYTHING YOU NEED TO KNOW BEFORE YOU GO

TRAVEL SPECIALS

First-Time Asia
First-Time Europe
More Women Travel

PHRASEBOOKS

Czech
Dutch
Egyptian Arabic
European
French

Seattle
Sydney
Tokyo
Toronto

German
Greek
Hindi & Urdu
Hungarian
Indonesian
Italian
Japanese
Mandarin
  Chinese
Mexican
  Spanish
Polish
Portuguese
Russian
Spanish
Swahili
Thai
Turkish
Vietnamese

Vietnamese

DICTIONARY PHRASEBOOK

AVAILABLE AT ALL GOOD BOOKSHOPS

ROUGH GUIDES:
Reference and Music CDs

REFERENCE
Classical Music
Classical:
  100 Essential CDs
Drum'n'bass
House Music

World Music:
  100 Essential CDs
English Football
European Football
Internet
Millennium

**ROUGH GUIDE
MUSIC CDs**
Music of the Andes
Australian
  Aboriginal
Brazilian Music
Cajun & Zydeco
Classic Jazz
Music of Colombia
Cuban Music
Eastern Europe
Music of Egypt
English Roots
  Music
Flamenco
India & Pakistan
Irish Music
Music of Japan
Kenya & Tanzania
Native American
North African
Music of Portugal

Jazz
Music USA
Opera
Opera:
  100 Essential CDs
Reggae
Rock
Rock:
  100 Essential CDs
Techno
World Music

Reggae
Salsa
Scottish Music
South African
  Music
Music of Spain
Tango
Tex-Mex
West African Music
World Music
World Music Vol 2
Music of Zimbabwe

AVAILABLE AT ALL GOOD BOOKSHOPS

100

Essential
CDs

*Eight titles,
one name*

ROUGH
GUIDES

Will you have enough stories to tell your grandchildren?

©2000 Yahoo! Inc.

Yahoo! Travel

DO YOU YAHOO!?

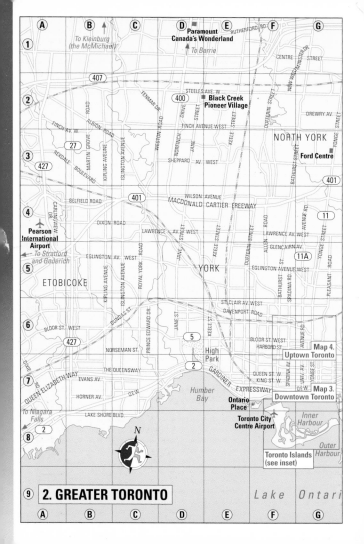

2. GREATER TORONTO

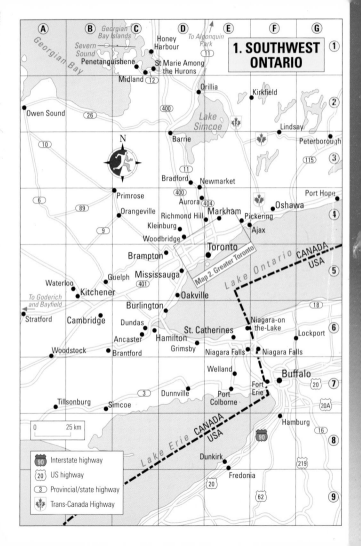

1. SOUTHWEST ONTARIO

Legend:
- **90** Interstate highway
- **20** US highway
- **3** Provincial/state highway
- Trans-Canada Highway

0   25 km

Rough Guides
on the Web

www.travel.roughguides.com

We keep getting bigger and better! The Rough Guide to Travel Online now covers more than 14,000 searchable locations. You're just a click away from access to the most in-depth travel content, weekly destination features, online reservation services, and an outspoken community of fellow travelers. Whether you're looking for ideas for your next holiday or you know exactly where you're going, join us online.

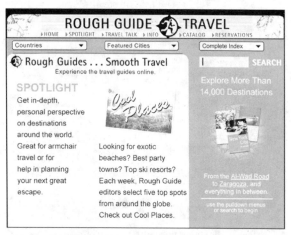

You can also find us on Yahoo!® Travel (http://travel.yahoo.com) and
Microsoft Expedia® UK (http://www.expediauk.com).

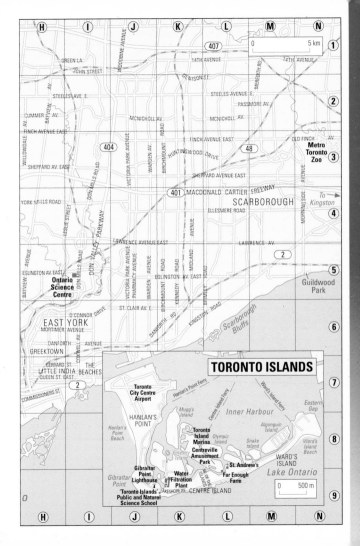

TORONTO ISLANDS

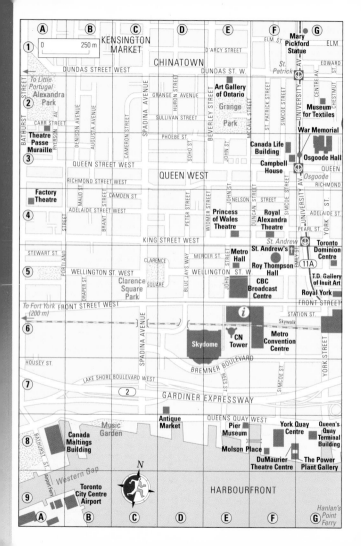

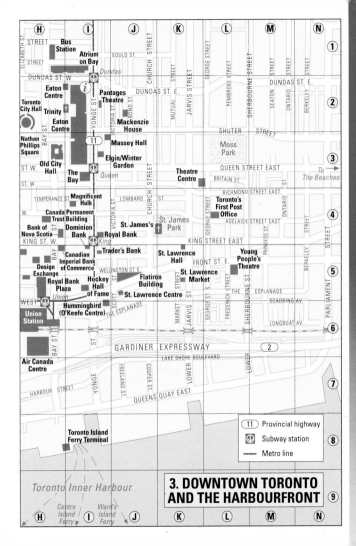

3. DOWNTOWN TORONTO AND THE HARBOURFRONT

- 11 Provincial highway
- Subway station
- — Metro line

Toronto Inner Harbour

Centre Island Ferry / Ward's Island Ferry

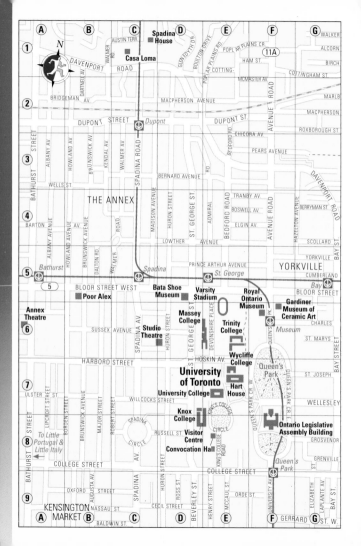